Indigenous Civil Society in Latin America

Indigenous Civil Society in Latin America

Collective Action in the Digital Age

. . . .

PASCAL LUPIEN

The University of North Carolina Press Chapel Hill

This book was published with the assistance of the Anniversary Fund of the University of North Carolina Press.

Library of Congress Cataloging-in-Publication Data
Names: Lupien, Pascal, 1978– author.
Title: Indigenous civil society in Latin America : collective action in the
    digital age / Pascal Lupien.
Description: Chapel Hill : University of North Carolina Press, [2023] |
    Includes bibliographical references and index.
Identifiers: LCCN 2022027349 | ISBN 9781469672618 (cloth ; alkaline paper) |
    ISBN 9781469672625 (paperback ; alkaline paper) | ISBN 9781469672632 (ebook)
Subjects: LCSH: Indians of South America—Political activity—Case studies. |
    Indians of South America—Political activity—Ecuador. | Indians of South
    America—Political activity—Bolivia. | Indians of South America—Political
    activity—Chile. | Indians of South America—Government relations. | Civil
    society—South America. | Digital communications—Political aspects. |
    South America—Politics and government—21st century.
Classification: LCC F2230.1.G68 L86 2023 | DDC 305.898—dc23/eng/20220622
LC record available at https://lccn.loc.gov/2022027349

Cover design and illustration by Jason Alejandro.

Contents

Figure and Tables

Figure

Tables

Acknowledgments

This book represents the combined efforts of hundreds of people. It would not exist without the knowledge, time, and generosity of the Indigenous leaders, activists, and community members who contributed to its development. It is not possible to name all of them here, and many asked not to be identified, but I would like to offer my sincere thanks to all of the individuals who agreed to share their stories with our research team. I hope that I have interpreted and presented their diverse perspectives as faithfully as possible. Any errors in this book are my own.

The research presented in this book would not have been possible without the support of three exceptional research assistants. Soledad Machaca, an Aymara scholar based in La Paz, Bolivia, was recommended to me by the director of the Social Communication department at the Universidad Mayor de San Andrés, where she was completing her MA at the time. This was one of the best recommendations I have received; Soledad is a dedicated and skilled researcher and has become a good friend. Alberto Lagos is a Mapuche researcher at the University of Temuco's Institute of Indigenous and Intercultural Studies (IEII) in Wallmapu. His knowledge of Mapuche politics and society, and his passion for achieving social justice in Wallmapu, greatly enhanced the results of the fieldwork. I first met Gabriel (Gabo) Chiriboga when he was an undergraduate in Social Development at the Universidad Técnica del Norte in Ibarra, Ecuador. I was inspired by his keen intelligence and his dedication to social justice. Gabo, who identifies as *campesino*, has since become a good friend and an invaluable research assistant. I could have not asked for better co-researchers for this project.

The online content analysis was supported by two talented and dedicated scholars: Adriana Rincón, who completed her PhD at the University of Massachusetts Boston in 2021, and Andrés Lalama, a PhD student at the University of Toronto. At the time of the research, both were visiting scholars at the University of Calgary's Latin American Research Centre (LARC). I am indebted to Pablo Policzer and others at the LARC for the logistical support and expertise they provided. I must also thank a number of other scholars who have provided various forms of encouragement and expertise that supported this project, from the development of the original funding proposal to comments on the manuscript itself: Janine Clark, Jordi Díez, David MacDonald, Roberta Rice, Philip Oxhorn, Ron Deibert, Irene Poetranto, Tamara Small, Leah Lavac, and Candace Johnson.

The research was carried out in three extraordinary countries: Wallmapu (called south-central Chile by settlers), Bolivia, and Ecuador, my beloved adopted land that holds a special place in my heart. I am fortunate to have had the opportunity to meet so many fascinating, dynamic people who are dedicated to the improvement of democracy in their countries. I would like to express my deep gratitude to all those who offered their time and perspectives. For their help and the contacts they provided, a special thanks to Ricardo Carrera (UDLA, Quito), Natalia Caniguan (IEII, Temuco), Edgar Pomar (UMSA, La Paz), Wilma Mendoza (CNAMIB, Santa Cruz), Karina Herrera (SIFDE, La Paz), and Miguel Posso (UTN, Ibarra).

I would also like to offer my thanks and appreciation to my editor, Elaine Maisner at UNC Press. I had heard very good things about Elaine before submitting the first draft of my manuscript, and I have to say that her excellent reputation as an editor is well deserved. Her expert advice, constructive criticism, and attention to detail greatly enhanced the final product. I must also thank Andreina Fernandez, who took over from Elaine as editor following her retirement from UNC Press, for her professionalism, efficiency, and willingness to help.

This research was made possible by generous funding from the Social Sciences and Humanities Research Council of Canada (SSHRC).

Indigenous Civil Society in Latin America

Introduction

Indigenous Civil Society in Latin America:
Continuity and Change

· ·

In late 2019, communities across South America erupted in protest. Hundreds of thousands of citizens engaged in acts of resistance and civil disobedience. They marched, blocked roads, and occupied public spaces. They chanted slogans such as "El pueblo, unido, jamás será vencido" (the people, united, will never be defeated) and antigovernment rallying cries. Some broke windows, burned tires, and destroyed symbols of colonial rule. Both violent and peaceful protesters were met with force by riot police and soldiers. For Bolivia, Ecuador, and Chile, these were the largest uprisings in a generation.

While Latin American history is characterized by turmoil and unrest, prior to these uprisings, the three countries had experienced over a decade of political stability and economic prosperity. Latin America emerged from the 2008–9 financial crisis relatively unscathed, benefiting from a prolonged resource boom. The left-leaning governments elected as part of the so-called Pink Tide (from approximately 2000 to 2017) implemented sweeping reforms that included redistributive economic policies and participatory democracy initiatives (Cornia 2014; Ellner 2012; Larrea and Greene 2018; Weisbrot 2008). Latin American social movements, once among the world's most dynamic, appeared to recede as social investment and a strong economy satisfied the basic needs of their traditional base. From Brazil to Bolivia, these reforms—at least in the early years—are credited with raising the standard of living for millions of Latin Americans (Calderón and Castells 2020). They also raised expectations beyond what most states were able to deliver in the long term. The collapse of oil prices in 2014 dealt a devastating blow to Venezuela, the cradle of the Pink Tide movement under populist president Hugo Chávez (1999–2013). Bolivia and Ecuador also saw their economies sputter by the second half of the decade. The region's sharp economic decline, and the inevitable cuts to social spending that this entailed, played a key role in the 2019 protests.

A defining feature of the 2019 uprisings in Bolivia and Ecuador, and to a lesser extent in Chile, was the presence and influence of Indigenous peoples. The wave of democratization that swept Latin America in the 1980s and 1990s provided new political opportunities and Indigenous social movements engaged in diverse forms of collective action and political participation. At the height of the protest cycle in the 1990s and early 2000s, Indigenous actors in Ecuador and Bolivia achieved notable victories, drawing on a sense of collective identity, strong organizations, and new political opportunities. Their remarkable achievements, particularly given the enduring social and political marginalization of Indigenous peoples throughout the Americas, resulted in a wealth of literature addressing the emergence and development of Indigenous social movements (Albó 2004; Brysk 1994, 2000; Lucero 2008; Paige 2020; Postero 2007; Rice 2012; Van Cott 1994, 2005; Yashar 1998, 2005).

With the relative decline of the Indigenous protest cycle by the mid-2000s, research turned elsewhere. Scholars interested in Latin America began to critically assess the political, social, and economic transformations ushered in by charismatic Pink Tide presidents such as Chávez, Bolivia's Evo Morales (2006–19), and Ecuador's Rafael Correa (2007–17). Large-scale collective action seemed to subside as these leftist governments met many traditional demands of Indigenous and marginalized sectors. They promulgated new constitutions that recognized Indigenous rights and invested in social programs that addressed pressing socioeconomic needs of their poorest citizens.

This period coincides with the emergence of social media and a dramatic upswing in the use of digital technologies for political action. Scholars argue that by the 2010s, the use of social media in Western countries and among urban middle-class citizens in the Global South had begun to transform the very nature of political activism (Bimber 2017; Castells 2009, 2015; Lilleker and Koc-Michalska 2017; Shirky 2008; Tufekci 2017). Because interest in Indigenous collective action began to wane at this time, we still know relatively little about how Indigenous communities use information and communication technologies (ICTs) to engage in the political arena.

This book examines how Indigenous civil society organizations (CSOs) are adapting to a globalized, technology-centered world. It addresses the gaps in our knowledge by reengaging with Indigenous collective action in the twenty-first century. In the context of increasing recognition of global indigeneity, along with the growing internationalization of Indigenous political and cultural rights through the United Nations Declaration on the

Rights of Indigenous Peoples (UNDRIP) and other mechanisms, this book contributes to updating and expanding our understanding of contemporary Indigenous politics in Latin America.

Questions, Significance, and Rationale

The following chapters take the reader into the heart of Indigenous civil society in Ecuador, Bolivia, and Chile in the latter half of the 2010s. They explore continuity and change within and across the three countries. The research presented in this book was conducted with the help of over 100 Indigenous leaders, activists, and communications specialists. It focuses on how Indigenous CSOs are pursuing political action in the twenty-first century and it is guided by the following questions: In what ways have social, political, and technological changes over the past decade influenced the evolution of Indigenous civil society? How and why have the strategies and tactics of Indigenous CSOs evolved over the past decade and what have been the most successful approaches? Why did Indigenous peoples return to large-scale resistance in late 2019 after more than a decade of relative calm? How, and in what direction, do ICTs shift the balance of power between Indigenous civil society and the state or other powerful actors? The comparison of cases across and within three countries will serve to interrogate the contextual factors that enhance or diminish the capacity of Indigenous actors to achieve their goals.

There are a number of developments that compel us to pursue answers to these questions. First, the relative decline of the Indigenous protest cycle by the mid-2000s meant that research on collective action turned elsewhere following a surge of widely cited monographs in the 2000s (Mijeski and Beck 2011). Even the most recent works tend to focus on the late twentieth-century "Indigenous Revolution" (see, for example, Paige 2020). This book picks up where a number of core works left off. It tells the story of Indigenous collective action in the second decade of the twenty-first century and examines how it has evolved, adapted, and—in some cases— remained consistent.

Second, there is a lack of recent comparative work that would reveal how and why Indigenous forms of action evolve over time, as well as the most and least effective tactics for engaging in the political arena. This book examines the ways in which Indigenous organizations are pursuing sustained civic action and taking advantage of institutions they helped to shape at the end of the last century. It will explain why collective action has shifted from disruptive to more "civic" forms of participation—and back again—in the twenty-first century. The analysis within and across countries sheds light on why some approaches have been more successful than others in terms of achieving tangible political outcomes. The book focuses on five key activities identified through the research: political participation and influencing policy, resource mobilization, communication and public relations, identity promotion and socialization, and mobilizing supporters.

Third, academic attention to Indigenous movements in the region waned just as the social media era began to take off. Studying how Indigenous CSOs use twenty-first-century ICTs will shed light on how some of society's most excluded groups can use the affordances of these tools to support their work, and how these technologies shift the balance of power. Addressing these questions contributes to collective action theory by examining how digital technologies fit into resource mobilization and political opportunities with respect to Indigenous peoples. It also helps us to update theoretical frameworks that aim to understand the use of digital technologies by integrating the perspectives of some of the world's most traditionally marginalized communities—theory has made certain assumptions based on studies of Western and middle-class actors—and developing a better understanding of their unique realities. A comparative study helps us to better understand the contextual factors that produce barriers or more favourable conditions for Indigenous civil society.

Methodology and Cases

This book draws on rich data collected over a four-year period with ninety Indigenous organizations in Bolivia, Ecuador, and Chile. It uses a unique approach that combines interviews with online content analysis to produce a comprehensive perspective on Indigenous movements in the twenty-first century. The research was supported by the invaluable work of three research assistants: Soledad Machaca (Aymara, based in La Paz, Bolivia), Gabriel Chiriboga (based in Northern Ecuador), and Alberto Lagos (Mapuche, based in Temuco, Chile). Each contributed to the project expertise, knowledge, and contacts with Indigenous civil society.

In collaboration with Indigenous leaders, we developed a sample of ninety cases (CSOs)—including thirty-six in Bolivia, thirty-two in Ecuador, and twenty-two in Chile—according to a diverse case method, which involves the purposive selection of cases to represent a range of important variables (Seawright and Gerring 2008). The cases provide variation along

TABLE I.1 Cases: Indigenous CSOs studied

Size	Bolivia	Ecuador	Chile
Large/national	2	2	0
Medium/regional	4	5	2
Small/local	30	25	20
Urban	6	5	2
Rural	30	27	20
Regions represented	Highlands (21); Eastern lowlands (15)	Highlands (24); Amazon (6); Coast (2)	North (2); Santiago Area (3); South, Araucanía, and Biobío (17)
Positive relationship with the state*	20	10	2
Total cases	36	32	22

*As reported by the CSOs

key dimensions: size, cultural differences, urban versus rural, and relationship with the state, which is closely related to political opportunities (see table I.1). Large, national CSOs represent Indigenous communities across the country (or aspire to do so) and many regional organizations are members. Midsized regional organizations represent political subdivisions such as provinces, or specific Indigenous nations. Small, local CSOs are by far the most common type. These may represent Indigenous peoples in a specific community or municipality. Most local organizations have very limited resources. In all three countries, Indigenous CSOs are primarily rural, although large and midsized organizations are often headquartered in cities. Relationships with the state vary between and within the three countries.

Bolivia, Ecuador, and Chile provide variation that allow for important comparisons of these variables within and across countries (table I.2). The three countries have significant Indigenous populations that have all engaged in some type of collective action in recent decades.[1] There are also important differences. Indigenous movements in Ecuador and Bolivia were considered the most powerful in their respective countries in the 1990s and early 2000s, and achieved significant gains (Rice 2012; Yashar 2005). In contrast, Mapuche peoples in Chile did not create these types of strong national organizations and have seen less progress on the political front. But Mapuche CSOs have made great strides in other areas, including identity promotion, education, and the use of digital technologies. Chile also has a higher level of development and stronger formal institutions, although the related benefits rarely extend to Indigenous peoples (Richards 2013).

Indigenous Civil Society in Latin America   5

TABLE I.2 Countries: Bolivia, Ecuador, and Chile (2021 data)

	Bolivia	Ecuador	Chile
Population*	11,809,000	17,872,451	19,255,125
Percentage of Indigenous**	40–70	7–35	9–12
Per capita GDP ($)*	9,111	11,879	24,928
HDI ranking	0.718	0.759	0.851
Internet access (percentage)*	44	54	82
Main regions	Altiplano (highlands), central valleys, eastern tropical lowlands (Media Luna)	Highlands (Sierra), coast, Amazon (Oriente)	North, Central (Santiago), South (Wallmapu/ Araucanía)
Indigenous nations	Quechua (49 percent), Aymara (41 percent), Guaraní, Mojeño, others	Kichwa (96 percent), Shuar, Achuar, Cofán, Huaorani, others	Mapuche (84 percent), Aymara, Quechua
Indigenous living in poverty (percentage)***	45	58	30

* https://datacatalog.worldbank.org/
** Range provided based on different sources (government statistics at the lower end, Indigenous CSO estimates at the higher end)
*** World Bank 2015

Research Design and Methods

This study draws on a community-based participatory research (CBPR) approach that incorporates the perspectives of Indigenous participants into the research design. This involved four steps. First, we established local advisory groups of Indigenous leaders in each country to articulate some of the goals of the research before the fieldwork began. Second, we narrowed down the focus of the study to the tasks that Indigenous leaders deemed most important. For example, it became clear that Indigenous CSOs prioritized a number of key activities, to differing degrees depending on the organization. We aggregated these activities into five categories that capture the range of work that CSOs engage in: political participation and influencing policy, resource mobilization, communication and public relations, identity promotion and socialization, and mobilizing supporters. Our questions and data collection tools were tailored based on the categories that emerged from this process, and those categories serve to structure the empirical chapters of this book. Third, the advisory groups were consulted during the course of the fieldwork to ensure ongoing alignment with community needs. Finally, we prepared reports for the participating CSOs, and the local research assistants delivered the results to communities through a series of meetings and workshops. This was a bidirectional process that involved asking participants if our interpretation of the results accurately reflected their perspectives. At the same time, we provided Indigenous leaders with information that they felt could help them to rethink or adjust their tactics. For example, given that most CSOs were relatively inexperienced with using ICTs, many leaders were particularly interested in learning more about how Indigenous CSOs across the region are using social media. They sought to develop new ideas based on a comparative analysis of more and less successful tactics for using ICTs. See figure I.1 for a summary of the CBPR approach.

Soledad, Gabriel, Alberto, and I conducted most of the fieldwork with Indigenous organizations in the three countries from June 2016 to March 2019. The data include a survey and a series of semistructured interviews. Questionnaires were distributed to 106 participants from the ninety Indigenous organizations in the three countries. We then conducted interviews with the same 106 individuals; these were intended to elicit in-depth perspectives that could not be captured through questionnaires. Some of these interviews were conducted one-on-one, while others took place as part of a discussion circle based on preferences determined during the consultation stage. Participants include leaders, communications agents, activists, and other representatives from the ninety organizations. We engaged in participant observation with a smaller number of cases, two or three in each country, by attending regular meetings over a period of several weeks. Interviewees are cited by their first or last names depending on their preference, while some chose to remain anonymous.

We conducted follow-up interviews in December 2019 (Ecuador), June 2020 (Chile), and July and August 2020 (Bolivia) with a subset of our participants (six or seven individuals in each country) in order to understand the role of Indigenous organizations in the late 2019 uprisings that affected all three countries. Due to the COVID-19 pandemic which gripped South America throughout 2020, follow-up interviews in Bolivia and Chile were conducted by telephone, using videoconferencing software, or anonymous questionnaires when subjects did not feel comfortable communicating through those means. I have also included a handful of responses from fieldwork

Local Advisory Groups	Consultations	Research Design	Consultations	Knowledge Mobilization
Establish an advisory group of Indigenous leaders in each country:	Initial consultations with advisory groups:	Develop representative sample of CSOs	Consult advisory groups every 2–3 weeks during the fieldwork to ensure ongoing alignment with community needs	Author and research assistants prepare reports for the participating CSOs
Ecuador: 6 advisors (4 highlands, 2 Amazon)	Identify cases (CSOs)	Tailor interview questionnaires		Meetings and workshops
Bolivia: 6 advisors (4 altiplano, 2 lowlands)	Develop relationships	Determine data collection methods for each CSO (e.g., one-on-one interviews vs. discussion circles)		Sharing results with participants
Chile: 5 advisors (4 Araucania, 1 Santiago)	Determine most important CSO activities to investigate			Question for participants:
	Develop interview questionnaires			Is our interpretation of the data accurate?
	Discuss appropriate research methods			

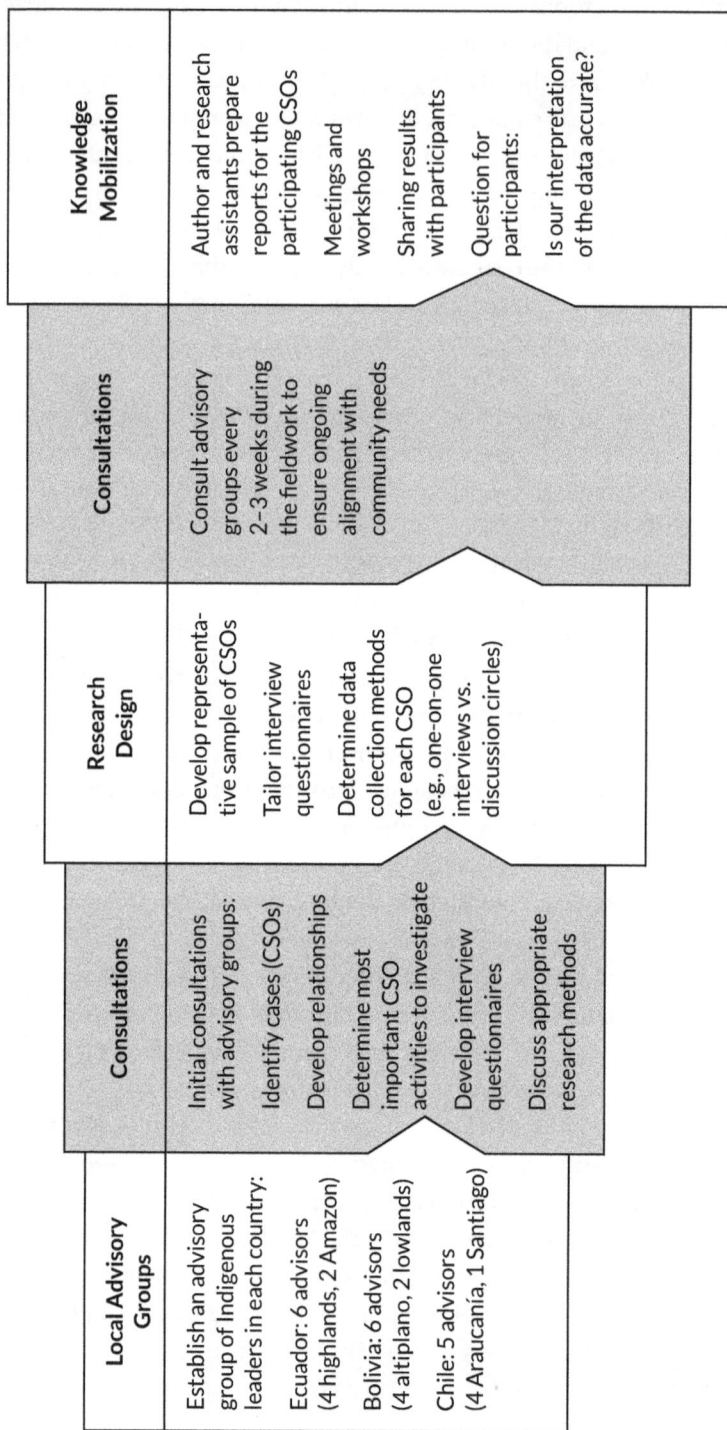

FIGURE I.1: Community-based participatory research (CBPR) process

that I carried out in 2009 in Ecuador and Bolivia, and in 2013 in Chile to highlight instances of continuity and change.

In early 2020, we conducted a qualitative analysis of social media content produced by Indigenous organizations, state agencies, and the mainstream media in each of the three countries. Data include social media publications and online news items collected during two specific protest events in each country. For Bolivia, these were the August 2018 demonstrations over development in the Isiboro Sécure National Park and Indigenous Territory (Territorio Indígena y Parque Nacional Isiboro-Sécure, TIPNIS)—a conflict that exacerbated existing tensions between opposition factions grouped under the Confederation of Indigenous Peoples of Bolivia (Confederación de Pueblos Indígenas de Bolivia, CIDOB) and Indigenous sectors aligned with the government of the Movement toward Socialism (Movimiento al Socialismo, MAS)—and the protests demanding the restoration of Evo Morales following the contested election of late 2019. For Ecuador, we examined the January 2019 protests in the province of Cotopaxi led by the Confederation of Indigenous Nationalities of Ecuador (Confederación de Nacionalidades Indígenas del Ecuador, CONAIE), and the larger nationwide uprisings that took place in October 2019. For Chile, we studied a series of protests in response to the murder of an unarmed Mapuche activist by state security forces in November 2018 and the antigovernment mobilizations that rocked the country in October and November 2019.

We analyzed 2,732 online publications, including 1,712 social media publications (1,236 tweets, 476 Facebook posts) and 1,020 online news articles. These data were collected from the ninety Indigenous CSOs, forty-six state agencies, and sixty media outlets. We selected government departments based on their level of interaction with Indigenous issues and/or matters related to national security. For example, in all three countries we analyzed social media content from the office of the president, the Interior Ministry, ministries related to security and natural resources, and so forth. We established a representative sample of media outlets in each country, with variation according to size, ownership, audience, ideological orientation, and level of government support. We focused on Twitter and Facebook content as these are the platforms Indigenous CSOs in South America use most frequently (Lupien 2020).

The analysis involved a two-step process. First, we collected the data using Netlytic and NVivo software. Netlytic is a cloud-based social network analysis tool developed by Toronto Metropolitan University's Social Media Lab. It allows us to automatically collect and analyze large amounts of text-based online content (Gruzd, Mai, and Kampen 2016). We also used NVivo to collect data from websites, particularly from media outlets. Second, we conducted a comparative qualitative analysis of the social media content retrieved to determine how Indigenous peoples, and their CSOs political and civic action, were framed. We developed an inductive coding scheme to identify linguistic and rhetorical mechanisms that could shed light on the questions discussed above. We used keyword analysis to identify recurring words surrounding Indigenous peoples, their activities and demands, to determine the extent to which these are used and normalized (Williams 1983). We used thematic analysis to look at questions, problems, and actors to see how they were framed. Two researchers reviewed content to create initial (inductive) thematic categories for the data (Were they framed positively, negatively, as noble, as violent, and so on? Where did they fit in categories such as the security/terrorism frame, social justice frame, etc.). We also identified the most popular hashtags (see Saxton et al. 2015). Two different Spanish-speaking research assistants then reviewed the analysis to reduce the amount of redundancy by merging the thematic categories and creating a detailed codebook that allowed for comparisons across the different actors involved (Indigenous CSOs, state actors, mainstream and alternative media). This allowed for an interrogation of the extent to which social media allow traditionally excluded groups such as Indigenous peoples to get their messages across. A summary of the results is provided in chapter 5, table 5.2, which compares the results of the analysis across the three jurisdictions.

Structure

The first chapter sets the stage for the reader by introducing the subject matter, engaging with relevant theory, and situating Indigenous collective action within the broader Latin American sociopolitical context. It includes a discussion of different forms of political action, identity politics, citizenship regimes, resource mobilization, political opportunities, and the use of ICTs by social movements. It also introduces my conceptualization of *Indigenous civil society* as a framework through which we can better understand Indigenous collective action in the twenty-first century. I present the problem to be studied throughout this book: How have Indigenous civil society and the sociopolitical context evolved, and what has been the impact of social media and ICTs? Drawing on relevant theoretical frameworks, I present the concept of *multiscalar positioning* to understand the complexity and diversity of their tactical repertoires.

The following three chapters explore Indigenous civil society in the three countries from the perspective of those who have been engaged in political and civic action on a daily basis. We learn how Indigenous CSOs are pursuing their goals, how and why their strategies have evolved over the past decade, and how ICTs affect their activities. We consider recent developments, including the 2019 events that mark the largest uprisings in the three countries in a generation. Following the three country chapters, the book reexamines the evidence presented in comparative perspective to shed light on what this research tells us about Latin American Indigenous political action in the twenty-first century. The book focuses on comparing the strategies and tactics used by Indigenous CSOs in the three countries, the mechanisms through which they engage with the state, and their use of ICTs. This involves delving more deeply into the variables that explain why some movements have been more successful than others. The conclusion discusses the broader implications of the book's findings for our understanding of collective action in the twenty-first century, including the impact of technologies such as social media.

1 Collective Action and Indigenous Civil Society
Theoretical Frameworks and Background

. . . .

On the morning of June 4, 1990, a large delegation of Huaorani people from Ecuador's Amazon region marched to the capital at Quito to demonstrate their anger over concessions granted by the government to oil companies. They were joined by thousands of Kichwa-speaking peoples from the Andes. They blocked roads leading to the capitals of seven provinces and prevented vehicular traffic on the Pan-American highway. Demonstrators occupied key locations in Quito and the Confederation of Indigenous Nationalities of Ecuador (Confederación de Nacionalidades Indígenas del Ecuador, CONAIE), which had coordinated the nationwide uprising, released a series of demands, including the granting of land titles to Indigenous communities. Within days, President Rodrigo Borja (1988–92) officially recognized CONAIE as a legitimate representative of Indigenous peoples and instructed his ministers to negotiate with its leaders. Two months later, on August 15, 1990, a group of Indigenous peoples from Bolivia's tropical lowlands marched to the Andean capital of La Paz. They were joined by communities from the highland *altiplano*, gathering supporters along the 650-mile trek. The size of the so-called March for Territory and Dignity was impossible to ignore. President Jaime Paz Zamora (1989–93) not only recognized Indigenous leaders by agreeing to meet with them but signed a series of decrees recognizing more than seven million hectares of Indigenous territories (Brysk 2000).

In Chile, the year 1990 marked the end of a brutal military dictatorship. While Indigenous organizations in Bolivia and Ecuador were demanding recognition and transforming their relationship with the state, Mapuche activists were building a network of associational spaces. By the end of the decade, organizations such as Coordinadora Arauco-Malleco (CAM) were engaging in a sustained, low-intensity conflict that challenged the hegemony of the state in Wallmapu, the Mapuche territories that the settlers gradually incorporated into Chile and Argentina.

Nearly three decades later, Indigenous protesters once again took over the streets of Quito, this time to contest a package of austerity measures introduced by the government of President Lenín Moreno (2017–21). In October 2019, Moreno and his cabinet were forced to flee the capital and to withdraw the unpopular set of policies. The national uprising, which involved both peaceful protest and violent disruptive action, did not end until the government reached an agreement with Indigenous organizations, clearly demonstrating their mobilizing capacity. At about the same time, the largest demonstrations since the transition to democracy spread across Chile. While Indigenous peoples did not assume a leadership role in these events, Mapuche civil society organizations (CSOs) encouraged their members to participate and observers noted the unprecedented appearance of Mapuche flags in the streets of Santiago. A month later, in November 2019, Bolivian cities were paralyzed by marches and roadblocks led by supporters of Evo Morales. The country's first Indigenous president had been forced to resign a month earlier following a contested election. He was subsequently replaced by a right-wing opposition leader who resorted to repression against Indigenous protesters, but disruptive collective action continued to threaten the stability of the interim administration. Morales's Movimiento al Socialismo (Movement toward Socialism, MAS) party returned to power through a landslide electoral victory in late 2020.

If we were to juxtapose aerial shots of the 1990s protests with footage from October and November 2019, we may conclude that little had changed in thirty years. From a distance, the protests looked very similar: streets filled with thousands of people, many wearing traditional Indigenous clothes and bowler hats; colorful Wiphala flags (a banner adopted by Aymara and Quechua communities in the Andes); placards representing various Indigenous organizations; roadblocks, fires, and smoke; and riot police carrying shields. But if we were to zoom in and look more closely, we would note important differences. In 2019, many of the Indigenous protesters would be glued to their cellphones. Some would be posting their perspectives on Twitter or Facebook, perhaps inviting friends to join them in the streets. Others would be filming the actions of security forces or the injuries of their fellow protesters. They would later upload these videos to YouTube. But the differences run much deeper than this. Less visible, but equally important, is the experience that Indigenous actors had gained, as well as the broader social and political changes that had shaped their countries in the twenty-first century.

The 1990 protests in Bolivia and Ecuador launched a protest cycle that lasted until the mid-2000s. Indigenous CSOs in both countries achieved significant policy concessions and by the late 2000s, they were participating in the drafting of new constitutions that enshrined many of the rights they had fought for. In Chile, the democratization process that had begun in 1990 opened political spaces. By the 2000s, Mapuche civil society had generated a panoply of new CSOs dedicated to reasserting identity, cultural expression, land rights, and autonomy.

But what has happened since these momentous events? The relative dearth of comparative research produced since the decline of the late-twentieth-century protest cycle leaves a gap in our knowledge of recent Indigenous collective action. While the cycle that began in 1990 had waned by about 2005, Indigenous civil society continued to develop, evolve, and to engage with and against the state. While not abandoning disruptive action, organizations diversified and expanded their strategies and tactics. This period witnessed the maturation of Indigenous organizations, fluctuating political opportunities, shifting citizenship regimes, and the expansion of the use of technologies for political engagement. These transformations have profoundly affected Indigenous civil society.

Historical research demonstrates that Indigenous actors have developed sophisticated forms of contention that incorporate both disruptive and "civic" strategies and tactics (Albó 2004; Colloredo-Mansfeld 2009; Platt 1982; Stern 1987; Tapia 2007). This book reveals how these two sides of Indigenous collective action have continued to evolve as CSOs build on their experiences in previous decades. In the twenty-first century, Indigenous movements have used an increasingly diverse repertoire of interconnected tactics. They have focused less on large-scale mobilization and disruptive action. They have concentrated on exercising the rights they gained "on paper" through previous struggles and on using the institutions they contributed to building in the 1990s and 2000s. Some, though not all, have been successful in pursuing their goals. These are exciting developments that provide significant lessons on how traditionally marginalized groups can make their voices heard. I demonstrate that Indigenous actors have developed a strong, diverse, and complex *civil society* that is distinct from but increasingly connected to the broader civil society in their respective states. Yet organizations have not abandoned the disruptive tactics that they relied on in the past. In 2019, Ecuador and Bolivia witnessed the largest Indigenous-led uprisings in a generation. These events demonstrate that Indigenous movements are still capable of large-scale mobilization and resistance when other approaches fail.

My comparative analysis reveals that organizations that successfully build on existing institutions and political opportunities and develop an interlocking repertoire of tactics across various scales (geographic, institutional, technological)—or what I call *multiscalar positioning*—are better able to achieve their desired outcomes. I also demonstrate that in addition to building on insights from the recent past, Indigenous movements have adapted to the evolving nature of political engagement in the twenty-first century, which increasingly centers on smartphones, social media, and other technologies. Indigenous organizations have enthusiastically adopted and adapted information and communication technologies (ICTs) for a variety of strategic purposes, while maintaining the traditional structures and practices that have served them well in the past. While ICTs create additional threats for marginalized actors, Indigenous organizations are becoming increasingly savvy users of these tools. This is demonstrated by the extensive use of social media in the 2019 uprisings. But Indigenous collective action has not morphed into the primarily online "networked" movements we have seen elsewhere, and this may in fact be one of Indigenous civil society's greatest strengths.

Collective Action and Indigenous Peoples: Conceptual and Theoretical Frameworks

Collective Action: Emergence and Development

In the late twentieth century, scholars rejected earlier conceptions of collective action as spontaneous occurrences of individuals reacting emotionally to circumstances they could not control (Della Porta and Diani 2006). McCarthy and Zald (1977) posit that movements emerge and grow where there are structures and resources in place that facilitate mobilization. These *mobilizing structures* include already existing organizations (formal and informal) such as churches and unions, as well as a range of everyday social spaces such as voluntary associations (Tilly 1987). Groups that wish to pursue a common goal build on the financial resources, leadership, organizational structure, technology, and social relationships already developed through these structures. *Political opportunity* theory posits that certain conditions foster the emergence of collective action. These include openness of the political system, stability of political alignments, the presence of allies or divisions within the elites, and the capacity of the state to repress mobilization (Tarrow 1998, 77–80). The concept has been broadened to demonstrate that in a globalized world, political opportunities may be available at the international level, where marginalized actors may be more likely to find sympathetic allies (Tarrow 1996).

Deborah Yashar's groundbreaking work (1998, 2005) notes that preexisting networks present in many parts of Latin America facilitated Indigenous mobilization by providing them with structures and resources on which to build. Movements emerged where political opportunities allowed them the associational space to mobilize. Brysk (2000) argues that mobilizing structures and political opportunities also included transnational networks that allowed Indigenous groups to develop international collaborations in the 1990s. These allies provided them with (among other things) information, financial and legal support, and access to international norms they could use to frame their discourse.

Collective action also entails the strategic construction of *collective identity*, a process that requires ongoing negotiation but allows activists to unite diverse individuals based on a shared vision (Kauffman 1990; Melucci 1989; Snow and Benford 1988). The identity that drove Indigenous collective action at the end of the twentieth century did not reemerge from a pre-Colombian past. Rather, it was strategically developed by Indigenous leaders through discourse, performances, and symbols such as the colorful Wiphala flag (Canessa 2014; Lucero 2007; Paige 2020). Yashar's work suggests that Indigenous collective action was most successful when the construction of a sense of collective identity was combined with efficient resource mobilization strategies and favorable political opportunity windows (Yashar 2005, 2007). But she also recognizes the centrality of citizenship to identity and collective action.

Citizenship is a contested terrain in Latin America, where Indigenous peoples have been excluded from full citizenship for the past five centuries (Antileo Baeza et al. 2015; Rivera Cusicanqui 2012, 2020). Citizenship is a multidimensional concept that encompasses membership in a nation or ethnic group, identity, and a series of rights and duties. T. H. Marshall's still influential (1950) essay conceives of three types of citizenship rights: *civil rights* (the first to be established in modern democracies, including free speech, freedom of religion, property ownership, and equal treatment under the law); *political rights* (the right to vote, run for office, and engage in civil society); and *social rights* (having one's basic human needs met, reflected in the rise of the welfare state). The liberal model of citizenship, formulated by thinkers such as Hobbes and Locke, emphasizes individual civil and political rights but relatively limits social rights (Rawls 1993; Walzer 1989). In contrast, the republican tradition, with its roots in Ancient Athens and further developed by Rousseau, establishes the concept of the "common good," and affirms that citizens must play an active role in the political arena, which can happen only when there is some degree of social citizenship (Miller 2000; Pateman 1970).

Yashar (2005) argues that the shift from corporatism, a citizenship regime that provided links between groups and the state, to neoliberalism, with its focus on individual autonomy, encouraged mobilization by simultaneously expanding political opportunities while restricting access points to the state. The corporatist regime that emerged in Bolivia and Ecuador in the 1950s to 1970s provided some measure of social citizenship. The following neoliberal era not only withdrew social rights but challenged local autonomy by threatening collective land rights, which are an essential part of Indigenous identity.

While the liberal conception is reflected in the design of Latin America's political institutions, Indigenous activists have sought to redefine citizenship from the 1990s onward (Lupien 2011; Postero 2007; Postero and Zamosc 2004; Rivera Cusicanqui 2020). One dimension of this struggle is the expansion of citizenship rights, from (neoliberal) political and economic to social. The following chapters demonstrate that Indigenous CSOs share this goal with other popular sector actors and are often able to expand political opportunities by forging alliances around demands for social citizenship. But the CSOs have increasingly challenged the fundamental premise of the liberal regime that imposes a single, unifying identity within state boundaries. They demand a more inclusive citizenship that recognizes the plurinational nature of their societies. Aymara intellectual Silvia Rivera Cusicanqui (2020) argues that Indigenous peoples have been offered conditional inclusion that confines them to cultural minority status. Neoliberal multiculturalism, she writes, allows Westernized elites to make nonthreatening concessions to cultural recognition while maintaining their power and leaving intact the citizenship regime upon which it is based. For Luis Tapia (2006, 2007), the historical process that constructs citizenship includes different sets of rights but also the design of institutions that support the exercise of those rights. A "monocultural state" limits democratization; full citizenship entails recognizing the equality of different forms of governance and the right to self- and cogovernance. This requires reforming the state to include different forms of governance, including communitarian models. For Manuela Picq (2018), an inclusive citizenship would require not only social rights, but the recognition of collective rights that challenge the liberal regime and its institutions, and the recognition of autonomous forms of governance outside of the liberal state.

Latin American states have long situated Indigenous populations outside of citizenship, which has had the unintended consequence of encouraging the development of local, autonomous governance structures and practices (Hoetmer 2017). Indigenous collective action from the final decade of the twentieth century to the present has disrupted the citizenship regime of neoliberal multiculturalism. It combines a struggle for social citizenship for all with demands for a new, inclusive, multi-faceted citizenship regime. As Rivera Cusicanqui writes, Indigenous citizenship does not favor liberal homogeneity, but the recognition of difference. Yet it also seeks to reshape the state according to Indigenous worldviews (Rivera Cusicanqui 2012, 2020). This book sheds light on how Indigenous civil society has pursued these goals in the twenty-first century, and how shifting citizenship regimes, political opportunities, and resource mobilization capacities have affected their strategies and tactics.

Forms of Collective Action

Collective action takes many forms and occurs in multiple, overlapping spaces. The concept of *civil society* refers to autonomous associations that operate in the public sphere. These are situated between the state and private individuals and serve to mediate between the two (Meyer and Tarrow 1998; Tarrow 1994). Studies of civil society emphasize the role it can play in working with the state to address problems through institutional channels (Cohen and Arato 1992; Collier and Handlin 2009; Oxhorn 2010, 2011, 2012; Seligman 1992; Taylor 1990). *Social movements* are broad campaigns that include networks and individuals with similar values and goals (Della Porta and Diani 2006). Social movements are often presented as the contestatory face of civil society; della Porta (2014) notes that while social movements are associated with radical claims, civil society organizations are considered moderate and reasonable.

These two forms of political participation roughly map onto another framework for understanding forms of political action. In the Latin American context, Alvarez and her colleagues (2017) describe two "faces of cultural-political struggles": "uncivic" activism and civic participation through Third Sector and state mechanisms, or what they call the "civil society agenda." Civic participation is associated with rational actors and respect for liberal democratic norms; those who play by the state's rules are legitimate and worthy of being invited into its spaces. "Uncivic" action is discursively linked to violence and disorder; those involved are subjected to criminalization and repression (Alvarez et al. 2017; Hale 2004).

The normative discourse that shapes our understanding of these two faces of political action is often reproduced and interpreted through an intersectional lens. Light-skinned middle-and upper-class opponents of leftist governments, for example, frame themselves as civil society while labeling marginalized and racialized actors as irrational mobs (Duno 2011; Fernandes 2010; García-Guadilla 2007). When applied to Indigenous peoples, the civic/uncivic dichotomy distinguishes between the *permitidos* (literally, "permitted ones") who do not challenge the established order or its institutions, and the dangerous, unauthorized *no permitidos*, who refuse to play by these rules (Gustafson 2017; Hale 2004; Hale and Millamán 2006; Lucero 2008; Richards 2010). According to Alvarez and her colleagues, the civil society agenda promotes institutional arrangements that provide multiple invited spaces for private interests and "authorized" sectors of civil society (the *permitidos*) to participate in the policy process while simultaneously disciplining citizens who refuse to play by the rules (Hale and Millamán 2006). It is part of a "new rationality for governance" through which the state can channel participation, lower the cost of implementing policies, promote citizen self-regulation, and depoliticize conflict (Alvarez et al. 2017; Baiocchi 2017).

But scholars note that in Latin America, collective action straddles the line between uncivic disruption in the streets and participation in state institutions, and many of these studies draw extensively on the tactical innovations of Indigenous peoples (Alvarez et al. 2017; Canessa 2012; Colloredo-Mansfeld 2009; Picq 2018). Indigenous communities have been aware of the benefits of combining different forms of contention for centuries (Mallon 1992; Platt 1982; Stern 1987; Thomson and Hylton 2007; Thomson 2002). Students of Andean politics in particular note how Indigenous actors have been trailblazers when it comes to engaging in institutional practices while contesting these same structures from the outside through land occupations, marches, and other forms of civil disobedience. Leaders understand the value of using a combination of unruly actions and civic participation (Albó 2004; Colloredo-Mansfeld 2009; León 2001; Rivera Cusicanqui 1987, 2012; Tapia 2007).

Indigenous Collective Action: Contention and Resistance

Indigenous peoples in postconquest Latin America have never been passive subjects. They have adapted their identities to evolving circumstances and have developed unique and complex forms of collective action. Historians have documented more than 100 uprisings in the region during the eighteenth century alone, including the 1780–82 Túpac Amaru uprising in the viceroyalty of Peru (Becker 2008; Lucero 2008). These uprisings tend to rise and fall in waves, or what social movement theorists describe as protest cycles. Modern examples in Latin America include the Indigenous uprisings of the 1990s to early 2000s, as well as the antineoliberalism movements that culminated in the election of Pink Tide governments in the 2000s (Silva 2009). Della Porta (2013) divides protest cycles into an ascending phase, a peak, and a declining phase. Decline may occur for a variety of reasons: state repression, efforts to divide a movement (often through co-optation of certain sectors or through selective repression of some actors and acceptance of others), or simply due to participant fatigue or disillusionment (Della Porta and Diani 2006; Della Porta and Rucht 2002).

The literature produced on the 1990–2005 Indigenous protest cycle in the Andes demonstrates that Indigenous movements achieved significant outcomes through mass mobilization and other forms of "uncivic" action (Paige 2020; Yashar 2005). In Ecuador, regional organizations such as Confederation of Indigenous Nationalities of the Ecuadorian Amazon (Confederación de las Nacionalidades Indígenas de la Amazonia Ecuatoriana, CONFENIAE) and the highlands Ecuador Runakunapak Rikcharimuy (ECUARUNARI) launched CONAIE in 1986 as the first national umbrella Indigenous organization in Latin America (Tibán and Ilaquiche 2008). The CONAIE led the 1990 Indigenous National Uprising, then the largest mobilization in Ecuador's modern history. This and subsequent revolts achieved significant policy outcomes and demonstrated the power of Latin America's strongest Indigenous movement of the 1990s (Selverston-Scher 2001; Yashar 2005).

In Bolivia, highland and lowland peoples developed two strong national-regional bodies, respectively, the Syndical Confederation of Rural Workers of Bolivia (Confederación Sindical Única de Trabajadores Campesinos de Bolivia, CSUTCB) and the Confederation of Indigenous Peoples of Bolivia (Confederación de Pueblos Indígenas de Bolivia, CIDOB). Numerous other organizations are dedicated to specific issues, such as the right to grow coca. Bolstered by a series of victories in the 1990s, and the related expansion of mobilizing structures and political opportunities, Indigenous organizations played a key role in the so-called Water War (1999–2000), which forced the right-wing administration of Hugo Banzer (1997–2001) to reverse course on a decision that would have privatized water in the city of Cochabamba (Dangl 2007; Fabricant and Hicks 2013). In both countries, Indigenous movements led cross-sectoral uprisings that resulted in the resignation of several presidents.

Ever since Spanish *conquistador* Pedro de Valdivia's first incursions into what is now southern Chile in the 1540s and 1550s, Mapuche history has been marked by fierce resistance. For the next three centuries, the Mapuche continued to successfully resist Spanish rule, engaging in a low-intensity war against the colonial regime with regular attacks on its forts and settlements in Wallmapu (Millalen Paillal 2012; Pichinao Huenchuleo 2012). Their relative autonomy constitutes a sharp contrast to the Andean peoples of Bolivia and Ecuador, who were conquered and incorporated into the Viceroyalty of Peru from the 1500s (Bastías Rebolledo 2009; Richards 2013). The Pinochet era (1973–90) was a trying time for Indigenous peoples. The state seized millions of hectares of Mapuche land in the Araucanía (a region of present-day Chile which contains a signification part of Wallmapu) and turned it over to forestry and timber companies. This exacerbated the poor socioeconomic conditions of the local population (Bastías Rebolledo 2016; Richards 2010). The modern Mapuche Conflict emerged following the restoration of liberal democracy in 1990 (Antileo Baeza et al. 2015; Cayuqueo 2018). CAM has been one of the most polarizing Mapuche political organizations. Since its first attack on forestry industry property in 1997, CAM and its territorially based militant groups (OTRs) have engaged in highly "uncivic" forms of resistance, including land occupations and sabotage (Cayuqueo 2018; Richards 2010). This period marks the beginning of a shift from taking back land to a struggle over territory, autonomy and "national liberation" (Millalen Paillal 2012; Pairicán 2013). But while CAM has received considerable attention from media and security forces, other sectors of Mapuche civil society have continued to deploy a more diverse set of tactics to pursue their goals.

Indigenous Collective Action:
Civic Participation and Invited Spaces

Some have argued that by the end of the twentieth century, protest had become a defining characteristic of Indigenous identity (Field 1994; Urban and Sherzer 1991). But Indigenous collective action has never been limited to the "uncivic"; Indigenous actors have claimed rights through colonial legal institutions as far back as the sixteenth century (Picq 2018). Indigenous peoples remained disenfranchised in the new Latin American republics founded in the nineteenth century but were heavily involved in unions and leftist collective action projects that sought to organize rural workers in the twentieth century (Paige 2020).

Indigenous civil society comprises a diversity of organizations that have developed an increasingly varied repertoire. These include legal action, media campaigns, and international lobbying, as well as involvement in state institutions and participatory mechanisms (Hoetmer 2017; Lupien 2011). In Bolivia and Ecuador, Indigenous peoples have long sought to be included in the state, rather than to exclude themselves from it (Canessa 2007, 2012). Bolivian scholar Luis Tapia notes that organizations that participate in marches and other disruptive tactics identify as contestatory social movements; but many of the same collectivities (syndicates, neighborhood councils, Indigenous assemblies) operate in civil society and engage with state mechanisms on a daily basis, moving between the two spheres (Tapia 2007). Indigenous communities have also become adept at adopting state discourse and conventional institutional design to local circumstances (Colloredo-Mansfeld 2009; Lyall, Colloredo-Mansfeld, and Rousseau 2018; Picq 2018).

There are different approaches to civic participation between and within the three countries. Highland communities in Bolivia and Ecuador have been shaped by contact with the state through corporatist incorporation as peasants and through unions and class-based organizing. The weak presence of state and other actors in the lowlands has left room for the emergence of collective action based more on ethnic identity than on class, which influenced the development of distinct organizations, although in Bolivia mobilizing structures were afforded less room than in Ecuador because the Bolivian lowlands are also the site of that country's economic elites (Lucero 2008). Liberal reforms implemented by neoliberal administrations in the 1990s had the unintended consequence of opening political opportunities for Indigenous actors (Postero 2007; Yashar 2005). In Bolivia, the Sánchez de Lozada government's 2004 Popular Participation Law (Ley de Participación Popular, LPP) delegated power and resources to local levels of government, creating 300 new rural municipalities (many of which were majority Indigenous) and directing 20 percent of state revenues to this level, to be distributed according to population numbers. The LPP recognized already existing traditional and popular forms of organization; the so-called territorial base organizations (organizaciónes territoriales del base, OTBs) could be governed according to the local customs (*usos y costumbres*). The law also created local governance roles for Indigenous communities through oversight committees. Mechanisms such as the OTBs provided Indigenous actors with political experience at the local level (Postero 2007). Bolivia is unique in Latin America in that it witnessed the rise to power of a social-movement-based, Indigenous-led political party, the MAS, founded in 1997 by Aymara leader Evo Morales with activists from the CSUTCB and other CSOs. Under the MAS, Indigenous CSOs aligned with the government have increasingly inserted themselves into bureaucratic spaces, while maintaining and expanding local governance practices based on both traditional and state-supported institutional arrangements (Gustafson 2017; Paige 2020).

In Ecuador, highland Indigenous communities adapted the 1937 Ley de Comunas following a period of land reform in 1964–73. The law supported the recognition of peasant communes, creating a set of "standard" tools and institutions for administering community affairs, including regulating internal conflicts (Becker 1999; Colloredo-Mansfeld 2009). Communes provided Indigenous communities with a recognized form of local governance through which they could interact with the state as "legitimate" actors. This also created mobilizing structures which CONAIE and other CSOs would later rely on to build a strong civil society.

In Wallmapu, and in particular the Araucanía region most frequently associated with political violence, Mapuche organizations have engaged across the spectrum of civil society and disruptive social movements. Mapuche journalist and activist Pedro Cayuqueo (2018) reminds us that Mapuche political violence is a recent phenomenon that began with the founding of CAM in 1998. In the preceding centuries, the political-institutional route was the norm for Mapuche activists. Prior to the "pacification" of the region by the Chilean state in the 1880s, a series of parliaments served as mechanisms for mediation between Mapuche leaders and the government in Santiago. Territorial autonomy was negotiated and recognized through these institutions (Pichinao Huenchuleo 2012). In the twentieth century, mechanisms included organic base organizations of direct democracy such as communal peasant councils, created in the 1970s to support rural mobilization and to integrate people into a (class-based) movement (Cárcamo Hernández 2016). Yet even in the CAM era, civic participation has continued. Cayuqueo (2018) points to the growing number of Mapuche mayors; arguing that capturing local governments is key to learning how to govern. But Mapuche civil society includes a growing and diverse set of associational spaces, both urban and rural, and some of which involve the appropriation of state-favored models (Curivil Bravo 2012).

Indigenous civic participation in all three countries was closely related to unions and leftist social movements in the twentieth century. In the 2010s, the terrain of Indigenous political activity is far more diverse and includes both invited state-society interface spaces and Third Sector organizations. In the 1990s, Latin America witnessed an explosion of institutions designed to encourage popular participation in decision making, prompting some observers to contend that the source of democratic innovation has moved from North to South (Fung 2011). The Pink Tide governments in Bolivia (Morales) and Ecuador (Correa) claimed a strong ideological commitment to participatory democracy and created mechanisms to implement this vision at the local level (Lupien 2018a; Ramírez and Welp 2011). In Chile, often cited as a model of liberal representative democracy but one of the least participatory countries in Latin America, President Michelle Bachelet (2006–10) declared citizen participation to be an important goal, although participation in the Chilean context tends to be framed as an instrument for effective governance and policymaking, and not as an alternative to representative democracy (Cameron, Hershberg, and Sharpe 2012; Cleuren 2007). Her administration promoted concrete changes, including the adoption of a new national law that recognizes citizen participation as a right and provides stronger legal recognition and support to institutions such as neighborhood councils (Lupien 2018). Some authors argue that participatory mechanisms can lead to an improvement of material conditions, more equitable policy outcomes and greater access to public goods and services for marginalized sectors (Avritzer 2002; Cohen and Fung 2004; Goldfrank 2011). Others focus on the "spillover effects" of citizen participation. They argue that direct involvement in decision making leads to an improved perception of the legitimacy of democracy and an increased sense of political efficacy among participants (Altschuler and Corrales 2012; Barber 1984; Pateman 1970).

As Alvarez and her colleagues (2017) note, the new participatory architecture in Latin America has provided opportunities for traditionally excluded actors to interact with the state. Invited spaces for collaborations between state actors and civil society allow the latter to combine strategies, tactics, and logics of social movements with the administrative and participatory practices of local governance, which can disrupt the state-civil society dichotomy (Pallares 2017). But some warn that participatory democracy initiatives are aligned with the "civil society agenda" that, rather than facilitating decolonization of the public sphere, serves to discipline and depoliticize social actors (Avritzer 2017; Laó-Montes 2017). According to this perspective, we must critically interrogate normative assumptions about the intrinsic good of public participatory spaces, as they may in fact constrain democracy through clientelistic practices, compliance, and dividing actors in to "civic" and "uncivic" categories. But Pallares (2017) takes a nuanced approach, arguing that civil society groups use participatory practices as a means of gaining legitimacy while continuing to oppose the state from the outside.

Indigenous actors have not simply integrated their political practices into state institutions; they have adapted and reshaped them to serve their communities' needs. In so doing, they do not seek to dismantle the state, but to pursue deterritorialized forms of sovereignty, or pockets of legal autonomy within the state (Picq 2018). What Colloredo-Mansfeld (2009) refers to as "vernacular statecraft" involves the adaptation of conventional institutional design to local circumstances. Beginning with the creation of legally sanctioned communes in the 1960s, Kichwa peoples in the Ecuadorian Andes gradually positioned these structures along the lines laid out by the state, appropriating and adjusting institutional design features so that they are "readable" to each other and to the state (Colloredo-Mansfeld 2009). At the same time, Indigenous communities have sought to relocate authority to the local level (through Indigenous justice, for example) and to disrupt the state-centric view of sovereignty. In this way, community and the state become deeply intertwined. This represents strategic appropriation rather than full commitment to state-led development projects (Lyall, Colloredo-Mansfeld, and Rousseau 2018). It is one of the key features and unique characteristics of Indigenous civil society.

Indigenous Collective Action in the Twenty-First Century

Social and political changes in the late 2000s and 2010s have had a profound impact on Indigenous civil society. These are explored throughout this book and include the development of a new citizenship regime in Bolivia and Ecuador, the digital revolution, and the legislative context that shapes the ability of civil society to use new technologies to pursue their goals.

Indigenous civil society is constantly acquiring new forms, crossing blurred lines, and negotiating fluid spaces. CSOs deploy diverse tactics and occupy different spaces at different times (or at once); they consist of both the civic and contestatory, and can complement each other or sometimes work at cross-purposes. Engaging in state-sanctioned participatory mechanisms may incorporate and depoliticize participation but while these concerns are not unfounded, they overlook how shrewd and politically savvy Indigenous civil society actors have become. They are increasingly adept at taking advantage of "civic" participation spaces and appropriating state discourse to advance their agenda. Even when they are not in control, Indigenous actors can use these spaces to have influence or adapt them for their own purposes. Their engagement in these mechanisms introduces alternative cultures of participation; these can in turn reshape the invited spaces. Their deliberate efforts challenge labels of co-optation to describe the relationship between political actors and civil society. Before expanding on the characteristics and evolution of Indigenous civil society, I will explore the changing nature of collective action in the twenty-first century, and in particular the extent to which ICTs have transformed the nature of political and civic action.

Collective Action in the Social Media Age: Digital Technologies and Networked Movements

Indigenous peoples have actively appropriated technologies, particularly radio and video, for collective action, cultural revitalization, and self-representation (Ginsburg 2000, 2008; Salazar 2002, 2011). The literature provides a rich portrait of the variety and diversity of purposes for which Indigenous actors have used these tools. Some argue that these technologies are imbued with Western worldviews that shape how they can be used for representation (Faris 1992). Others respond that Indigenous media can be used to create alternative public spheres (Salazar and Córdova 2008), foster agency and self-determination (Córdova 2014), and promote narratives made invisible by hegemonic discourse (Wortham 2013).

Indigenous community radio has long been an important tool for the creation and dissemination of local content and alternative narratives (Cárcamo-Huechante 2013; Cárcamo-Huechante and Paillan Coñuepan 2012; Lozada and Kúncar 2004). In contrast to the tightly controlled content creation process of commercial media, community radio involves a high level of participation from local communities. It is a relatively inexpensive technology to set up and use, it allows for communication among population groups that lack access to infrastructure, and it supports oral cultural practices (Lupien 2017). Bolivian miners' radio stations were pioneers in creating a space for counterpower. They were strongly local in character and focused on events of everyday life including local meetings, sporting events and social celebrations, but also engaged in the political sphere (O'Connor 1990). In Ecuador, Indigenous community radio stations have played a key role in the recovery of public spaces, the decentralization of information, and the dissemination of a critical pedagogy influenced by liberation theology (Cerbino and Belotti 2016; Matrone 2019). Community radio and popular communication pedagogy helped to foster the development of the country's Indigenous movement and played a key role in the 1990 uprising in rural provinces such as Chimborazo (Torres 2019). Mapuche radio has also served as a site of counterpower by disseminating cultural traditions and alternative narratives in the context of a media market dominated by private conglomerates (Cárcamo-Huechante and Paillan Coñuepan 2012).

Terence Turner (2002) demonstrates how remote communities have used video technology to raise awareness of their causes, to document state-community relations and instances of repression, and to ensure accountability by recording agreements made with government actors. Turner sees Indigenous media as a political project to leverage greater agency. Low-cost and accessible visual media provide tools for self-representation, reaching global publics and transforming Indigenous identities on their own terms (Turner 1995). Demonstrating how Indigenous peoples apply their own aesthetics and epistemologies to the use of video, Turner rejects narratives that view technologies as a threat to culture. He insists that Indigenous communities are less concerned with cultural conservation than they are with maintaining sovereignty over representation (Turner 1992).

Faye Ginsburg (1991) posits that Indigenous peoples appropriate and transform media tools to their own ends. She argues that rather than posing a threat to culture and values, technology can reinforce and transform cultural identities. Other scholars agree that Indigenous media can have transformative effects through both the process of production (which is empowering) and impact on the public sphere. The documentary has become the "weapon of choice" for Mapuche activists against extraction and development; they use it, among other goals, to make human rights violations visible (Córdova 2018). Dominant narratives confine Indigenous peoples to an imagined past; technology can help to reposition these temporal imaginings (Lempert 2018; Schiwy 2009).

This literature demonstrates that Indigenous peoples have long taken on a proactive role in using technology to pursue collective goals. As Ginsburg (2016) argues, Indigenous media alone cannot overcome unequal power relationships but they can be used to "speak back to structures of power that misrepresent Indigenous peoples." But Salazar (2015) points out that the Indigenous media literature has not engaged enough with collective action and stresses that more attention to political activism is needed.

Perhaps the biggest impact on collective action between the 1990s and the 2010s has been the advent of the Internet age and, more recently, of social media. Observers argue that digital technologies have transformed the very nature of collective action. Political engagement has increasingly moved online (Bennett and Segerberg 2013; Biekart and Fowler 2013; Bimber 2017; Castells 2015; Lilleker and Koc-Michalska 2017; Murschetz 2018). Digital technologies allow organizers to mobilize large numbers of unrelated people quickly and cheaply, an affordance Bimber (1998) calls "accelerated pluralism." Diffusion and use of these tools, according to cyber optimists, favor democratization, citizen engagement, and autonomy of civil society (Castells 2015; Howard 2010). Digital technologies can help activists to spread information and emotional appeals, coordinate logistics, disseminate news about conditions and events, and reach international audiences, which may alter the political opportunity structure by putting pressure on governments (Larson 2019).

Authors such as Manuel Castells (2015) and Zeynep Tufekci (2017) believe that digital technologies have created an entirely new type of social movement: participatory, nonhierarchical, and "networked" through new technologies. These networked movements reject formal leadership and organizations, distrust political parties, and seek to circumvent the mainstream media. Castells, one of the most influential and prolific writers on the subject, has long argued that the Internet embodies the culture of freedom, as it was built to withstand control by elites who seek to disrupt the flow of information (Castells 2001). Drawing on cases such as the Arab Spring and the Spanish Indignados movement, he paints a vibrant picture of leaderless, horizontal, decentralized networks interacting across different nodes. Activists make decisions though participatory assemblies—conceptually connected to free spaces on the Internet—but do not produce formal political programs, although they are unified by their desire to transform the democratic process. They view formal organizations as constrictive and they eschew electoral and other forms of civil participation (Bennett 2014; Castells 2015).

Castells believes that the ability to reach a wide audience at low cost facilitates collective action. But he goes a step further, arguing that digital technologies are a site of counter power where social actors can challenge established institutions and discourse, demand representation, and promote their own demands. Counter power requires autonomous communication and spaces free from those who hold power. The institutional public sphere is occupied by the powerful; social movements must construct a new public space. Social media facilitate horizontal networks that are difficult for governments to control; they provide spaces for unfettered deliberation and coordination. Castells acknowledges that "the influence of these movements on policy is usually limited" (Castells 2015, 236). But he believes that they are able to raise consciousness and perhaps eventually have an impact on politicians.

Tufekci (2017, xi) agrees that a new era of collective action has emerged in the 2010s. She describes this as a "historical transition, a shift in how social movements operate and in how powerful actors respond. . . . A reconfiguration of publics and movements through the assimilation of digital technologies." In this "networked public sphere," ordinary citizens can debate ideas, document incidents, spread news, and respond to corporate or state media. In the past, it was difficult for actors to organize and mobilize without formal organizations and hierarchical leadership. In these "new" movements, very little is accomplished through traditional organizations. Tools such as Twitter facilitate and accelerate this process, encouraging ad hoc action by whoever shows up.

But Tufekci offers a more critical and nuanced analysis of the impact of digital technologies on collective action. The Internet, she argues, allows movements to grow rapidly, but without building formal and informal mobilizing structures and collective capacities that prepare them for the challenges they will inevitably face. In contrast to the past, when movements were built up over a long period and involved meticulous and sustained organizing work, today's movements are organized online. New movements can scale up quickly and deal with logistics without building up this prior organizational capacity. But she claims that with speed comes a particular weakness: their ability to pursue goals and change tactics beyond the original protest event is limited as they are unable to sustain the momentum. Their lack of experience and collective decision-making capacity renders them fragile in the longer term. For these reasons, they tend to rely on the same tactics to recapture their initial success, and the lack of leadership means that there is nobody to negotiate with the state and press claims in a sustained manner. Tactical innovation, she argues, is the key to maintaining momentum and pursuing long-term goals.

We have seen that throughout the twentieth century, Indigenous communities adopted and appropriated technologies such as radio and video to engage in the public sphere and to create sites of counterpower. In the twenty-first century, Indigenous groups have built on "older" twentieth-century technologies to pursue some of the same goals using new digital tools. While most studies on the use of ICTs by social movements focus on Western democracies (Breuer and Groshek 2014), a growing body of literature examines how Indigenous peoples have actively appropriated digital platforms. Tufekci (2017) identifies Indigenous Zapatistas in Mexico as the earliest global movement of the Internet era. Studies have looked at using digital media a tool of self-representation to communicate messages independently of the mainstream media, and to challenge dominant stereotypes (Basanta 2013; Petray 2013; Soriano 2012; Wilson, Carlson, and Sciascia 2017); communicate with other Indigenous groups and mobilize supporters and allies (Virtanen 2015); create new forms of cultural expression (Landzelius 2006); produce news and information that cover issues that matter to Indigenous people (Wilson, Carlson and Sciascia 2017); engage in political campaigning (Basanta 2013; Budka 2019; González Lorenzo 2009; Monasterios 2003; Wagner 2018); and support participatory democracy initiatives (Cruz and Gravante 2018). Indigenous communities seek to use digital tools for both cultural preservation and change, and as part of an ongoing strategy of resisting and rewriting colonial narratives (Ginsburg 2016; Hinzo and Clark 2019; Landzelius 2006; Wilson, Carlson, and Sciascia 2017). But this does not mean that they have or will become the types of "networked movements" that supposedly characterize collective action in the twenty-first century.

Indigenous Collective Action:
A Different Kind of Networked Movement

Students of collective action in the 2010s posit that networked movements are fundamentally different from those of the past and operate under a different logic (Bennett and Segerberg 2013; Castells 2015; Howard and Hussain 2013; Larson 2019; Tufekci 2017). But they focus on primarily "born digital" movements rather than on existing movements that adopt digital technologies as an "add on." They also study high-profile, but generally ephemeral movements such as Occupy, the Arab Spring, or the Spanish Indignados. This literature rarely engages with Indigenous collective action and many of the characteristics they attribute to "new" movements do not apply to contemporary Indigenous CSOs. Indigenous civil society demonstrates both strengths and weaknesses that do not conform to understandings of how collective action has evolved in the Internet age.

When I first met with members of the Indigenous advisory group who had agreed to support my research in Ecuador, I expressed my interest in focusing on the use of digital technologies by Indigenous CSOs. Their first response was to warn, "You may not have much to write about. ICTs make up a small part of who we are and what we do" (meeting, Quito, June 2016). Members of the advisory council I worked with in Bolivia were also adamant when I met them nearly two years later. The youngest member, a leader from the eastern Beni department, insisted, "If you want to understand Indigenous organizations and politics, you should really focus on all the things we do and try to see how ICTs fit into our work, rather than starting with ICTs. You will get a much richer picture this way" (meeting, El Alto, May 2018). These suggestions set me on a different course from the one I had originally intended, and this theme—that ICTs are a relatively small part of a much bigger picture—played out throughout the course of my fieldwork.

Indigenous CSOs are increasingly adopting digital technologies but look nothing like the diffused networked movements discussed in the literature. They continue to rely on strong organizations and traditional social movement tactics, yet they have evolved considerably since the peak of the 1990–2005 protest cycle. They are thoroughly "modern" despite their (relatively) limited reliance on ICTs and social media. In Latin America, Indigenous collective action is bolstered by strong mobilizing structures, experienced leadership, in-person contact, sense of place, and a strong collective identity. Much of the literature on new movements suggests that these are the very characteristics that distinguish movements of the "past" from those of the present.

As the following chapters demonstrate, formal organizations and strong leadership continue to play a key role in Indigenous civil society, and these are among its greatest strengths. Tufekci (2017) writes of the collapse of gatekeeper organizations and applies this broadly to social movements. Both she and Castells distinguish between "new" (networked) movements and "old" organization-based collective action. Networked activists distrust formal leadership and vertical organizations, which are no longer needed because digital technologies can now be used to coordinate action and distribute information (Castells 2015). But inherent in these observations is a normative assumption that formal organizations are always top down. While some Indigenous CSOs do operate according to a vertical organizational structure, many others do not and in fact are designed to ensure that decisions are made in community assemblies and communicated up to higher levels. Castells, Tufekci and others write of citizens' assemblies that rely on horizontalist meeting techniques and consensus decision-making process in movements such as Occupy and the Indignados. But in many Indigenous communities, these communitarian governance practices were common long before the Internet age (Curivil Bravo 2012; Rivera Cusicanqui 2020; Tapia 2006, 2007).

The networked movements are described as diffuse and unstructured; they have succeeded in bringing together potentially powerful coalitions with limited identity and ideological ties (Bennett 2013; Biekart and Fowler 2013; Langman 2005). Participation is far more individualized, with collective identity and ideology taking a back seat to personalized action frames (Bennett and Segerberg 2011). This "networked individualism" is replacing not only hierarchical organizations, but collective social narratives (Bennett 2014; Calderón and Castells 2020). The overreaching theme of these movements is a call for new forms of political deliberation, representation, and decision making. Indigenous actors have been pursuing these goals for decades. The following chapters will demonstrate that collective identity remains at the heart of Indigenous political action. But this does not mean, as is often assumed, that Indigenous identity draws its inspiration from the past. To the contrary, we will see that Indigenous identity continues to evolve and to adapt to changing circumstances.

Networked communities are based on affinities rather than on geography; digital technologies can build connections between disparate actors with an overreaching societal vision (Tufekci 2017). In contrast, Indigenous identity is attached to place, territory, and natural resources (Canessa 2012, 2014; Ginsburg 1991). In Latin America, relationships within and between Indigenous communities are already strong. They may be enhanced or facilitated by technologies, but these connections have been carefully constructed by CSOs over the past few decades (Gustafson 2017; Paige 2020). We will hear from Indigenous leaders in the following chapters who stress the importance of relationships and the need for face-to-face contact. Among Indigenous people of all ages, there is a strong belief that talking to people over a computer screen does not reproduce these types of bonds, but rather diminishes the nature of these interpersonal relationships.

Most of the studies of networked movements describe activists as young, urban, educated, and technologically savvy individuals (Castells 2015; Howard and Hussain 2013; Larson 2019; Tufekci 2017). This rather narrow demographic does not fit the profile of many Indigenous communities. While many Indigenous youth have migrated to large urban centers and a growing number are pursuing postsecondary education, communities are often situated in rural or poor urban neighborhoods. When engaging with Indigenous CSOs, we must also consider the role of Elders in community governance, decision making, and knowledge production. While the networked movements are characterized by youth, Elders continue to play a key role in Indigenous CSOs as they are viewed as knowledge holders. In any case, community leaders point out that due to a lack of resources and infrastructure, even Indigenous youths often lack technology skills (Lupien 2020).

We must also keep in mind that even when they do use ICTs, Indigenous CSOs may be faced with certain barriers in comparison to the state and other powerful actors. Authors recognize that the potential of ICTs to empower marginalized social groups may be hindered by unequal access (Eckert 2018; Flores-Yeffal, Vidales, and Martinez 2019; Linabary and Corple 2018). Access issues remain a problem for Indigenous communities in Latin America at the dawn of the third decade of the twenty-first century (Lupien 2020; Lupien and Chiriboga 2019).

And then there are barriers that go deeper than access and training. Online platforms and search engines are typically infused with Western or East Asian cultural codes that frequently ignore or devalue Indigenous ways of knowing, and can generate barriers to use (Srinivasan 2013; Wagner 2018; Wagner and Fernández-Ardèvol 2019). As Tufekci (2017) acknowledges, status, race, gender, and class still matter online. The capitalist market structure within which social media platforms are embedded may also threaten to commodify Indigenous knowledge, limit the participatory nature of online activism, and reproduce "real world" colonial logics (Budka 2019; Fuchs 2009; Hinzo and Clark, 2019). And Indigenous scholar Marisa Duarte (2017) points out that fiber optic cables and Internet towers, like previous communications infrastructure, are built on land from which Indigenous peoples have been displaced, and they serve to further entrench state sovereignty. In this sense, digital information is confined within a colonial information infrastructure created by and for settlers. Duarte questions to what extent tools over which Indigenous peoples have no control can facilitate self-determination. These questions shift our understanding of the digital divide from inequality differentiated by a simple measure of access to multiple dimensions of digital inequality.

Finally, researchers note that governments use social media against civil society actors by generating content to muddle information, confuse logistical details, counterargue, promote fake news, and threaten (Larson 2019; Lupien, Chiriboga, and Machaca 2021; Tufekci 2017). Historical frames can also be perpetuated through social media to generate moral panic and racial scripts that seek to criminalize and to "other" Indigenous actors (Flores Yeffal, Vidales, and Martinez 2019). While Castell's networked public sphere can provide spaces for ordinary citizens to debate ideas, spread news, and respond to media, this only matters if others are listening.

In the following chapters, I argue that Indigenous CSOs have not morphed into primarily online movements. But many of the weaknesses of networked movements may be strengths for Indigenous collective action. Indigenous organizations and their tactics have been carefully developed over several decades. While the new movements are characterized by what Tufekci calls "tactical freeze," the remainder of this book demonstrates that Indigenous CSOs are characterized by tactical innovation, which supports their pursuit of long-term goals. The new movements prefer horizontalism without formal hierarchies or leaders but they are confronted by a state that is built on hierarchical leadership and structures. The goal of new movements is not to develop a political platform (Tarrow 2011). Indigenous CSOs, at least the more politically oriented ones, have detailed plans, usually based on extensive community feedback, in which they lay out their claims and an action plan for pursuing their goals. Leaderless, horizontal movements may benefit from flexibility and they are more difficult to co-opt, but Indigenous CSOs benefit from organizational depth, a culture of collective action rooted in years of experience, clearly defined decision-making processes, and strategic, long-term plans. Networked movements can choose to ignore institutions and to avoid creating their own formal mechanisms, but the institutions of power will continue to operate regardless. Indigenous leaders recognize this, which is why CSOs continue to work through them.

ICTs, Security, and the State:
Political Opportunities in the Digital Age

Digital technologies have a significant impact on political opportunities, but civil society's ability to use them is in turn shaped by the political context. Latin American constitutions confer on their citizens an extensive set of civil and political rights that match those enjoyed by citizens of established Western democracies, including freedom of speech and assembly, and the right to receive and disseminate information freely. But most countries, including Bolivia, Ecuador, and Chile, have adopted legislation that negates the rights and freedoms enshrined in their constitutions (Lupien, Chiriboga, and Machaca 2021). On and off the Internet, Indigenous CSOs must navigate a complex set of laws and informal practices that can be used to punish dissent and silence their voices. States have a wide array of antiterrorism and related laws at their disposal that can serve to repress groups that they deem to pose a security threat (Weisenhaus and Young 2017). In Chile and Ecuador, these were developed under dictatorships prior to the Third Wave democratization processes. These laws once served in the fight against leftist guerrilla groups but are increasingly being applied to environmental activists that challenge extractive activities. Indigenous activists and organizations have frequently been labeled as "terrorists" by state actors, as well as by mining and oil industry interests.

Since the fall of the authoritarian regimes in the 1980s (1990 in Chile), most Latin American countries nominally allow for freedom of expression. In practice, however, there are a number of pieces of legislation that effectively limit these freedoms. Many countries in the region have laws in place that make it an offense to "insult" public figures. Known as *desacato* (contempt) laws, they serve to criminalize criticism against politicians who can successfully argue that it constitutes "slander" (Mason 2012). Convictions can result in prison sentences that range from a few months to several years.

More recently, the Pink Tide governments (including Bolivia and Ecuador) have promulgated legislation intended to ensure that information disseminated is "socially responsible" or "truthful." Such provisions are intended to break the monopoly of powerful interests over the circulation of ideas, but critics claim that in countries with weak formal institutions, presidents may have too much control over what is deemed to be "truthful" (Lupien 2017). Information pluralism laws are also designed to distribute broadcasting licenses more equitably (to include civil society and Indigenous communities, for example). While diversifying media ownership may certainly produce positive benefits, the power that such laws give the state over content may also pose a threat to Indigenous communities who are deemed to be a threat to national interests.

Despite their own sensitivity to criticism, governments in the region appear willing to engage in cyberattacks and the spread of "fake news" against opponents. A team of researchers from the University of Toronto's Citizen Lab have identified a network, which they have dubbed "Packrat," that has systematically targeted opposition figures, journalists, and activists, particularly in the Pink Tide countries (Scott-Railton et al. 2015). The tactics have included distributing malware and conducting phishing attacks through fake opposition group websites and news organizations. In other cases, politically themed fake news websites are developed to appear as credible news organizations in order to spread disinformation.

Latin American states also have an extensive set of laws directly related to communications surveillance, although observers note that these were created during the age of landline wiretapping and have not kept up to date with the evolving scope of ICTs (Rodríguez 2016). Governments are spending significant sums of money to purchase and maintain security software, including surveillance systems, biometric data and identification registries, and CCTV. State intelligence agencies appear to be using these technologies without regard for the law or constitutional provisions (Pérez De Acha 2016). The majority of countries in the region have either purchased or are investigating Remote Control System (RCS) software. This came to light thanks to an information breach at one of the largest producers of RCS programs, the Italian-based firm Hacking Team. The breach, which included emails, financial data and invoices, revealed that Mexico (the company's largest client), Chile, Ecuador, and several others had purchased RCS software (Ragan 2015).

While there is evidence that Latin American governments are using RCS and other software—often illegally—to spy on actors considered subversive, we know relatively little about the targets of these attacks or how the programs are being used. With a handful of exceptions, such as Ecuador's CONAIE, Indigenous organizations are rarely mentioned in reports produced by digital rights organizations, although their research has uncovered attacks on journalists and opposition political figures. There may be a number of reasons for this. Journalists and political actors may be more aware of state intelligence agency practices and legal frameworks. They may have access to more resources and better-developed networks, which provide them with the capacity to determine whether or not they are being targeted. Still, given the conflict between many Latin American states and Indigenous organizations, as well as the perceived threat that the latter pose to natural resource-based economic interests, it is difficult to believe that RCS and other software are not being used to spy on their activities.

There is a need to further theorize the role of Indigenous actors in the age of online collective action. While the relatively limited use of digital technologies among Indigenous CSOs may be presented as a disadvantage, it may also mean that they can avoid some of the risks discussed above. If powerful actors can cause inaction by creating fear and confusion, and if governments are fine-tuning their online surveillance and sabotage tactics, are primarily offline movements less vulnerable to attack?

Indigenous Civil Society and Multiscalar Positioning

The literature on Indigenous collective action explores both disruptive social movements and how Indigenous actors engage across a wider terrain, but we need to more fully develop the concept of Indigenous *civil society* and how it has evolved in the twenty-first century. Contemporary Indigenous civil society is unique in that it encompasses a world that is both distinct from but intertwined with broader civil society. It involves resistance, civic participation, electoral politics, participatory democracy, a distinct worldview, unique practices, and a vast service sector. It increasingly draws on digital technologies, while maintaining many of the features that have made it strong: formal organizations, adept (but not necessarily hierarchical) leadership, in-person relationships, strategic plans, and a deep sense of identity. It draws from the past but evolves and matures with experience.

Indigenous civil society is rooted in identity and a unique set of claims that draw on the past while remaining firmly grounded in the present. It is not homogeneous, it consists of various nations and ethnicities, it is often fragmented, but we can recognize common goals, demands, and practices rooted in indigeneity. Actors call for full civil, political, and social citizenship, but on their terms and recognizing their lived history as colonized first peoples (Lupien 2011). Land rights are at the heart of Indigenous peoples' claims throughout the region and are related to the right to inhabit and use ancestral territories according to traditional ways of being. This includes the right to engage in Indigenous modes of agricultural production, and communal land use models, as opposed to private property or the public ownership model preferred by segments of the non-Indigenous left. Natural resource rights are closely related to land rights and include the protection of natural resources, such as water and hydrocarbons, and the right to use these resources for local development. Indigenous movements also insist that any decisions about resources on their traditional territories be made according to the principle of free, prior, and informed consent (FPIC). Cultural rights include the right to live according to traditional cultural values and practices, promotion of Indigenous languages and bilingual education, and enjoyment of full citizenship while retaining these practices. They also include recognition that the state comprises distinct nations (plurinationality). Economic rights are related to social citizenship and include redistributive economic policies, investment in social programs, and the rejection of neoliberalism. Political and legal rights vary from one jurisdiction to another but generally include autonomy and self-governance, collective rights, and recognition of customary law within Indigenous territories. Many of the demands and claims pursued by Indigenous movements were recognized by the international community and enshrined in the United Nations Declaration on the Rights of Indigenous Peoples (UNDRIP) in 2007.

This book demonstrates that Indigenous civil society consists of a more diverse architecture than any other public sphere Latin America. It is distinguished by the existence of communitarian structures and self-government mechanisms based on participatory and consensual decision-making processes. Power structures are generally not shaped like a pyramid with larger organizations at top presiding over a base; they are diffuse and porous. Within Indigenous civil society, there is a high level of local engagement and deliberation, and a preference for participating in micro-level organizational spaces. Local mechanisms tend to be more respected and valued than national or subnational-level liberal representative institutions. This is not only a question of the proximity of these spaces to daily life. As Tapia (2007) notes, liberalism imagines democratic participation only at the moment of casting a vote, which he astutely points out is in fact a "predemocratic state." Indigenous civil society seeks to disrupt this pattern and to relocate participation into the governing process itself.

Indigenous civil society has created a comprehensive system of institutions where populations have a political life separate from elite-dominated liberal institutions. Many of these CSOs have evolved into parallel authority structures. These function primarily at the local level, and are accountable to communities, but their mobilizing resources can also be used to speak to and collectively interact with the state and other actors external to Indigenous civil society. Some CSOs may serve, at least in practice, as parallel governments with some state-like functions. This broad array of mobilizing structures and institutions includes village councils, *ayllus* (traditional community governance structures in the Andes), unions, trade organizations, cooperatives, political parties, and social service organizations.

In Ecuador, organizational structures are not rooted in pre-Colombian models; they are based on "Western" models such as communes (Lucero 2008). In Bolivia, the corporatist tradition influenced the structures that developed (*sindicatos* such as CSTUCB and its affiliates) but did not eliminate competing pre-Colombian models. *Ayllus* and *sindicatos* continue to be part of Indigenous civil society, although the latter often function according to a communal form of government similar to *ayllus*. In Chile, most contemporary Mapuche organizations emerged following the return to democracy in

1990; they range from community associations, to state-society dialogue tables, to militant paramilitary cells (Cayuqueo 2018; Curivil Bravo 2012; Pichinao Huenchuleo 2012). But Mapuche civil society is also rich with sophisticated media organizations, educational institutes, and cultural centers, many of which function online (Córdova 2018). In all three countries, Indigenous civil society institutions operate both parallel to and in dialogue with the state, bypassing the state when it serves their needs, working with the state when that is more beneficial.

In Latin America, civil society often fills the vacuum for a weak or absent state by providing a range of social services. Alvarez and her colleagues (2017) perceive of the Third Sector as part of the "civil society agenda" that seeks to contain and depoliticize popular sectors. But this perspective overlooks both the distinct nature of Indigenous civil society, the diversity of its components, and the political acumen of its leaders. While foreign and domestic NGOs and religious associations have long engaged in providing various services to Indigenous communities, often with ideological strings attached, Indigenous civil society has developed its own independent system that combines social service provision and community work in the territories (*trabajo en territorio*) with identity promotion, political action, and sometimes even protest. The community service–oriented function is yet another unique feature of Indigenous civil society. It often fills in gaps left by the state, sometimes works with the state, and frequently contests it all at the same time.

Despite this complex system, Indigenous civil society generally does not challenge the existence of the state itself. With the exception of some Mapuche organizations, most Indigenous groups in the region do not seek to create a new independent state. Even when they control devolved subnational jurisdictions, calls for full political independence are almost unheard of in Ecuador and Bolivia (Filipe Quispe's movement in Bolivia, which sought to establish an Aymara republic in the Andes, was a rare exception). This too distinguishes Indigenous civil society from the many "ethnic" movements that fight for political sovereignty across the globe. Instead, politically oriented Indigenous CSOs seek to establish what Picq (2018) refers to as nonexclusive, deterritorialized forms of sovereignty, relocating decision-making power to the local level while demanding greater inclusion in the national state through an expanded and differentiated citizenship regime.

But we must also avoid romanticizing Indigenous civil society; communities and their members experience conflicts and may separate into factions. While participatory democracy is preferred to liberal institutions and governance practices often strive to meet these ideals, hierarchies and decision-making mechanisms that exclude some members can and do develop. Political polarization and class divisions exist within Indigenous civil society as well (Colloredo-Mansfeld 2009).

Multiscalar Positioning

Indigenous actors and organizations move seamlessly between forms and scales of collective action. Even more so than other sectors, Indigenous civil society is remarkable for the porousness that makes up its sphere of action. Researchers who study the state-civil society dynamic argue that activists can play a strong role in policy development by having "overlapping memberships" (Banaszak 2010; Beckwith 2000). Beckwith (2000) refers to this strategy as double militancy which she describes as the location of activists in two political venues, with participatory, collective identity and ideological commitments to both. The concept of double militancy involves participation from both the inside and the outside of the formal political realm. This book draws on my expansion of the concept of double militancy to understand Indigenous movements' tactics and strategies. "Double" refers to a binary, while "militancy" implies confrontational or violent methods in support of a political or social cause. I use the term *multiscalar positioning* because political action takes place on multiple, overlapping scales (within and between communities, nationally and internationally, within state institutions and semiautonomous participatory mechanisms, and increasingly in the virtual world) and because Indigenous CSOs are as likely to deploy nonconfrontational forms of participation and blend various forms of action (traditional and online). Positioning implies the type of deliberate, strategic participation that characterizes Indigenous civil society.

Multiscalar positioning includes participating—often simultaneously—in disruption (outside), directly in institutions of the state (inside), mechanisms that straddle institutional and extrainstitutional involvement, and in cyberspace (not really inside or outside). Multiscalar positioning also includes the service provision and community work (*trabajo en territorio*) functions that many Indigenous CSOs fulfill.

Twenty-first-century Latin America is characterized by shifting power dynamics and a new participatory architecture exemplified by innovative state-society interface mechanisms such as participatory budgeting. This adds a layer of complexity to Indigenous organizations' strategies and tactics, as the lines between institutional and extrainstitutional action are more blurred. As Wampler (2012) points out, "The principal consequence of the broadening of the democratic process is that community activists are no longer forced to choose between contentious politics or clientelism, between autonomy or co-optation, between party politics and social movement organization. Rather, the participatory architecture now allows citizens and leaders to deploy a wider range of political strategies" (Wampler 2012). Local (municipal) politics is also important as a space for multiscalar positioning. Given the devolved nature of some Indigenous local governments, these forms of engagement cannot be defined as either inside or outside. While Indigenous communities sometimes build on state-sanctioned models to develop local governance mechanisms, they infuse these with their own ways of doing and use them in ways that were not intended by state architects. While it would be naïve to deny that the state can and does co-opt segments of Indigenous civil society, it is just as problematic to overlook the many instances where Indigenous civil society captures state-society mechanisms at the local level. But I also challenge the notion, common in the literature, that any action that does not take place on the "outside" inevitably leads to co-optation, particularly as leaders of Indigenous civil society become more politically savvy.

Multiscalar positioning also includes reaching out to and engaging with non-Indigenous sectors by promoting mutual demands or by framing Indigenous demands in ways that resonate with other sectors. Indigenous CSOs in Ecuador have become particularly adept at doing this, although even Mapuche organizations, which have been more inclined to remain separate from Chilean civil society, have adopted this strategy over the past few years. And finally, multiscalar positioning involves the use of ICTs, which allows organizations to engage with and against the state in cyberspace. Chapters 2 to 4 of this book examine what all of this looks like on the ground.

The Arguments

In the following chapters, I expand on the arguments put forward at the beginning of this chapter. I discuss the evolving political, social, and technological context in which Indigenous CSOs must operate, the impact of these changes on their tactical repertoires, and how they have adapted in the twenty-first century.

Indigenous Civil Society and Forms of Contention:
Political Opportunities, Citizenship Regimes, Mobilizing Structures

I began this chapter with a brief description of pivotal events that demonstrated the potential power of Indigenous civil society. In Chile, the year 1990 marked the end of the continent's most brutal dictatorship and the beginning of a low-intensity conflict between that country's largest Indigenous nation and the state. The protest cycle that began in 1990 produced historic changes in Bolivia and Ecuador, culminating in the election of leftist governments and the adoption of progressive constitutions that offered unprecedented sets of rights to Indigenous peoples in the mid-2000s. But the cycle appears to have waned from that point onward. The relative lack of media and academic attention in the period after 2005 may give the impression that Indigenous CSOs became less active, but this book demonstrates that quite the opposite has happened.

Political opportunities in Bolivia and Ecuador shifted during the presidencies of Evo Morales (2006–19) and Rafael Correa (2007–17). The political opportunity structure in these two countries represent a paradox of the Pink Tide governments, which simultaneously expanded possibilities for political participation while seeking to channel and control popular movements. But the new participatory spaces, even if limited, created opportunities that encouraged many CSOs to adapt their tactical repertoire. The popularity of both governments, sustained by high levels of social investment and rising living standards, also forced CSOs to rely less of disruptive action. The general satisfaction among lower-income social sectors limited their ability to call on civil society allies and lessened the appeal of protest even for many Indigenous communities. Public support also provided more room for these governments to use repression against those who could be labeled as being in conflict with the majority.

In Chile, the lack of change in the political opportunity structure and very limited public support meant that disruptive action continued to be the primary tool used by the larger Indigenous CSOs, but Mapuche civil society is developing a panoply of CSOs dedicated to promoting culture and building a Mapuche nation. In all three countries, the political opportunities available to Indigenous CSOs shifted again in 2019, sparking a return to large-scale disruption. But the political opportunity structure throughout the region was also profoundly transformed during this period by the expansion of social media and other ICTs. We will see that these technologies have both expanded and constrained political opportunities for Indigenous CSOs.

Citizenship regimes also shifted dramatically in the two Pink Tide countries and demonstrate a paradox. Social citizenship was expanded as never before while civil rights were slowly curbed throughout the period. Political rights were expanded more in discourse than in practice, although there were tangible reforms with respect to participatory democracy, especially in Bolivia. This postneoliberal citizenship regime, particularly as regards the social rights afforded to marginalized communities, responded to many demands of Indigenous CSOs. Even if some were not fully satisfied, many of those they represent were. Chile's (neo)liberal citizenship regime remained deeply entrenched throughout the period, although it is increasingly being contested by non-Indigenous sectors, providing Mapuche CSOs opportunities for collaboration. In all three countries, the use of social media has changed how younger Indigenous people interact with the types of traditional mechanisms that promoted and reproduced Indigenous identity and citizenship in the recent past.

By the early 1990s, Indigenous movements in Bolivia and Ecuador had built strong and well-organized CSOs on the foundations of preexisting mobilizing structures. Throughout the first two decades of the twenty-first century, these remained stable. They had already developed considerable political experience and skill, and continued to build on this. But the CSOs also evolved during this period. They increasingly began to adopt the practices and tactics generally associated with civil society. In Chile, CSOs had less experience to build on and the structures and practices of most prominent organizations have developed to support resistance and to defend against state militarization in their territories. ICTs have affected the work of CSOs in all three countries and have forced organizations to adapt their tactics. But we will see that leaders have prioritized building and adapting the "traditional" formal and informal mobilizing structures that served them well in the past over developing ICT-focused strategies.

That Indigenous actors are skilled at blending contentious and civic action is well established in the literature. This book shines a light on how Indigenous actors move back and forth between forms of action during certain periods and based on certain variables that include resource mobilization, political opportunities, and identity. Despite the relative decline in the use of disruptive protest during the Pink Tide period, Indigenous groups were not idle. Rather, they were building on previous experience and structures, as well as seeking ways to engage with new political opportunities, international allies, and state-society mechanisms.

I use the term *multiscalar positioning* to describe the complex, shifting repertoire of strategies and tactics employed by Indigenous civil society actors. CSOs operate across *multiple scales* that include local communities, state institutions, transnational civil society, and virtual networks. They strategically and deliberately *position* themselves within and between these scales depending on a number of variables. The forms that this multiscalar positioning takes, the strategic ebbs and flows, depend on political opportunities, resource mobilization capacity, and citizenship regimes. These factors facilitate engagement on some scales and render others less accessible.

Indigenous CSOs in Bolivia gained far greater access to power, which would set the movements in the two Pink Tide countries on different paths from the late 2000s onward, but there are also commonalities. Shifting political opportunities and citizenship regimes forced Indigenous CSOs in Bolivia and Ecuador to revisit strategies and tactics for political participation, communication, resource mobilization, and education. The focus of their efforts moved from disruptive (and costly) protest cycles to a more sustained, ongoing, and multifaceted approach that is generally associated with civil society. Political opportunities and the nature of citizenship did not evolve in Chile during this period. The most prominent Mapuche CSOs were structured around disruptive action and resistance; due to the absence of meaningful change, they had little reason to adapt their approach. Yet there is a growing crop of newer CSOs that are starting to adopt alternative tactics, and at the beginning of the 2020s, a new multiscalar positioning approach seems to be emerging. In all three countries, those with the means to do so are exploring new ways of mobilizing resources and are using ICTs to reach a wider audience and to engage in the virtual public sphere on their own terms. The sustained multiscalar positioning approach pioneered by Indigenous CSOs, but now expanded to include online political action and a more diverse array of tactics and mechanisms, will likely have the most significant long-term impact in terms of advancing these groups' claims.

Return to Large-Scale Resistance: Late 2019

By late 2019 and continuing into 2020, it was apparent that Indigenous CSOs had not abandoned disruptive action. Why did Indigenous movements return to large-scale resistance in late 2019 after more than a decade of relative calm?

I argue that in Bolivia and Ecuador, political opportunities shifted again as the postneoliberal citizenship was threatened. Social citizenship, which has been expanded during the Pink Tide period, created expectations among Indigenous peoples and lower-income mestizos. The withdrawal of these social rights (coupled with the removal of the MAS from power in Bolivia) caused the multipositioning strategy to break down and led CSOs to turn back to disruptive action. But the political opportunity structure looked very different in the two countries and this helps to explain why one uprising (Ecuador) was successful while the other (Bolivia) was not. In Ecuador, the Indigenous movement demonstrated solidarity. Faced with a highly unpopular government, it also found allies across civil society. In Bolivia, the movement was deeply divided, making it more difficult to secure the support required to tackle a right-wing interim regime that was prepared to use repression. The Chilean state has never extended social citizenship and has sought to limit political rights and curtail citizen participation in politics. The massive demonstrations of late 2019 reminded Mapuche CSOs that they have common grievances with nonelite Chileans. This encouraged many of them to jump on board in an effort to expand social and political rights. But it also demonstrates the increasing diversity and sophistication of Mapuche civil society, a segment of which seeks to move beyond conflict and to collaborate with potential Chilean allies. I also argue that mobilization is more likely when social rights (rather than civil or political rights) are threatened or withdrawn, because attacks on social citizenship create political opportunities that allow Indigenous CSOs to build alliances with non-Indigenous popular sector actors. We will also see that the impact of ICTs on capacity of Indigenous actors to engage in protest varies considerably based on a number of variables, as well as the extent to which actors are able to align their demands with a broader civil society identity.

Indigenous CSOs and Twenty-First-Century ICTs

Throughout this book, we will see that the increasingly complex tactical repertoire employed by Indigenous movements includes the use of ICTs such as cellphones, laptops, and social media. Most Indigenous movements are concerned with preserving culture and tradition, but this does not mean that they are static or resistant to change. They have moved steadfastly into the twenty-first century and this includes the use of digital technologies, although they seek to use these tools on their own terms. Indigenous leaders are aware of the role that social media plays in disseminating messages and influencing public opinion. They also understand that groups that oppose Indigenous claims, from state agencies to extractive industries, have an online presence. ICTs have become an essential tool in their multiscalar positioning work and were used successfully by some CSOs during the 2019 protests.

ICTs affect Indigenous CSOs and communities in different ways depending on size, resources, relationship with the state, and skill level. Still, while social media have become an integral part of the strategical repertoire of the larger CSOs, Indigenous civil society does not resemble the type of "networked" collective action that many authors have come to associate with "modern" movements. The implications of this are complex. Indigenous civil society operates primarily offline, and while this may create certain disadvantages in an increasingly online public sphere, this should not be read as a rejection or lack of "modernity."

Indigenous civil society retains many of its traditional strengths: well-organized mobilizing structures, experienced leadership, a wide and diverse range of tactics, detailed proposals and plans, and the capacity to mobilize based on a sense of collective identity.

Social media and other ICTs complement the tactics used by Indigenous civil society, but they do not replace traditional collective action strategies. They also create new threats and barriers that affect the key activities carried out by CSOs. For this reason, I decided to weave Indigenous CSOs' use of ICTs into the narrative rather than focusing exclusively on or dedicating entire chapters of the book to technologies. I believe that this allows the story to remain faithful to what Indigenous participants told me: that ICTs are just one (significant but relatively small) part of their multiscalar positioning.

Comparing Strategies and State-Society Mechanisms

By comparing CSOs within and across the three countries, I examine the most (and least) successful strategies adopted by Indigenous organizations in the 2010s. This also involves considering the types of state-society mechanisms that allow for Indigenous CSOs to effectively interact with the state while maintaining the autonomy required to pursue their constituents' interests.

Defining relative success or failure in collective action studies is notoriously difficult. This book follows Gamson's (1990, 2003) analysis, which considers two sets of outcomes to determine success: the concrete advantages secured by a movement for its constituents (this may include beneficial policy concessions) and recognition from the state, which confers legitimacy on a movement or organization (also see McVeigh et al. 2003). From this perspective, Indigenous civil society in Ecuador is frequently considered the strongest in Latin America (Rice 2012; Yashar 2005). But as Lucero and García (2007) warn, it is important to conceive of alternative ways of evaluating Indigenous collective action beyond the "strong" and "weak" case dichotomy. I also consider Meyer and Whittier's (1994) argument that even when these more tangible outcomes are not achieved, collective action can produce "spillover" effects. These may influence other segments of civil society, who may adopt values, incorporate tactics, or promote common goals. Spillover effects may also affect individuals by instilling in them a sense of pride or political efficacy (Amenta et al. 2010; Diani 1997; Ferree and Hess 1994; McAdam 1999).

I argue that Indigenous CSOs are most successful at achieving policy outcomes when they develop a structure that is integrated and organized yet encourages bottom-up participation and democratic internal decision making, and that reflects the need for regional representation and accountability. The development of political skills on the part of Indigenous leaders has a significant influence, particularly when they are facing less experienced government officials. Long-term success also depends on continuing with a multiscalar positioning repertoire that blends civil society and social movement approaches and tactics. Solidarity across Indigenous CSOs is key: unity produces strength in numbers, fragmentation leads to weakness. The ability to reach beyond core constituencies and frame issues in a way that resonates with other sectors is also important. Finally, the strategic use of ICTs can help to support Indigenous CSO efforts by contributing to resource mobilization, public relations, and socialization.

Engaging in state-society interface mechanisms, including in the new participatory architecture established in the Pink Tide states, provides Indigenous CSOs with more options and is an important part of the multiscalar positioning strategy. While I argue that fears around co-optation are both overblown and condescending, too much integration with these mechanisms may be a weakness, particularly when the state is dominated by a single party such as the MAS. As we will see with the Bolivian case, CSOs may end up orienting their strategies and tactics entirely around the MAS architecture, making them vulnerable when that party is no longer in power.

There is, however, considerable variation with respect to strategies and tactics used within and across the three countries. This is based on variables related to resources and political opportunities, such as size of the organization (smaller, local organizations tend to focus on local issues and avoid national politics), relationship with the state, geography (the more natural resources in a given territory, the more conflict), and capacity to benefit from ICTs.

· · · · · ·

The next three chapters present evidence based on four years of fieldwork. They examine how the rapidly evolving political and social context has affected the work of Indigenous social movements in the 2010s. They consider how changes in the political opportunity structure, available resources and mobilizing structures, and citizenship regimes have enhanced or hindered the ability of Indigenous organizations to advance their goals. Through my conversations with Indigenous leaders and community members, I demonstrate how Indigenous organizations have adapted their strategies and tactics. Following the case studies, I compare and contrast CSOs in the three countries to determine the most effective strategies and tactics, and the overall impact of ICTs on Indigenous collective action.

2 Ecuador

Decline or Strategic Realignment?

· ·

In the early morning of October 15, 2019, Salomé Quishpe looked out over the rooftops of her working-class *barrio* in the hills above Quito's colonial center. As she made her way down from the modest dwelling she shares with her daughter and grandchildren, Salomé picked her way through piles of burnt tires, broken glass, and chunks of pavement. Originally from Chimborazo, a province in the central highlands known for its majestic volcanoes, the Puruhá woman was heading to a plaza where she spends her days selling *chicharrón* (fried pork rinds) and other snacks to passersby. She mused about the need to make some money after two weeks without income. But Salomé had not been idle during the uprisings that had rocked the country over the previous two weeks. The sixty-two-year-old grandmother had first begun organizing for Indigenous women's rights as a teenager in the small town of Alausí. She participated in the CONAIE-led uprisings in the 1990s, and she took to the streets again in October 2019. She quietly observed that "we [Indigenous Ecuadorians] don't always agree, but we come together when we need to. I am proud of what we have done. They said that the Indigenous movement is weaker now than before, but we showed them that we still have power, and the will, to resist. When the people are united, we cannot be defeated" (Salomé, interview with the author, October 15, 2019).

For the first two weeks in October, Salomé was one of thousands of Indigenous Ecuadorians who occupied the streets of Quito, the country's colonial capital. The protests had begun days earlier when transportation workers blocked roads in response to an economic austerity package introduced by the administration of President Lenín Moreno on October 1. Since his election in early 2017, Moreno had begun to reverse the "Twenty-First-Century Socialism" legacy of his predecessor, leftist president Rafael Correa (2007–17). The latest measures, adopted at the behest of the International Monetary Fund (IMF) in return for credit, included the elimination of gas subsidies, cuts to public-sector benefits and wages, and the removal of certain import tariffs that favored Ecuadorian goods. Moreno stood his ground at first, stating that his government would not back down, and security forces were deployed to restore order. The union representing transportation workers came to an agreement with the government and for a fleeting moment, it appeared that the protests would subside.

Then the situation abruptly shifted. As in previous crises (1990, 1997, 2000, 2005), Indigenous CSOs took on a leadership role, marking a major turning point in the protests. By the second week of October, Quito looked like a war zone. Streets were littered with broken glass, debris, and burning tires. Major roads and bridges across the country were blocked, bringing the country to a standstill. The armed forces were deployed on October 7, resulting in violent clashes. Demonstrators briefly occupied the National Assembly building on October 9 while CONAIE leader Jaime Vargas insisted that there would be no dialogue with the government unless the austerity measures were reversed.

President Moreno and his cabinet abandoned the temperate Andean capital and moved the seat of government to the sweltering coastal city of Guayaquil, although protests had erupted there as well. This was a remarkable development, but the political upheaval was not unprecedented for the small nation. In the previous two decades, three presidents had been overthrown as a result of popular uprisings opposed to neoliberal austerity measures (in 1997, 2000, and 2005). Indigenous movements were the undisputed leaders of the first two and key players in the third. But while the 2019 uprisings had much in common with the previous events, there were differences. Indigenous leaders drew on provisions of the constitution they had helped to draft just over a decade earlier. They made extensive use of social media to coordinate mobilization efforts, to denounce what they believed to be excessive force by the state, to disseminate images of injured civilians, and to condemn Moreno and interior minister María Paula Romo as oppressors.

On Sunday, October 12, the government and Indigenous leaders began negotiations aimed at defusing the conflict that had by now paralyzed the nation's economy. Moreno's concession, after days of refusing to back down, demonstrated that the Indigenous movement in Ecuador remained too powerful to ignore. The fact that three of his predecessors had been forced to resign and flee the country for implementing unpopular economic policies was not lost on Moreno. By October 14, the unpopular bill was rescinded, ending the most significant upheaval since the 2005 ouster of then-president Lucio Gutiérrez.

For a time after 2005 it appeared that Indigenous civil society, led by CONAIE, was somewhat diminished. Many of the Indigenous participants we interviewed prior to the 2019 protests said as much, with many looking back nostalgically to the 1990s. The alliance between the Gutiérrez administration and Pachakutik, an Indigenous political party, severely strained the relationship between social movement organizations and elected Indigenous officials. While Pachakutik members eventually broke with Gutiérrez, the damage had been done, and the country's most powerful social movement appeared to recede. CONAIE and other organizations clashed regularly with the Correa government, but their efforts failed to reach the scale—or achieve the outcomes—of the previous two decades. Yet if observers questioned the capacity of CONAIE and other Indigenous organizations to mobilize as they were able to do in the past, these doubts were extinguished in October 2019. Indigenous organizations assumed the leadership of a mass movement that included people from diverse social sectors and they succeeded at achieving their primary goal.

This chapter demonstrates that this was not a "relaunch" of Ecuador's Indigenous social movement. Rather, it was an affirmation that Indigenous civil society remains strong in Ecuador. Following the ill-fated Gutiérrez alliance, and especially under Correa, Indigenous CSOs were forced to adjust to a new political context and citizenship regime that simultaneously extended social citizenship and provided new (but limited) opportunities for participation while imposing limitations on civil rights and restricting space for CSOs. They adapted their approach to political participation, resource mobilization, communication, and education to the changing context, and they have continued to develop an expanding repertoire of strategies and tactics. They turned their attention to the "civic" practices that the state accepts as *lo permitido*. When the gains they had achieved over the years were threatened, and the political opportunity structure shifted again, they were able to build on their experience to assume a leadership role within Ecuadorian civil society. The relative solidarity and cohesive structure of Indigenous civil society, supported by the skillful use of ICTs, demonstrated that Indigenous CSOs remain a strong political force in Ecuador.

Mobilizing Structures, Political Opportunities, and Citizenship: Continuity and Change

In the 1990s and early 2000s, Ecuador held the dubious distinction of being one of Latin America's most volatile countries (Solimano 2005). Much of this was due to the ongoing conflict between Indigenous civil society and the state. The election of Rafael Correa and his Alianza PAIS coalition in 2007 ushered in a decade of relative political and economic stability. Correa's victory marked the beginning of a shift in policy; his agenda included nationalizations, unprecedented investments in infrastructure, healthcare and education, and wide-ranging redistributive programs. Dubbed the "Citizens' Revolution," Correa's program also promised to introduce a new model of participatory democracy and expand Indigenous rights.

But while socioeconomic rights were significantly extended during Correa's time in office, much of the promised agenda remains unfulfilled, according to the majority of Indigenous leaders I spoke to. This had a complex impact on Indigenous civil society. On the one hand, the Citizens' Revolution appeared to expand political opportunities by creating more access points to the state. On the other, while the Correa administration encouraged citizen participation in decision making, it required them to engage in the public sphere through state-sanctioned mechanisms while simultaneously reducing space for participation outside of this system.

Despite ongoing conflict with Indigenous organizations, Correa's redistributive policies earned him widespread and sustained popularity, thereby undercutting support for protest mobilization. This was certainly a factor in the tactical shift adopted by Indigenous leaders, as was the increasing frequency of repression. Correa's successor and former vice-president Lenín Moreno reemphasized political and civil rights, but his neoliberal agenda weakened social rights. This broke the pact between lower-income sectors and the state, and the result was a return to large-scale resistance.

Mobilizing Networks and Resources

From the 1960s to 1990s, Indigenous groups had built on preexisting structures and networks to create some of the continent's strongest CSOs (Paige 2020; Yashar 2005). In the Andes, these included rural workers' unions focused on land reform and Catholic organizations committed to social development in the countryside. The church was a key player in the launch of ECUARUNARI, which united Kichwa communities across the Ecuadorian Andes. Catholic organizations and rural unions provided ECUARUNARI and other Indigenous associational networks with the technical support, training, and resources they required. Rural unions and church-based organizations provided this support with the intention of advancing their own agendas: respectively, class and ecclesiastical mobilization. But by the

1980s, leaders of ECUARUNARI and affiliated networks had asserted their independence. They began to promote Indigenous identity and make claims related specifically to the historical experiences of Indigenous peoples (Colloredo-Mansfeld 2009; Lucero 2007; Paige 2020). They also started to develop close alliances with organizations in the Amazon.

The Ecuadorian state demonstrated little interest in the Amazon until the 1960s and Indigenous peoples in that region were left to their own devices. This began to change as the state encouraged colonization of the region as a means of relieving land pressure in the highlands and these efforts accelerated with the discovery of oil in 1967. Given that churches, and church-related schools and medical centers, were the only existing institutions in the sparsely populated region, Indigenous leaders used them to build new mobilizing structures such as the Shuar Federation, founded in 1964 (Selverston-Scher 2001). This led to the formation of provincial organizations such as the Federation of Indigenous Organizations of Napo (Federación de Organizaciones Indígenas de Napo, FOIN) and eventually CONFENAIE, formed in 1980 to coordinate activities between Amazonian organizations. ECUARUNARI and CONFENAIE agreed to create CONAIE in 1986, which became Latin America's first nationwide Indigenous umbrella organization (Rice 2012).

Many of Ecuador's local and regional Indigenous organizations followed CONAIE's lead in the uprisings that rocked the country during the 1990s. The solidarity and level of coordination provided by this integrated, cohesive network produced unprecedented policy victories. But the ill-fated political alliance between CONAIE, Pachakutik, and the short-lived Gutiérrez administration ended when the government signed an agreement with the IMF. CONAIE participated in the 2005 uprising that ousted Gutiérrez, but a rift had already developed within Indigenous civil society, as many had warned about the risks of participating in electoral politics and government.

While some observers claim that these developments weakened the movement (Mijeski and Beck 2011), this chapter demonstrates that the relative lack of visibility after 2005 represents more of a strategic shift. By 2005, Indigenous mobilizing structures and networks were already well developed. In the 2010s, Indigenous civil society did not need to build new institutions as it did in the 1960s to 1990s; leaders continued to work with the structures that had served them well over the previous two decades. They also began to engage with emerging mechanisms and tools, including new participatory institutions and, increasingly, ICTs.

Indigenous civil society in Ecuador is diverse and characterized by a complex structure. At the higher levels, it comprises large to medium-sized organizations such as CONAIE and ECUARUNARI, as well as provincial-level associations (I engaged with those representing Imbabura, Cotopaxi, Bolívar, Chimborazo, Tungurahua and Azuay in the highlands, and Napa and Pastaza in the Oriente). But Indigenous civil society also includes hundreds of community-level Indigenous governance councils, state-recognized communes established according to the 1937 law, participatory mechanisms established under Correa, committees dedicated to specific issues (such as water or education), organizations that provide social services, and cooperatives uniting various categories of workers or producers.

The sheer number and heterogeneousness of Indigenous CSOs posed a challenge as I sought to develop a representative list of organizations to work with for this research. The Ecuador-based advisory council of Indigenous knowledge holders I asked to participate as part of the CBPR approach supported Gabriel and me with this momentous task. They developed the typology of organizations mentioned above and helped us to narrow our cases down to thirty-two by working with us to establish a representative sample. The typology includes size (large/national, medium/regional, small/local), geography (highlands, coast, Amazon), and primary function (political, service provision, cultural, cooperative). Participants felt that a complete picture of Indigenous civil society requires an engagement with organizations representing all of these variables.

During the course of my fieldwork, many leaders insisted that their structures are parallel to the state. They see CONAIE and affiliated regional organizations as a type of Indigenous government that functions alongside, and often in opposition to, state institutions. The organizational landscape in the 2020s looks much as it did in 2005, and in the 1990s for that matter. However, the political landscape changed significantly during these years, and this has had an impact on the associational space available to Indigenous organizations and on how they do their work.

The evolution of technologies available to Indigenous actors from the mid-2000s onward is another key factor in the mobilization of resources. ICTs, particularly community radio, have served as tools for social, educational, political, and intellectual development of Indigenous civil society. Indigenous actors have used radio in innovative ways to create alternative spaces that favor participation and emancipation, sometimes supported by progressive sectors of the Catholic Church. In 1962, Monsignor Leonidas Proaño, bishop of Riobamba (Chimborazo Province) and an influential figure in Ecuadorian liberation theology, founded the Popular Radio Schools of Ecuador (Escuelas Radiofónicas Populares del Ecuador, ERPE). ERPE was established with a clear set of educational goals, including the development of a pedagogical praxis aimed at the economic, social, psychological and intellectual liberation of marginalized peoples; the creation of decentralized communication practices for democratizing the public sphere and encouraging popular participation; and to give voice to the "voiceless" (Cerbino and Belotti 2016; Matrone 2019). Torres (2019) documents how the ERPE played a central role in the development of Indigenous civil society in Chimborazo and helped local organizations to mobilize their communities during the 1990 uprising. She argues that radio not only served as a tool for disseminating calls to action but had a much more profound effect on civil society by supporting the construction of an alternative discourse. Influenced by liberation theology, this counterhegemonic discourse ultimately transformed Indigenous identity. While community radio remains an important resource for rural communities, some segments of civil society are using the Internet to construct a virtual public sphere. This chapter demonstrates that in Ecuador the results of these efforts have been mixed, and shows the possibilities and limits of "newer" ICTs for Indigenous civil society.

Political Opportunities

In 2008, Ecuadorians voted in favor of adopting a new constitution spearheaded by Correa. It established a progressive set of rights and mechanisms that, at least on paper, profoundly altered the country's political opportunity structure in favor of Indigenous peoples. The constitution also responded to many of the demands that Indigenous civil society had fought for over the previous two decades. Indigenous leaders participated in the Constituent Assembly charged with drafting the new Magna Carta (Lupien 2011).

While these reforms suggest a deepening of democracy, the vast majority of Indigenous leaders and activists I spoke to insisted that these rights are rarely recognized in practice. More concerning from their perspective, however, are various laws that restrict freedom of expression and criminalize protest. As a Shuar Elder observed, "It's easy to say that participation is a right and to create citizen councils and other institutions. But defending our rights requires working with the state sometimes and against it at other times. And despite the language of the constitution and the Law of

Participation, there are still many laws in Ecuador that restrict our rights" (anonymous interview with the author and Chiriboga, April 13, 2018).

The Elder was referring to antiterrorism legislation and *desacato* laws, which were used extensively by Correa to target critics. They allow for prison sentences of up to two years for "offending" the president. Many Indigenous leaders and communication specialists told me that these measures encouraged self-censorship, particularly as organizations expanded their online and social media presence. Ecuador's criminal code does not specifically mention ICTs but the provisions are broad enough to ensure that offences can be committed via the Internet.

In 2013, the National Assembly, dominated by Alianza PAIS, passed a new Communications Law (Ley Orgánica de Comunicación, LOC) that further reflects the often contradictory nature of the Citizens' Revolution by opening the marketplace of information to a much broader spectrum of the public while at the same time giving the state significant control over content. The stated purpose of the law was to democratize the circulation of information and ideas by breaking the media monopoly of traditional elites. This is a goal long supported by Indigenous actors. As in much of Latin America, media ownership in Ecuador is highly concentrated. When Correa came to power in 2007, over 95 percent of television, radio, and print media outlets were in private hands. The majority were under the control of a few wealthy families; 287 out of 348 television licenses were controlled by nineteen families and six of the eight national channels were directly linked to banking interests (Kitzberger 2017). These media outlets tend to support conservative political parties and neoliberal economic policies. Not surprisingly, they have not been particularly sympathetic toward Indigenous CSO. The hostility of the country's mainstream media was brought up by most of the participants I spoke to, and the examples they provided ranged from the media depicting Indigenous protesters as threats to national security to their ignoring state violence against Indigenous communities. A communications specialist who worked for CONAIE during the 1990s put it bluntly: "The Ecuadorian media has never been our friend" (Vilma, interview with the author, December 12, 2019).

The 2013 LOC contains a number of progressive measures to address the problem of media concentration. It provides a formal legal framework for establishing, supporting, and encouraging community media, as well as an "affirmative action" provision that requires the state to support "diversity, interculturality, and plurinationality" in the media. The LOC also states that media licenses will be divided evenly between private, public, and community actors. These provisions were welcomed in principle by all the Indigenous participants I spoke to. They have the potential to shift the political opportunity structure in favor of marginalized actors by providing them with a means of challenging the messages of corporate interests that control private media and with a platform for expressing their own perspectives to the general public.

Interviewees pointed out that the promises of the LOC had not been fulfilled in practice due to a lack of financial resources and expertise. Willy, an Indigenous leader from Cotopaxi, summed it up as follows: "Creating a more equal media landscape where Indigenous peoples can compete with private interests requires more than just passing nice laws. Setting up a television station requires resources, financial and human, it requires training and equipment" (Willy, interview with the author, August 17, 2016).

Another concern for Indigenous and non-Indigenous civil society actors is that the LOC gives the government broad powers to limit the circulation of ideas. The law requires all information to be "verified, contrasted, precise, and contextualized," and prohibits "media lynching," defined as "disseminating information with the purpose of discrediting or harming the reputation of a person or entity." While these provisions are not necessarily problematic per se—Indigenous organizations and activists have often been the target of racist, fearmongering attacks by the private media—the LOC established a state agency as the final arbiter of what constitutes "truthful" information. The Superintendency of Information and Communication (SUPERCOM) was given vast powers to monitor media content and enforce the LOC. It has conducted investigations of media outlets or individual journalists, imposed fines, and ordered retractions or apologies for perceived violations. SUPERCOM has also leveled censorship charges against media outlets who refuse to publish stories that the regulatory body deems to be in the public interest. Journalists responsible for "media lynching" of the president or other public officials may be investigated and charged with an offense. From 2013 to 2017, the agency launched over 1,000 investigations, the vast majority of which resulted in sanctions (Fundamedios 2017).

While the more restrictive aspects of the LOC and the mandate of SUPERCOM concentrate on the media, they have also resulted in a climate of self-censorship among Indigenous organizations. Many leaders pointed out that definitions in the LOC are vague and may apply to the use by civil society organizations of social media and other ICTs to disseminate information. As Rodolfo, an Indigenous communications agent from Pastaza, pointed out: "We are using tools like Facebook and Twitter more and more . . . but if we send out political messages using social media, will this be considered journalism according to the LOC? It's not clear, but many of us don't want to take the risk, at least not under our own names or the name of the organization. We see what happened with some journalists. And even if the law cannot be used against us, saying something against the government, especially the former government, may provoke online threats" (Rodolfo, interview with the author, February 22, 2018).

Rodolfo was not alone. There have been various reports of journalists, media outlets, and social media users being subjugated to online harassment from anonymous sources. Many such incidents occurred after Correa himself publicly attacked those who criticized him and encouraged his supporters to "fight back." Many of the individuals I spoke to reported similar incidents following a public disagreement with the former president. Some also showed me fake social media profiles that had been created in their names and used to discredit them. Following his election, Moreno announced his intention to amend the LOC, stating that some elements of the law violated international standards of press freedom. The changes addressed some critics' concerns, such as repealing the "media lynching" clause, but retained vague requirements such as the dissemination of "quality information." The Indigenous leaders we interviewed remained concerned about how the LOC could be used to silence them, while lamenting that the more positive aspects of the legislation, such as support for community media, have not yet been put into practice.

The political opportunity structure for Indigenous civil society in Ecuador is also shaped by the discourse of national security, and antiterrorism laws have frequently been used against Indigenous activists, particularly when their protests appeared to threaten extractive industries. The criminal code adopted under a dictatorship in 1971 and in force until 2014 contained numerous provisions against "terrorism," "sabotage," and "national security," but these terms were not adequately defined and were often interpreted in an arbitrary manner for political purposes. The new criminal code adopted in 2014 provides more precise definitions. For example, it defines subversive activities as "promoting, directing or participating in organizations, armies, combat groups, or cells, destined to subvert public order or interfere with the normal performance of security forces." Article 366 defines terrorism as "acts that endanger the life, limb, or liberty of persons or endanger buildings, means of communication, or transportation." These offenses can be committed individually or as part of an "armed group." While less vague than the previous version, the 2014 criminal code still allows prosecutors and judges considerable room for interpretation. It also allows authorities to access personal communications, including ICTs such as laptops and social media accounts. Ecuadorian legislation states that surveillance cannot be conducted for political purposes, yet there is evidence that Hacking Team software has been used to spy on opposition political actors and journalists, as well as CONAIE (Scott-Railton et al. 2015).

The Correa government frequently linked natural resources to national interests and security, and used articles from both the 1971 and the 2014 criminal codes to prosecute Indigenous activists for various offences. The CONFENIAE and other organizations, in an attempt to halt the growing expansionism of oil drilling in the Amazon region, have engaged in various forms of protest, often using disruptive tactics. In 2013, Pepe Acacho, a Shuar leader, was charged with terrorism and sentenced to twelve years in prison for leading protests against water privatization and mining projects. Prosecutors latched on to the "armed groups" language in the criminal code, noting that Acacho and his followers carried spears during their protests. His defense team pointed out that spears are traditionally used by Shuar men; protesters were carrying them as a cultural symbol and could certainly not have used such simple weapons against the heavily armed soldiers that were sent to contain the protests. On appeal, the National Court of Justice downgraded his sentence to eight months in 2018 and he was released shortly after, following a pardon by President Moreno. In 2016, the Interior Ministry charged Shuar leader Agustin Wachapá with "inciting discord" based on his Facebook posts encouraging Amazonian peoples to resist the military presence on their territories. Wachapá, who opposed a local mining project, was acquitted in 2018 by an Ecuadorian court. But while the Moreno government initially adopted a more conciliatory approach, it also used these provisions against Indigenous leaders following the 2019 uprising. Days after the end of the protests, the state prosecutor's office announced an investigation into CONAIE leader Jamie Vargas for promoting "subversive" activities.

In addition to this complex legislative framework, the Pink Tide president's unprecedented popular support created another political opportunity barrier for Indigenous CSOs. Correa was elected in 2007 with 57 percent of the vote and reelected twice by a large margin (in 2009 and 2013). His approval rating remained high throughout his terms and never dropped below 51 percent. Moreover, his support was particularly strong among lower-income and working-class Ecuadorians. During the 1990s and early 2000s, Indigenous movements were successful in part because strong organizations such as CONAIE were able mobilize large numbers of non-Indigenous citizens against neoliberal austerity packages and a declining standard of living. They forged alliances with leftist parties and labor unions. Achieving this kind of cross-sector solidarity is far more difficult when living standards and revenue are improving for the majority of the population. Under Correa, Indigenous organizations continued to engage in protest, particularly against oil drilling in the Amazon, but they were unable to successfully reach beyond groups of supporters to engage the broader public. Indigenous leaders recognize this. A Shuar leader who had joined Acacho's protest put it this way: "It became much harder with him [Correa] in power. The economy was strong and, yes, a lot of money was put into roads, medical clinics, social programs, welfare programs. Of course, it is harder to get working-class mestizos to contest the government in these circumstances" (anonymous interview with Chiriboga, April 12, 2018).

But there is more to the story. Indigenous peoples tend to be presented as a monolithic political constituency. There are deep divisions within national Indigenous populations, just as there are within any ethnic or social group (Colloredo-Mansfeld 2009). Media and academic attention has focused on the hostility between the Correa government and prominent Indigenous organizations such as CONAIE, CONFENAIE, and the Shuar federations, leaving many observers with the impression that "Indigenous peoples" were at war with the government. The reality is far more nuanced and complex. Correa was popular with working-class voters, but many Indigenous citizens benefited from his socioeconomic policies as well. Unsurprisingly, this translated into support among some Indigenous communities, although this was less visible because the larger organizations tended to grab the headlines.

I regularly encountered evidence of this during my fieldwork. The larger, more politically active Indigenous organizations, as well as most of those in the Amazon provinces, remained critical of Correa. But in smaller, local organizations, as well as among community members not directly involved in large politically oriented CSOs, the picture was very different. This first struck me when I visited a small Indigenous women's organization on the outskirts of the northern town of Ibarra in 2016. I had just come from a discussion at the local chapter of the CONAIE where representatives reaffirmed the "persecution" they continued to endure under then-president

Correa. As I sat down in the circle of chairs set up to engage in a discussion with the women, I noticed a large portrait of Correa hanging on the wall to my right. Underneath the portrait was a table with flowers and candles. It looked almost like a shrine that one often sees in Latin American homes to honor deceased relatives. I commented to the women that I was surprised to see this, given that many Indigenous organizations accused the man in the portrait of political persecution. Several of the women responded vehemently to my observation. Carmen insisted that:

> You will hear that kind of thing from CONAIE and other big organizations. That is their experience and they can express their opinions. But please understand that they do not represent all, or even most, Indigenous people. Much of what they fight for is good, but they have a political agenda. Here, our goal [she gestured to the other women in the circle] is to live a dignified life, to feed our children, to send them to school, to get medical attention when we need it. Our president has done much to give us these things. We respect and support him for this. (Carmen, interview with the author and Chiriboga, June 16, 2016)

This meeting took place in 2016, at the beginning of my research. Over the next three years (including after Correa left office in early 2017), I continued to see his portrait on the walls of small, Indigenous CSOs throughout the Andean region and heard perspectives that echoed those of Carmen and her friends. These individuals expressed little interest in responding to calls from national Indigenous organizations to mobilize against the government. Even among larger organizations opposition to Correa was not unanimous; the National Confederation of Campesinos, Indigenous Peoples, and Afro-Ecuadorians (Confederación Nacional de Organizaciones Campesinas, Indígenas y Negras, FENOCIN) continued to (sometimes tentatively) support the government, a position which has occasionally led to tensions with CONAIE.

In contrast to his former boss, Moreno's approval rating took a nosedive shortly after his election and continued its downward spiral throughout his mandate. This is hardly surprising given that he campaigned on sustaining the social citizenship and redistributive policies of the Citizens' Revolution yet did exactly the opposite. While support for Moreno increased among those who opposed him during the election (upper-middle professional classes and the country's elite), it collapsed among the lower-income and working-class Ecuadorians who had voted for him. The latter group represents a much larger segment of the population, and this created new political opportunities for Indigenous CSOs. Despite Moreno's early overtures to Indigenous civil society, the deep cuts to social spending and declining living standards meant that the president would find few friends among these organizations. CONAIE, ECUARUNARI, CONFENAIE, FENOCIN, and others took advantage of this window to once again assume a cross-sectoral leadership role in the movement against Moreno's IMF-supported austerity measures.

Citizenship Regime

From the 1990s to the late 2010s, Ecuador oscillated between a neoliberal citizenship regime and an alternative "postneoliberal" model of social citizenship and back again. Correa's Citizens' Revolution and his 2008 constitution promised a new, postneoliberal citizenship regime. The constitution rejects the neoliberal model and establishes citizen participation in decision making as a fundamental right. Article 1 declares Ecuador to be a plurinational state, one of the primary demands of Indigenous civil society in Ecuador since CONAIE's first manifesto. The constitution also establishes social citizenship rights, declaring that state economic policy will aim first and foremost to achieve a more adequate redistribution of the national wealth. As organizations such as CONAIE and ECUARUNARI had demanded, the constitution recognizes Indigenous modes of communitarian production and affirms that the state will intervene to encourage a more equal distribution of the means of production.

Indigenous leaders and community members we interviewed fully embraced the new model, while insisting that the Correa and Moreno administrations have failed to put it into practice. But the new constitution and subsequent legislation altered the perception of citizenship and created expectations around the role of Indigenous peoples in the public sphere. Leaders frequently and consistently addressed themes such as the role of citizens in decision-making, participation as a right, and the relationship between citizens and the state. The perspective of Rosana, an Indigenous seamstress from the province of Imbabura is typical of respondents: "Being a citizen means being treated with dignity, with respect by the state and its representatives. It means we do not just vote every few years, it means we can have a voice in decisions that affect our lives. It is not just about individual rights, it is about our collective rights to live well according to our own ways" (Rosana, interview with the author, July 26, 2016).

The discourse of the Citizens' Revolution proposes the model of citizenship that Rosana and her colleagues envision. Following up on the constitutional provisions around citizen participation, the Ecuadorian government adopted the Citizen Participation Law (Ley Orgánica de Participación Ciudadana) in 2010. The law reaffirms participatory rights using collective language and creates various types of state-society mechanisms through which citizens and groups (such as Indigenous nations) have the right to participate in decisions that involve them. The legislation requires agencies and departments at all levels of government (central, regional, provincial and municipal) to establish a "system of citizen participation," which incorporates one or more of these mechanisms into planning and decision making. For example, citizens can form a local neighborhood assembly at their own initiative and, once it is established, they can put forward development plans and local policy initiatives, administer service and infrastructure improvements, promote education with respect to citizen rights, and exercise oversight over decisions made. The law includes specific provisions for Indigenous communities, allowing them to create local participatory mechanisms that conform to their own organizational forms developed in accordance with their internal traditional customs and practices.

For some, participation in these mechanisms had a positive impact on citizenship through more equitable access to public goods and services, as well as by encouraging people to develop a greater sense of political efficacy and confidence in their role as citizens. Typical of the perspectives expressed by interviewees, an Indigenous woman living near Quito told me: "Before the assembly, I was too shy to say anything, to express my opinions in front of strangers even though I had strong opinions about what my community needed. Really, I was terrified. But knowing that I have the right to participate, I started to speak and now it is hard to shut me up" (Rosario, interview with the author, July 14, 2016).

However, a careful analysis of the legislative texts reveals a consistent pattern of parameters around popular participation, both in terms of the scope of participation that is possible and the types of mechanisms in which citizens should participate. Citizens are encouraged to participate in the public sphere, but within the established "participatory system." Participation in one of the mechanisms established by the Citizen Participation Law is deemed legitimate; engagement in the public sphere beyond this system is not. These limitations placed around both the scope and arenas for public engagement appear to simultaneously expand and limit citizenship. Alfredo, an Indigenous leader from Imbabura, pointed out the inherent contradictions of the citizenship regime that developed under the Citizens' Revolution:

> Well, there are far more ways to interact with the state now. The constitution, and the Participation Law, they created all kinds of ways of participating in local and even national government institutions. This is good in theory. We have used some of them. But any other kind of participation, such as through our Indigenous organizations, well that is not seen as legitimate. In fact, they are increasingly seeking to criminalize it. It's paradoxical: more opportunities for participation, which is good, but it is controlled participation, which is bad. (Alfredo, interview with the author and Chiriboga, June 17, 2016)

Perhaps the most significant change ushered in by the new citizenship regime was the focus on economic and social rights. Article 284 of the constitution claims that state economic policy will aim first and foremost to achieve a more adequate redistribution of the national wealth and to encourage national production. Article 285 states that the focus of fiscal policy will be financing social services and public investment. This aspect of the Citizens' Revolution is less ambiguous than the citizen participation dimension and produced tangible results for the poor. Correa declared one-third of the country's debt to be illegitimate, raised taxes on the wealthiest Ecuadorians, and invested the additional revenue in health care, education, and infrastructure. Despite dire warnings from international financial institutions, Ecuador experienced low unemployment and significant annual growth (an average of 4.2 percent) from 2007 to 2015, a pattern that was sustained during the 2008–9 international financial crisis. His government invested over $20 billion in education over ten years, including the construction of schools that offer programs in Indigenous languages. The minimum wage was raised from US$170 per month in 2007 to US$375 by the end of his term in 2017, and he implemented a conditional cash transfer program for low-income families. In the same time frame, the national poverty rate decreased from 40 to 23 percent. Extreme poverty for Indigenous peoples dropped from over 70 to just over 30 percent (Masala and Monni 2019).

Many Indigenous CSOs take the position that democratic citizenship requires socioeconomic equality. A leader from Chimborazo affirmed that "being a citizen is about more than just voting in elections. It requires a certain level of equality. People cannot really exercise their rights as citizens if there are such inequalities that prevent them from participating on equal terms" (Hernán, interview with Chiriboga, September 17, 2018). In fact, among those Indigenous leaders interviewed during the course of my research, even Correa's harshest critics conceded that their communities had experienced improved material conditions and access to public services during his mandate.

These progressive economic reforms were largely dismantled by Correa's successor. The new government also continued to support oil drilling in the Amazon, although Moreno originally adopted a far more conciliatory style of politics than his predecessor. Shortly after taking office, he launched a National Dialogue intended to repair the relationship between the state and civil society. Moreno also assumed a far less hostile attitude toward the media and civil society actors, demonstrating a welcome degree of tolerance for contrary viewpoints. Among other measures, he reformed the Communication Law in 2018 by taking power away from the controversial SUPERCOM oversight body and eliminating some of the more restrictive articles that opponents referred to as "gag laws."

While Indigenous groups who had felt persecuted by Correa saw these as important peacemaking gestures, Moreno's continued support for extractive activities and the reversal of social spending policies quickly tarnished the relationship. The last straw was the October 2019 austerity package that, among other things, eliminated fuel subsidies dating back four decades. These measures were intended to put $1.5 billion per year back into state coffers, money that was to be used to service the deficit according to a deal with the IMF. They represented a direct threat to the postneoliberal citizenship regime that many Ecuadorians had come to embrace over the previous decade.

Indigenous Civil Society in Twenty-First-Century Ecuador: Adaptation and Challenges

In June 2016, I sat down with Ronaldo, an Indigenous activist based in Quito, at a café in the city's working-class south end. While we had remained in contact through social media, this was the first time we had met in person since 2009. Back then, I was primarily interested in the Indigenous movement's achievements in the 1990s and the apparent reversal of fortune they had experienced since 2005. As I began to reengage with Indigenous activists in 2016, it quickly became clear how much things had changed over the preceding decade. Ronaldo worried that the Indigenous civil society in general, and key organizations such as CONAIE in particular, had lost steam. He expressed concern that they were no longer able to achieve significant outcomes and that young people in particular were less politically engaged than previous generations. Ronaldo later acknowledged that what he was really talking about were the large-scale marches, roadblocks, and land occupations of the 1990s.

As I spent time with organizations across the country over the next few years, a clear trend emerged. Since 2005, they have shifted their efforts from disruptive (and costly) protest and focused on engaging in the policy process, promoting political participation in their communities, communication and public relations, alliance building, identity promotion, and education. Those with the means to do so are exploring new ways of mobilizing resources and are using ICTs to reach a wider audience and to engage in the "virtual" public sphere on their own terms.

Through my conversations with Indigenous leaders, I have identified four reasons why disruptive tactics were replaced with alternative forms of engagement from 2005 to 2019. First, the Correa government's redistributive social policies helped to meet the basic needs of large segments of the population, including Indigenous peoples. Reducing poverty and other dimensions of human insecurity directly addresses the types of economic grievances that encourage many marginalized actors to assume the risks involved in disruptive protest. This may make it harder to mobilize supporters who fear losing some of the benefits they have received. Rodolfo addressed this point: "It easier to get people to mobilize around basic necessities like income, food, water, than around more abstract things like identity, or even rights. You can't blame people, I guess. But when a government makes life better for people, they are less willing to fight for other goals" (Rodolfo, interview with the author, February 22, 2018). Correa's consistent popularity among working-class and lower-income Ecuadorians also shaped the political opportunities available to opposing groups. Leaders of politically oriented organizations spoke of "co-optation" and insisted that this made it more difficult to bring non-Indigenous working-class sectors on board as they were able to do in the past.

Second, Indigenous Ecuadorians enjoy, at least on paper, a vastly expanded set of political and cultural rights following the adoption of the 2008 constitution. These rights are granted based on their status as precolonial peoples and align closely with UNDRIP: rights to ancestral territories and the resources on these lands, some local political autonomy, communal land-use models, and recognition of cultural practices, from Indigenous justice to traditional modes of agricultural production. This means that for many activists it made more sense to work through state institutions to ensure that these rights would be implemented in practice. As Marlon Santí, a former CONAIE president, had once told me following the adoption of the constitution in 2009: "We have worked hard to achieve what is in the constitution, now we must continue to work hard to ensure that officials do their duty, as public servants, by respecting the constitution and its provisions. But now, we have more to build on. We can use what we have gained to ensure that our rights are respected" (Santí, interview with the author, May 13, 2009). Related to this, the constitution and Citizen Participation Law created a wide array of mechanisms through which civil society actors can engage with the state and participate in the political process. While these mechanisms may be flawed and may fail to live up to expectations, Indigenous CSOs have more choices and entry points to state institutions, which allow them to diversify their approaches. In this section we can see that many organizations have taken advantage of this new participatory architecture.

Third, the reliance of some Indigenous organizations on various levels of government for financial support has led to self-censorship. A number of representatives from organizations that do not receive public money argued that those who do are effectively co-opted. While this is debatable, it is clear that while state-funded actors may continue to pressure the state through institutional channels, they are less likely to engage in protest for fear of losing their *permitido* status.

Finally, the Correa government used various forms of repression against "unauthorized" Indigenous actors with increasing frequency. In the Amazon, the president sent the armed forces to confront Indigenous protesters who had mobilized to block oil companies and other extractive industries from developing projects on their territories. As discussed in this chapter, Indigenous leaders were charged with various offenses for leading protests or for "insulting" the president. In addition to this, Correa regularly used state media to publicly criticize and denounce opponents, including *no permitido* Indigenous leaders. This often led to further consequences, such as harassment by state agencies or by the president's supporters.

Ecuadorian Indigenous CSOs in the 2010s operated in a different political context and have adjusted their strategies and tactics accordingly. Yet their priorities have remained relatively consistent over the past three decades: land rights, environmental protection and control of natural resources on traditional territories, socioeconomic rights and redistribution, intercultural education, cultural rights, and the recognition of plurination-ality. The remainder of this chapter explores how Indigenous civil society pursued these goals from 2005 to 2020. It focuses on the core activities of Indigenous civil society as identified by leaders and activists: resource mobilization, intervention in the policy process, communication and public relations, identity promotion, education, and—when all else fails—disruptive protest.

Political Participation and Influencing Policy

Mobilizing structures are the building blocks for civil society but the ultimate goal is to have a say in decision making and to influence the policy process. This is one of the roles that has changed the most over the past two decades. When I first visited Ecuador in 2009, I spoke to many individuals who had been active during the 1990s. Luis Macas is one of the most prominent Indigenous leaders in Ecuador. He led CONAIE during the peak of the 1990s protest cycle. He was elected to the National Assembly under the banner of Pachakutik, appointed Minister of Agriculture by Lucio Gutiérrez in 2003, and ran for president of Ecuador in 2006. During a brief conversation in 2009, he argued that Indigenous peoples had achieved significant gains through disruptive action, but that it was time for Indigenous CSOs to diversify their strategies. Macas stated that politics can also be about working through civil society and institutions such as the courts and cited the need to take on oil and mining companies through these means (Macas, interview with the author, May 13, 2009).

During the course of my fieldwork from 2016 to 2019, it became clear that Macas had accurately predicted the future. Indigenous organizations, particularly CONAIE and the large regional associations, were engaging in an ongoing, sustained multiscalar positioning strategy. This includes dialogue with all levels of government, working through formal and informal institutions, and developing strategic relationships.

By the late 2000s, and particularly following the adoption of the 2008 constitution, which formally recognized the rights they had been fighting for, Indigenous groups had more options available to them. This evolved into less reactive and more proactive but sustained political action. While some of the basic demands have been met on paper, the focus during the 2010s has been to work through various channels and mechanisms to ensure that they are implemented in practice. The overall guiding strategy for Indigenous organizations seeking to promote political participation and influence policy has three dimensions: shoring up support at the community level, engaging with the most effective state-society mechanisms for a given objective, and building on previous achievements to legitimize their claims.

The first and most important task for Indigenous CSOs is sustaining and deepening relationships with the communities they represent through *trabajo en territorio* (community work within a territory). The importance of this work was highlighted by almost every leader, activist, and community member I spoke to and is a distinct feature of Indigenous civil society. It consists of three facets. The first involves providing training and educational workshops. This is discussed in more detail later in this chapter. The second entails engaging with local residents on community development projects. This varies from one community to another, but according to Marco of the Indigenous and Peasant Association of Bolívar, "responding to needs of our base is the best way to forge engagement with our organization" (Marco, interview with the author and Chiriboga, March 8, 2018). Community work is not only important for local and regional organizations. CONAIE, which is headquartered in central Quito, cannot afford to distance itself from rural communities. According to communications agent Apawki Castro, "addressing the problems and needs of the communities, attending to the demands that emerge from the base, working on these problems with them, this is how we strengthen the organizational process of CONAIE." But he added that these projects also allow CONAIE representatives to foster political support by rallying community members (Apawki, interview with the author and Chiriboga, March 23, 2018). FOIN representative Rosita also prioritizes this work not only because social development is a worthy goal in itself but also because it provides leaders with the opportunity to make isolated communities aware of threats related to mining activities and to solicit support to fight incursions into their territories (Rosita, interview with Chiriboga, April 12, 2018). This facet of *trabajo en territorio* clearly has both a development and a political objective and is a fundamental element of Indigenous civil society.

Finally, community work also helps organizations to develop their policy agenda through traditional governance practices. The decision-making process for each organization begins in the villages and leaders are expected to travel around the territory to meet with locals. This includes calling community meetings to gather feedback about the organization's work, identify needs and priorities, solicit preferred solutions, and collect ideas about how to proceed. According to Indigenous governance practices, these meetings are conducted in a participatory format that invites engagement from all members of the community. Once they have collected ideas from the villages on their territory, leaders call a larger assembly at a centralized location and invite people to attend. An effort is made to achieve consensus whenever possible, and the decisions made at these assemblies guide the leaders moving forward. It is also important that this process not be unidirectional. As described by a Shuar leader Pascual, it involves feeding priorities up from the villages, to the local organization, to the provincial body for Pastaza, and finally to CONFENAIE and CONAIE. The regional and national organizations then take this to the appropriate state agencies (Pascual, interview with Chiriboga, February 23, 2018).

This is a complex and time-consuming exercise for organizations, but leaders attach a great deal of importance to *trabajo en territorio* for two reasons. They see this work as a means of strengthening ties with the base. This is essential for any organization that seeks to play a role in the policy process, from political parties to NGOs. Leaders understand that the more support they have, the more likely officials are to listen to them. But they also strive to respect traditional governance by maintaining communitarian and participatory practices. As a leader from Chimborazo put it: "Our policy priorities and strategies for achieving them starts on our territories, in the communities. It is bottom up, not top down like the state. This is our way" (Eusebio, interview with the author and Chiriboga, February 8, 2018).

The community territory work informs Indigenous CSOs' policy priorities and strategies, but they must interact with the state and other external actors in order to advance their demands through the policy cycle. In Ecuador, this enterprise can take various forms and is carried out through both formal and informal institutions. Willingness to engage through formal institutions depends on the organizations' relationship with the state, but most of the large and midsized associations I studied do participate in various processes and mechanisms at all levels of government. They engage in dialogue with civil servants, politicians, and other social organizations. They look for policy window openings and strategically request meetings with officials from the relevant government ministry, or with municipal representatives depending on the issue to be addressed. Many organizations use tools such as petitions to support their requests. Larger organizations may have representatives with expertise in particular policy areas (environment, education, housing) that develop sustained (formal or informal) relationships with relevant government departments, while smaller ones may rely on one leader to do all of the work. A number of organizations also participate in mechanisms established by the executive, such as the President's Dialogue promoted by

Moreno shortly after he took office and again during the 2019 protests. These dialogues are an opportunity for Indigenous leaders to speak directly to the president. While there is much skepticism, some appear willing to take advantage of opportunities. Julián from the Pastaza Achuar Federation observed, "Our interests are usually only considered when it is convenient for authorities. But with the current [Moreno] government, there is an opening, there are more links being created with organizations" (Julián, interview with Chiriboga, February 23, 2018).

This work requires Indigenous civil society leaders to develop and refine their political skills. Experienced participants defined political skills as understanding how to seek political support for a given problem or initiative, knowing which institutions and agencies do what and who can get things done, being familiar with procedures for submitting a complaint (denuncia), understanding how procedures and institutions work at various levels of government, and knowing about legislation and Indigenous rights. Participants almost unanimously claimed that Indigenous organizations have gotten much better at this over the past decade. They also placed a great deal of importance on personal contacts and the unwritten and rules and subtleties of informal institutions. Leaders exert considerable effort on building relationships with local and state officials who are open to working with them.

Some representatives also pointed out that Indigenous leaders continue to participate directly in the political sphere by standing for elections to the National Assembly, regional prefectures, and municipal councils. Pachakutik remains active; it won a record twenty-seven seats in the 2021 election. A representative from a local organization in Tungurahua province summarized the sentiments I heard from a number of his colleagues across the country: "There are some benefits of participating in government, of course. But there are also risks. We saw that in 2005. I think we have been more successful participating through our organizations, from the outside, rather that participating on the inside, inside the system. The system is corrupt, and it corrupts. It is hard to hold power accountable when you are part of it" (anonymous interview with the author and Chiriboga, February 8, 2018).

Indigenous actors made limited use of the new participatory architecture created by the 2008 constitution and the 2010 Citizen Participation Law. Just under half of those I spoke to had participated in mechanisms such as the silla vacía (empty seat), reserved for citizens on various decision-making bodies, or the local citizens' assemblies. Community members and leaders who have participated in these mechanisms pursued various objectives, from obtaining land titles to promoting infrastructure and transportation projects. Most of these individuals complained about the absence of genuine citizen participation and argued that participatory mechanisms do not work in practice as they are promoted in the enabling legislation. Based on my findings, only participatory mechanisms located in Indigenous-majority communities served as efficient channels for influencing decision making, and even then, only at the local level. The citizens' assembly in Alausí, for example, achieved some success in normalizing land titles, creating an Indigenous knowledge program and a small business fund, installing utilities, and paving streets. While limited local resources constrain what the local assembly is able to accomplish, there has been some movement on all of these fronts, with several projects ongoing. But Alausí is a community with deep Indigenous roots and a history of activism. Respondents agreed that local Indigenous CSOs, or branches of the regional organizations, served as an essential resource. They provided guidance on traditional Indigenous governance practices as well as knowledge of Ecuador's citizen participation laws.

There is, however, considerable variation with respect to strategies and tactics used by CSOs. This is based on variables related to resources and political opportunities (such as the size of the organization), relationship with the state, and geography. CONAIE is the country's (and arguably Latin America's) most prominent Indigenous organization and its tactical repertoire reflects this. Its highly democratic structure reflects the need for regional representation and accountability. The CONAIE National Congress is held every three years. It consists of representatives from across Ecuador and is the highest decision-making body. Elected delegates make resolutions, develop plans and strategies, and elect the organization's leaders which form the Governing Council (Consejo de Gobierno). The Governing Council includes the president, vice-president, and the section heads. ECUARUNARI represents the (primarily Kichwa) people of the highlands and accounts for around 45 percent of the CONAIE delegates. CONFENIAE represents multiple smaller nations in Ecuadorian Amazon and holds 30 percent of delegate seats, while the Confederation of Indigenous Nationalities of the Ecuadorian Coast (Confederación de Nacionalidades Indígenas de la Costa Ecuatoriana, CONAICE) holds 25 percent. Each of these three organizations comprises various provincial and local organizations in their respective region. CONAIE section heads (*dirigentes*) are responsible for policy areas of keen interest to Indigenous peoples and perform the roles of "shadow" cabinet ministers. There are *dirigentes* for Education, Women and the Family, Territorial and Natural Resource, Health and Nutrition, Youth, Communication, and National and International Policy. CONAIE strives to achieve regional representation in the council. Other bodies include the Assembly, made up of representatives of the various nationalities and peoples of Ecuador, which evaluates the work of the council; and an advisory committee that provides technical advice.

The structure of CONAIE reflects its status as a form of Indigenous government and its organizational architecture functions much like a parallel state. As such, it pursues a wide range of tactics and engages with various state-society mechanisms. CONAIE is an excellent example of the multiscalar positioning approach. Its strategy focuses on addressing community problems and priorities, working with partner organizations, and not losing touch with the base. Once priorities have been established according to the bottom-up approach described above, CONAIE representatives write policy briefs, reports, and recommendation letters addressed to the appropriate government agency. The section heads for areas such as environment and education are likely to take the lead on this. Departments at all levels of government receive a frequent flow of representatives and documents from CONAIE and its affiliate organizations determined to keep the pressure up. *Asambleístas* (members of the National Assembly), particularly those representing constituencies with large Indigenous populations, are also accustomed to letters and proposals from the organizations. In some cases, CONAIE representatives develop close working relationships with bureaucrats and *asambleístas*. But these relationships can be tenuous and depend on shifting political opportunities and alliances. Humberto Cholango, the former CONAIE leader appointed to head the National Water Secretariat, provided a direct link to the highest levels of government and CONAIE officials met with him regularly. Cholango resigned during the October 2019 uprising. He had little choice; he could not support a government that was suppressing Indigenous protesters without destroying his legitimacy with Indigenous civil society. Yet the resignation of the only Indigenous minister in the Moreno cabinet closed an access point to the state.

Delegations from CONAIE also participate regularly in the various round-tables and consultative bodies set up by the government to solicit feedback. According to leaders, this can be an effective approach when the officials are open to integrating Indigenous perspectives into policy, yet they always have backup plans if this is not the case. As one environmental leader noted, "It is always best if we can have a good relationship with our *asambleístas* and with the Ministry (of the Environment). But if they don't listen to our concerns, we have other options" (anonymous interview with Chiriboga, April 15, 2018). One of these options is meeting with members of opposition parties or with officials from local or municipal governments not controlled by the national governing party. CONAIE and its leaders fully understand the notion of political opportunities, and how it can sometimes be useful to play politicians from different parties against each other. And of course, disruptive protest remains on the table as a last resort, as demonstrated by the events of October 2019. Representatives from CONAIE, ECUARUNARI, CONFENAIE, and various regional organizations emphasized that the political skills required to navigate the political landscape developed from years of experience and practice.

CONAIE and other large CSOs now work within two spaces: in person and online (Apawki, interview with the author and Chiriboga, March 23, 2018). The former remains far more common, and Indigenous representatives across the country emphasized that ICTs can complement but never replace person-to-person contact. But ICTs are becoming an increasingly important tool in the tactical repertoire. A communications official explained: "With social media, we can take our message to the world. We don't have to go through private media, who will only distort what we have to say" (anonymous interview with the author, September 14, 2016). But most of the individuals interviewed stressed that the fact that everyone can create social media posts does not in itself shift the balance of power. The state and corporate interests have greater resources to develop targeted social media campaigns and more practice when it comes to framing issues. Medium-sized organizations follow the same approach as their larger counterparts. They begin their work at the community level and engage with various state-society mechanisms, although generally at the provincial or municipal levels (Eusebio, interview with the author and Chiriboga, February 8, 2018). Engagement with the central government is more likely to happen through CONAIE, ECUARUNARI, or CONFENAIE. Leaders of the provincial organizations claim that they can position themselves more favorably by aligning with larger ones.

The smaller, local organizations are more likely to claim that they avoid politics and focus on community and sustainable development projects. Leaders tend to assert that political action is the domain of larger organizations. A representative from a community in the southern province of Cañar explained that "our role is to develop and administer social programs and services. In our communities, we have to fill the gaps where the state fails" (anonymous interview with Chiriboga, January 26, 2018). But when analyzing their responses, it becomes clear that leaders of these smaller organizations tend to associate politics with disruptive protest and that they are, in fact, politically active as members of Indigenous civil society. Thus, Fabian commented that "we prefer to hold meetings with relevant departments and authorities to get things done. Our goal is to make life better for our communities. We don't participate in marches and roadblocks. That is too political" (Fabian, interview with Chiriboga, January 25, 2018). In general, smaller organizations are more likely to receive state funding than larger and midsized organizations, which have a greater capacity to develop alternative sources of revenue. This limits the autonomy of small organizations, but their leaders pointed out that there is nothing to prevent them from working through larger bodies to pursue political goals.

While preferring to avoid confrontation, many smaller organizations do engage with local government and find municipal bodies to be more receptive than higher levels of government. A representative from a neighborhood women's organization argued that "there are some openings at the local level depending on the local government. Less at higher levels, they do not see us an important" (anonymous interview with the author, June 14, 2016). An example from rural Chimborazo demonstrates how small organizations can engage in decision making at the local level without support from regional organizations. In an Indigenous-majority village, a number of projects were spearheaded by a local community organization, including lighting and street paving, as well as beautification projects, such as a community garden. Street lighting was installed for a neighborhood of about twenty blocks. A needs assessment was conducted through a community forum; residents were invited to attend and to vote on priorities for improving their community. The organization established a list of priorities, prepared a report, and delivered its requests to the local municipal council, which in turn applied for funding through an infrastructure program administered by SENPLADES, the state development agency.

Indigenous CSOs have recognized for some time the importance of alliance building. But their approach to building their networks has evolved over the first two decades of the twenty-first century. ICTs allow isolated communities to strengthen ties with domestic and transnational networks, and to share information and strategies with partner organizations. Leaders noted that ICTs allow for faster and more efficient communication and help activists work in a more articulated way. They also allow organizations to have a better understanding and appreciation for what is happening in other communities, which helps to coordinate efforts. As Carmen said: "They help to bring us closer together, to make the territory smaller because we have a lot of isolated communities, and before we often didn't know what was happening elsewhere. By using ICTs we can communicate, we can know about activities happening in other parishes" (Carmen, interview with the author and Chiriboga, June 16, 2016).

Resource Mobilization

Indigenous CSOs require human, information, ICT, and, of course, financial resources in order to function. There was unanimous agreement among all of the individuals I spoke to that their organizations have limited resources but that they manage to pursue their goals through flexibility, creativity, and relying on the generosity of their communities.

Larger Indigenous organizations employ full-time staff, while smaller ones must rely primarily on volunteers. In most cases, however, limited budgets prevent organizations from hiring people with specialized skills and expertise. Leaders observed that to compete with state agencies and other powerful actors such as mining and oil companies, they need people with various skill sets: ICTs, political communication, marketing and promotion, ability to develop compelling press releases and public relations campaigns, and proficiency in creating captivating multimedia content. This was identified as a resource issue in that people who have developed these professional skills (Indigenous or not) expect a decent salary. The cost of postsecondary education is high in Ecuador and finding someone with the required expertise in ICTs or communications who is willing to work on a volunteer basis is nearly impossible. Within the communities, those who do have the necessary skills tend to be busy with their own work. Indigenous youth who receive a formal postsecondary education leave their communities to get jobs in the cities; those who already live in cities are lured away from Indigenous organizations by more tempting job offers.

Information is essential in order to make educated decisions and adjust strategies. Representatives claimed that ICTs have made their jobs easier on this front. As Willy stated, technology "brings us closer to what is going on. We are better informed, and we can get information directly without having a third party select and interpret it for us" (Willy, interview with the author, August 17, 2016). The Internet is primarily used for access to information about relevant legislation, data and statistics, social trends or current news that may impact the community or the organization's goals.

It is seen as a particularly valuable tool for information gathering because it provides access to sources that would otherwise be unavailable to activists. In the past, it was necessary to travel to the cities or rely on external allies to deliver information to rural communities.

ICTs constitute a resource that was relatively insignificant when Ecuadorian Indigenous peoples created these mobilizing structures, but they have become crucial. Computers, cellphones, and social media are essential components of any organization's resource mobilization strategy. Interviewees spoke to the value of technology in terms of making their work easier and more efficient. They felt that it was impossible for organizations to be completely integrated into the public sphere without using social media. Almost all expressed interest in innovative ICT-related projects in support of the communities. Willy put it this way: "We want to preserve our customs and ways, but this doesn't mean we are stuck in the past. We cannot function in modern society unless we are online, or things will move on without us. This is especially important for our young people" (Willy, interview with the author, August 17, 2016).

Despite their leaders' recognition of the importance of ICTs, the overall picture is that the use of these technologies remains limited; Indigenous civil society looks nothing like the "networked" movements described by Castells (2015) and Tufekci (2017). There was considerable consensus among leaders that ICTs serve to complement their work and are an important part of their repertoire, but they can only support rather than replace the various activities they regularly engage in. Oswaldo summarized what may of his colleagues felt: "We are able to use computers, cellphones and social media effectively because we had already built a strong organization over the years: strong relationships, links with our community, an understanding of our rights and how to get things done with the relevant authorities. ICTs would be of much help if we didn't already have this" (Oswaldo, interview with the author, June 23, 2016).

Of course, the ability to acquire information and technology, or to hire experienced staff, depends on an organization's financial resources. Indigenous leaders, particularly in the highlands, reported that grants from domestic and international NGOs had dramatically declined over the previous decade. This obviously has a significant and wide-ranging impact on the capacity of Indigenous organizations to engage in the public sphere. While the reasons for this trend are not entirely clear, experienced activists I spoke to identified three possible explanations.

The first aligns with the argument made at the beginning of this book and that was succinctly described by a representative from the FENOCIN: "They lost interest in us" (Villamar, interview with the author and Chiriboga, December 5, 2017). Others pointed out that in the past, much of the funding available was provided by faith organizations from overseas. Representatives of the Federation of Evangelical Indigenous Peoples and Organizations (Consejo de Pueblos y Organizaciones Indígenas Evangélicas del Ecuador, FEINE) insisted that foreign missionaries were traditionally key players in Indigenous organizations' resource mobilization strategies, as they provided money, supplies, equipment, and training. They noted that over the past two decades, successive governments had made evangelical Christian groups feel unwelcomed in Ecuador. But representatives from secular organizations such as the CONAIE reminded me that they had campaigned against the presence of U.S.-based evangelical organizations for decades. One leader insisted that the religious groups "always offered resources with conditions, and those conditions involved allowing them to impose their religion, their values, and their culture. We are open to NGOs working with us if they respect us and want to support rather than change our communities" (anonymous interview with the author and Chiriboga, December 8, 2017).

Finally, some pointed out that under Correa, many NGOs not aligned with the government had left the country or faced harassment from state agencies. This was the most common perception among those I spoke to, particularly in the Amazon. Leaders felt that the political agenda behind this was to make life difficult for NGOs working with Indigenous organizations opposed to the government. The ultimate goal, they say, was to deprive their organizations of funding, a tactic that seems to have been largely successful. Rosita of FOIN explained that in addition to putting in place measures that "limited the ability of organizations to receive funds from nonprofits," the previous administration "also closed the government's doors on us" (Rosita, interview with Chiriboga, April 12, 2018).

Under half of the Ecuadorian organizations included in this project (40 percent) relied on funding from at least one level of government. But dependence on state subsidies limits political autonomy and puts organizations at a disadvantage vis-à-vis government and private entities. Leaders and representatives interviewed noted that they must use caution about what they say in a public forum or what they post on social media. They are hesitant to criticize elected officials in the name of their organization but note that even when expressing a personal opinion, they must think carefully about the financial repercussions for the organization. As one activist from the northern highlands indicated, this leads to self-censorship: "We are careful about taking positions because it can hurt us, and our responsibility is to respond to the needs of people we represent. We depend so much on the state, on funds from government agencies, we can't offend them by taking strong positions" (anonymous interview with the author, June 24, 2016). A number of leaders pointed out that this is not so different from accepting NGO funds. From an organization in Pastaza, Julián asserted that money always comes with conditions, and that NGOs have their own objectives, just as governments do. Many NGOs receive their own funding from private interests which may have a hidden agenda. Julián mentioned the example of mining companies that send in seemingly unaffiliated "charitable" organizations to prepare the groundwork in Indigenous communities (Julián, interview with Chiriboga, February 23, 2018).

Some of the more politically oriented CSOs are unwilling to self-censor and most Indigenous organizations rely on other means of acquiring resources. The term that came up most frequently when leaders were asked about this was *autogestión* (self-management). This refers to a system of resource mobilization that revolves around soliciting goods and services through contributions, donations, and pro bono work. Supporters of the organization, members of the community, or other organizations that do have the resources provide these free of charge, sometimes in exchange for something else. Often members of an organization use their own personal resources or those of their families and friends. They then manage these resources in collaboration with their communities. *Autogestión* allows organizations of all sizes to operate even when they lack a budget to purchase goods and services. Over 90 percent of the organizations that participated in this study use this system to some extent.

The Indigenous and Peasant Federation of Imbabura (Federación Indígena y Campesina de Imbabura, FICI) provided an interesting example of how this can work in practice. FICI is an organization based in the Kichwa market town of Otavalo. Its website (http://fici.nativeweb.org/) frames its work as a struggle against "discriminatory state policies and more than five hundred years of resistance in the face of colonial and neo-colonial exploitation and oppression." This is an ambitious goal that necessitates active engagement in the public sphere but FICI does not have a budget to purchase goods and services required to communicate with the public and promote their activities. Given the lack of access to ICTs in the rural communities they serve, FICI uses flyers to distribute information. The organization relies on the support of the many print and copy shops found in Otavalo These small businesses serve an important market in a country where few people have access to printers at home. In Otavalo, popular with foreign tourists for its Indigenous market, many of these shops are owned by relatively prosperous local Indigenous entrepreneurs. FICI has close relationships with some of these individuals, who agree to print flyers free of charge. They do this in exchange for the opportunity to promote their businesses at events and festivals organized by FICI (Rocío, interview with Chiriboga, November 27, 2017).

Other examples of *autogestión* abound, and the goods and services traded vary from one organization to another. A small women's organization in Imbabura trades clothing and other products of its members, most of whom are seamstresses. The regional federation of Indigenous organizations in the rural province of Bolívar asks all of its members to contribute agricultural products they produce on their land. These are then traded for resources that the federation (or its member organizations) need.

Some are addressing marketing deficiencies by creating producer cooperatives. The leader of a peasant federation in northern Carchi province explained: "We organize ourselves in order to eliminate the intermediary and to keep us united. With that corporation of producers, we can buy machines to pit the fruit, prepare the product, things like that" (Salomón, interview with Chiriboga, November 24, 2017). FENOCIN is developing a project, with the help of an international NGO, to train members on topics such as business entrepreneurship, procedures, and value product addition. Other organizations, such as the Pastaza Shiwiar Nationality Federation, take advantage of the support of domestic and international networks to improve their business model, or to broaden their promotional opportunities. In many communities, however, the marketing apparatus remains very basic. According to Oswaldo, a leader from Imbabura: "In the case of embroidery, there are one or two families that dedicate themselves to making clothing and have their internal businesses and sell to their circle of clients and more at fairs and festivals" (Oswaldo, interview with the author, June 23, 2016).

Over one-third (38 percent) of the organizations surveyed use ICTs to promote services and products, and many others are exploring the possibilities. Communities can announce their participation in a market or fair through social media, with information about what kind of goods will be available. ICTs can also be used to promote specific products on social networks or on a website. Some felt that technologies could help them to export their products internationally to consumers in Western countries who are interested in purchasing Indigenous handicrafts and clothing on-line. Others have started to use the Internet to help them make decisions about what potential consumers are looking for. For example, a women's cooperative that produces and sells traditional Indigenous clothing has a dedicated member who browses websites to find out about current styles and seasonal trends to think about how to market the cooperative's products (multiple interviews with the author, June 2016).

An interesting development is the use of social media to promote community tourism, and some of these initiatives have been quite successful. CSOs create pages on sites like Facebook to advertise services such as community tourism experiences. Pesillo (Olmedo), a small community north of Quito, has used Facebook as a tool to reach tourists who want to learn more about Indigenous lifestyles. The Pesillo Nuestro page, "promotes the natural and cultural beauty of the Region . . . in recognition of our identity and wealth." The small community of fewer than 4,000 had over 7,000 followers on Facebook in 2021, and it has seen a significant increase in tourism. The Shuar peoples, who live in the most isolated regions of the country, have also used Facebook to promote community tourism. José Vargas Moya, a young Shuar businessman, promotes his ecotourism company through his Facebook page, which offers videos of activities that tourists can do, articles about ecotourism, and photos of tourists enjoying the Amazon jungle. Although there are no reliable connections to the Internet in isolated towns, entrepreneurs who want to promote their services on social networks can go to the nearest city to access it from an internet café or a telecenter (José, interview with Chiriboga, February 24, 2018).

Communication and Public Relations

Indigenous CSOs must communicate regularly with various stakeholders: the communities they serve, other Indigenous organizations, state agencies, and the general public. In-person communication remains the preferred method for communicating with community members. Organizations strive to maintain ongoing, bidirectional channels of communication through *trabajo en territorio*, but they also hold regular meetings with communities and individual members to discuss problems and solutions. For example, Pueblo Kichwa Rukullakta's main line of communication is through regular community council meetings (Sanchiguango, interview with Chiriboga, April 13, 2018). Meetings are convened through the distribution of flyers, posters, and other printed documents. Particularly in rural areas, this may involve driving—or even walking—from village to village to meet with residents, although local radio has also been used for decades. This is not only more practical, but it also respects customary practices and oral tradition. Rosita from FOIN affirmed what many of her peers felt: "Technology can never replace in-person contact" (Rosita, interview with Chiriboga, April 12, 2018).

In more remote regions, in-person contact or radio are often the only means available for interacting with residents. Remote communities cannot afford to bring technology to their people. With government support, some administrative districts have been setting up *telecentros* (community centers where people can access computers and the Internet) but these are usually installed in the main town of each district. People from the rural communities do not have easy access and must frequently travel long distances on foot to access them. Organizations point out that the most isolated communities could benefit most from better access to ICTs, especially with respect to communication. Federiko of the Pastza Shuar Nation explained that "in the Amazon, communication is very difficult due to access and coverage, the use of cellphones is very limited, we can only communicate from village to village by walking there or through radio, community radio, which we have had since 2009" (Federiko, interview with Chiriboga, February 22, 2018). In some remote Andean communities, meetings are still called via sound-emitting instruments such as the *churo*, a spiral-shared conch that has been used for centuries in Kichwa territories.

Participating in the political arena requires the ability to reach a broad audience and frame issues in a way that resonates with publics beyond an organization's core membership. Indigenous organizations fully understand the role of the virtual public sphere in shaping public opinion. They use social media to communicate with domestic and international publics because "the state is on social media, the mining companies are there, the oil companies are there. They are reaching millions of people. If we are not there, then their messages are heard and ours are not" (anonymous interview with the author, April 14, 2018). Another leader captured what many of his peers expressed: "Things like Facebook pages can be used to provide more visibility and perhaps this can be important in terms of getting messages out there. Government agencies, as well as potential allies do tend to have a presence online, so it is important to be there too. Plus, we need the make sure the general public knows what we are doing from our own perspective; otherwise, we allow others to tell our story" (anonymous interview with the author, July 16, 2016)

Nearly three-quarters of the CSOs I worked with have active Facebook accounts, although some use them more frequently than others. Larger organizations such as CONAIE, ECUARUNARI, CONFENAIE, and FENOCIN have multiple Facebook pages for different purposes and aimed at diverse constituencies. For example, CONAIE has a public communications account (CONAIE Comunicación) and separate sites for women and for youth, in addition to the public page of its leader, Jamie Vargas. Less than one-third of CSOs use Twitter, although the number is growing. CONAIE and the larger regional organizations produce far more politicized content, regularly tweeting their positions on everything from government corruption to funding for public education.

Most participants stressed, however, that technology is a means to an end; they feel that it can be helpful only if Indigenous aspirations are taken seriously. As one director said: "Technology helps us, but some things remain constant: we need people to take us seriously and accept out proposals. If our proposals aren't accepted, technology or no technology, we're no further ahead" (anonymous interview with the author, September 14, 2016). But most were adamant that ICTs cannot replace "old fashioned" forms of communication, noting the importance of community to Indigenous culture. "It is always better to communicate directly, face to face, with the people. Technology can also be a good means, but it depends on how it is used. And there are limits to the quality of communication on the Internet, it loses the human touch. Its fine to use it, but sometimes human contact is needed." (anonymous interview with the author, December 11, 2017).

And some Ecuadorian Indigenous leaders, many of whom have been arrested or threatened in recent years, believe that ICTs provide yet another area for officials to engage in political persecution. As one leader stated: "Technologies have some benefits for us, but governments have the capacity to use them much more effectively than we do. ICTs make it easier to communicate with supporters, but they also make it easier for them [state and foreign agents] to monitor us, to know what we say and do" (anonymous interview with Chiriboga, February 22, 2018). Over three-quarters of interviewees in Ecuador expressed concern about cybersecurity and surveillance.

There is also evidence that governments or other powerful actors in the region, such as extractive industries, are supporting the spread of "fake news." Indigenous activists we interviewed, particularly those whose territories are located in the Amazon, where extractive industries are present, claim that they have been targeted by such campaigns. Most leaders in that region discussed examples of social media being used to frame them as terrorists or criminals. Said one leader, "The oil companies, they create fake accounts, they don't use their own. They use them to say we are engaging in acts of terrorism, that we are destroying things, that we are a danger to people. They just make things up, but it spreads over the Internet, on Facebook, and people believe it" (anonymous interview with the author and Chiriboga, April 14, 2018).

My content analysis of social media platforms demonstrates that large organizations such as CONAIE, ECUARUNARI, and CONFENAIE disseminate consistent messages that focus on social justice, Indigenous rights, denouncing corruption and violations of the constitution, and criticism of the government. Use of these platforms increases significantly during periods of unrest, such as during the January 2019 protests in the province of Cotopaxi and, of course, the October 2019 uprisings. On these occasions, the CSOs appear to direct their messages primarily to the Ecuadorian public and to the international community, along with responding to criticism from the government. But the analysis also reveals that these messages do not make it beyond the social media platforms of other Indigenous CSOs. The issues that Indigenous organizations promote via social media are rarely picked up by mainstream media or by government officials. When they are, they are framed in very different terms. I present an example of this later in the chapter.

Identity Promotion and Socialization

Those who studied Indigenous social movements at the height of the protest cycle in the 1990s argue that identity was key to mobilizing otherwise disparate Indigenous groups under a single mobilizing structure; the ability to do so successfully contributed to CONAIE's emergence as the region's most powerful Indigenous organization (Lucero 2008; Yashar 2005). But what has happened since then? Has Indigenous civil society managed to maintain a sense of unity constructed around identity? And what has been the impact of expanded access to the Internet and social media, especially among young people? On these questions, Indigenous leaders seem to be divided, although a majority feel that Indigenous identity weakened from the mid-2000s onward and that the Internet is at least partially to blame. But others see new opportunities that have yet to be fully exploited and point to the events of October 2019 to support their optimism.

All of the organizations involved in this study emphasized the importance of maintaining Indigenous identity, and most see a connection between a strong sense of identity and their ability to influence politics. Elders favor the kind of person-to-person exchanges that their ancestors relied on to convey local culture and traditions from one generation to another. Organizations hold festivals, ceremonies, musical performances, and storytelling events to enrich and strengthen local customs and identity. "There is so much cultural diversity here, our spaces are strengthened through cultural events and festivals, these are manifestations of our culture, supported by grassroots organizations" (Hernán, interview with Chiriboga, September 17, 2018). For many Elders, identity is also strengthened through spirituality, which can be promoted through festivals and ceremony but is essentially about one's relationship with nature. Others attribute identity to traditional practices such as the *minga*, where all members of the community cooperate to achieve a common goal (Flavia, interview with Chiriboga, March19, 2018).

Some organizations go further, arguing that like any population group, Indigenous youth must be deliberately socialized in a way that brings them closer to the ancestors' culture and values. As CONAIE's communication representative puts it, "Our people have been socialized for generations into adopting a foreign *cosmovisión* (worldview). This happens through the institutions of the colonizer, such as schools and political institutions, and it weakens our identity. Our job is to counter this by socializing youth into embracing our ways and customs, our values" (Apawki, interview with the author and Chiriboga, March 23, 2018).

Organizations have developed a number of mechanisms for achieving this goal. FOIN develops cultural activities for young people, which they bring directly to schools, while FENOCIN and Pueblo Kichwa Rukullakta have created their own schools and cultural programs to teach people of all ages about what it means to be Indigenous. Some local bodies "determine socialization priorities according to resolutions of regional or national organizations in order to develop a more coherent program to bring to the grassroots" (Federiko, interview with Chiriboga, February 22, 2018). Teaching activities are not always focused on traditional practices; Indigenous organizations strive to offer training that is both indigenized and relevant to contemporary issues. In early 2020, for example, many of the Indigenous organizations included in this study engaged in educating their communities about COVID-19, including how to protect themselves from the virus. In all cases, Indigenous leaders and teachers link a strong Indigenous identity to self-esteem and to their ability to mobilize communities. "When the people have a shared identity, they have a reason to work together to achieve a goal, they have a motivation to fight together, identity links individuals. They [the non-Indigenous majority] look for ways to weaken our identity by destroying our culture because they know that if this happens, self-esteem is lost and our organizations will be weakened" observed Marco (Marco, interview with the author and Chiriboga, March 8, 2018).

But all of these forms of cultural preservation require a sort of socializing proximity. For this reason, leaders express concern about the growing exodus of young people from rural communities to cities. Marco reiterated the fear that many Elders conveyed: "Due to internal and external migration, Indigenous identity isn't as strong as it used to be. It has been weakening due to migration, and this weakens us, it will make us weaker politically." Juan Carlos added that "once young people leave their communities, they are not exposed to any cultural activities, spiritual events or socialization . . . well, they are only exposed to socialization from outside sources. This makes them lose their identity, or even be ashamed of it" (J. C. Andes, interview with the author, April 13, 2018). And many leaders also point out that in addition to a weakening of identity, a dispersed Indigenous population makes it more difficult to mobilize people.

The verdict is split with respect to whether ICTs strengthen or weaken Indigenous identity. For some, Internet-based technologies can serve to enhance Indigenous identity across distances, while others (the majority) see these tools as a threat. Those who adopt the former position argue that ICTs can facilitate the spread of culture and the transmission of identity over a wider territory, which can counteract the negative effects of domestic and international migration. In the isolated Amazon region, the Federation of the Achuar Nation of the Province of Pastaza used digital material, videos, and social media to promote culture, music, and dance to those who have left their community (Julián, interview with Chiriboga, February 23, 2018). In this way, cyber optimists such as Marco argue that ICTs can "facilitate the recovery of Indigenous culture. This is important because young people use these tools, and they are exposed to foreign ideas, but as we start to use these tools to promote our culture, this has raised their self-esteem, and through seeing expressions of their identity online they are not ashamed to recognize their origins" (Marco, interview with the author and Chiriboga, March 8, 2018).

But a greater number of respondents believed that technological advances were a threat to cultural identity and they seek to counter this trend by putting more energy into in-person events, festivals, and educational activities. Rosita of FOIN declared: "With young people technology hurts identity, it changes their worldview. They have exchanged their Indigenous identity for a globalized one through the Internet" (Rosita, interview with Chiriboga, April 12, 2018). Flavia of the Pambabuela Women's Organization agreed: "[ICTs] have totally damaged identity; this is due to access to foreign ideas and ways that are promoted online as being better, the Indigenous and cultural essence of our area here has been lost" (Flavia, interview with Chiriboga, March 19, 2018). Again, leaders linked this perceived loss of identity to their capacity to mobilize supporters. An Elder lamented that "it is harder to mobilize than in the past because there is lack of interest, our Indigenous identity has become diluted. The Internet brings in foreign ideas that make people want to pursue a different lifestyle and leave their Indigenous culture behind. Without a strong sense of collective identity, people will not mobilize" (Hernán, interview with Chiriboga September 17, 2018). Another stated that "the strength in our movements has always come from close bonds and from a sense of Indigenous identity. If everything goes online, we lose this, this leads to more individualism and that takes away from our greatest advantage when it comes to mobilizing our people" (J. C. Andes, interview with the author, April 13, 2018)

Protest Redux: October 2019 and Beyond

In this chapter, representatives from Indigenous organizations across Ecuador outlined their multiscalar positioning approach to participating in the public sphere. In the 2010s, this involved a greater variety of tactics and engagement with a range of state-society mechanisms. The events of October 2019 make clear that Indigenous CSOs still have the power to mobilize large numbers of people, to take on a leadership role in protest movements, and to successfully pressure the state, but their success depended on certain conditions.

The austerity package introduced by the Moreno government in October 2019 was not a surprise to most Ecuadorians. Although he campaigned on a promise to pursue the decidedly postneoliberal agenda of Correa's Citizens' Revolution, Moreno changed course within months of the February 2017 election. Over the next two years, his agenda included a reduction in public investment and redistributive programs, increased labor flexibility, trade liberalization, and lower taxes for large corporations. These policies earned him the nickname El Traidor (The Traitor) and resulted in a steadily declining approval rating over the course of his mandate, from over 70 percent in early 2017 to under 30 percent by mid-2019, and as low as

7 percent by early 2020 (Reid 2019). The president's loss of credibility opened a window for Indigenous organizations to take a leadership role in opposing his policies.

The protests were originally spearheaded by transportation workers angry about the elimination of fuel subsidies, one of the measures in the government's austerity package known as Decree 883. They began on October 3, 2019, with the support of Ecuador's largest labor and student unions, as well as CONAIE. Thousands of taxi, bus, and truck drivers blocked roads and bridges, essentially paralyzing transport throughout the country. The government declared a state of emergency and mobilized the military. Having lost control of Quito and with protesters overwhelming security forces at the presidential palace, Moreno relocated the government to Guayaquil on October 8. By this time, roads into the capital and cities such as Cuenca (the country's third largest) were cut off by roadblocks, while in the Amazon, protesters seized major oil fields and shut down operations. Citizens occupied numerous provincial government buildings in both the highlands and the Amazon, the offices of various ministries and, for a short time, the National Assembly in Quito.

By the second week of the crisis, a movement that had started with transportation workers was clearly dominated by Indigenous CSOs. CONAIE declared that the demonstrations would continue until the government reversed Decree 883 and reinstated the fuel subsidies. Violent clashes between citizens and state forces were a daily occurrence throughout the country. A Human Rights Watch investigation conducted after the crisis had ended found that "During the October protests, security forces used excessive force against protesters and journalists, including firing teargas canisters directly at individuals and at close range and brutally beating and arbitrarily detaining protesters" (HRW 2020). October 10 was a particularly volatile day. Indigenous groups took refuge in Quito's House of Culture (Casa de la Cultura) where they detained several police officers. CONAIE president Jamie Vargas called for the end of repression, the return of the bodies of deceased protesters, and the repeal of Decree 883.

Indigenous groups were also responsible for calling an end to the uprisings, further demonstrating their leadership role. On October 13, CONAIE and a government delegation held meetings in Quito which resulted in the withdrawal of the unpopular decree despite Moreno's previous assertion that he would not back down. CONAIE called off the protests in response, and calm was restored. This was a humiliating defeat for the fledging Moreno administration, and a victory for CONAIE and its allies. While other sectors of civil society were involved from beginning, it was clear to all Ecuadorians who was calling the shots and who had the power to continue or to end the protests.

My research team and I conducted a series of follow-up interviews in December 2019 to solicit the perspectives of organizations that had participated in the protests. We talked to leaders and activists in Quito and Imbabura, which was one of the provinces most involved in the protests. We wanted to understand why Indigenous organizations decided to shift from institutional "civil society" strategies to large-scale disruptive action; the mobilizing structures, resources, and political opportunities that allowed them to do so; and the tactics used during the protests.

Indigenous protesters took advantage of the same mobilizing networks that had served them well over the past three decades. CONAIE largely coordinated the protests and spearheaded the political enterprise by acting as the representative of Indigenous civil society before the state. ECUARUNARI and CONFENAIE assisted with these efforts in their respective regions, but small and midsized organizations across the country participated. These networks were well developed, from the channels of communication used to the strategy behind the various disruptive tactics deployed. All of these organizations were familiar with coordinating mobilization and drew on institutional memory and lived experiences to plan their moves. But all of the leaders we spoke to agreed on one point: mobilization started in Indigenous communities and moved up through local and regional organizations to CONAIE. As one participant described it, "CONAIE doesn't control the people, they didn't come out because CONAIE asked them to, they came out because they knew the decree was going to affect them. But CONAIE channeled and represented the people's claims, it coordinated our strategies at the national level" (anonymous interview with the author and Chiriboga, December 17, 2019). They all agree that citizens rose up first, that the impetus came from the bases who, contrary to government claims, are not manipulated by their leaders but are rational actors who seek to protect their own interests. They were assisted by networks across the country and by community media outlets. The director of a Kichwa radio station in Imbabura province explained "We helped to socialize the population. The call came from CONAIE, from ECUARUNARI, and we helped to spread the word." He added that the uprising was "called at national level by these organizations, but this happened because communities asked for it, and each community here [in Imbabura] organized itself" (anonymous interview with the author and Chiriboga, December 17, 2019).

Still, leaders emphasized the need to "resocialize" Indigenous populations after a decade of relative compliance, which they attribute to repression under the Correa government. The theme of self-esteem was brought up many times during the interviews conducted after the 2019 uprisings, and this was linked to pride generated by success of the movement and the skill demonstrated by Indigenous organizations. Many leaders hope that more people will identify as Indigenous in the next national census, which they believe underestimates the Indigenous population due to a reluctance to self-identify.[1] In fact, the number of people identifying as Indigenous increased in the 1990s during the peak of the protest cycle. An organizer from FICI explained:

> For twelve years, we were weakened because of the previous government. The great force of the Indigenous movement was held back during the time. The former regime weakened us, people were afraid, but with this uprising we saw self-esteem return. Organizations worked to resocialize people to not be passive. With the knowledge provided by our fathers, and the collective experience of our organizations, we mobilized. (Anonymous interview with the author and Chiriboga, December 17, 2019)

This socialization process was made possible by the extensive network of Indigenous structures and institutions that were already in place, including the educational programs that had been developed to promote Indigenous identity.

Social media content produced by state agencies insinuated that Indigenous groups were not autonomous actors leading the protests but were being manipulated by non-Indigenous interests. Moreno and Romo accused Rafael Correa of orchestrating the protests in collaboration with Venezuelan president Nicolás Maduro. Correa, who was living in Belgium at the time, certainly made his support for the protests and his animosity toward his former vice-president clear through social media. Moreno used social media to declare that Indigenous groups were "keeping bad company" and were aligned with "dark forces linked to organized political crime, led by Correa and Maduro, in complicity with narco-terrorism, gangs, violent foreign citizens." The latter theme was repeated through the period under study, with various government officials accusing Indigenous groups of being manipulated by *correístas*. This is contrary to Indigenous CSOs' own social media narratives, according to which they are leaders of a legitimate citizens' movement. But the government's assertion that Indigenous groups were somehow manipulated by Correa is both condescending and ahistorical. Indigenous civil society's complex and effective structures, networks, resource mobilization capacity, and strategies are the result of years of experience, learning, and dedication. There is no evidence that the CONAIE and other Indigenous organizations are influenced by politicians on either side of the political spectrum.

Under Correa, the political opportunities of activist Indigenous organizations to mobilize protest were limited by a combination of factors: a heavy-handed government that was perfectly willing to use existing laws to limit mobilization in the name of security (and create new laws to control the circulation of information) and a favorable socioeconomic context that made it difficult to mobilize both traditional allies and large segments of the Indigenous population against a popular president. As we saw earlier in this chapter, Indigenous organizations of all sizes and political inclinations did not remain inactive during these years. Rather, they shifted their tactics away from protest toward other means of pursuing their objectives. By 2019, the political opportunity structure had shifted considerably.

But Moreno also threatened the social citizenship regime that Indigenous and working-class sectors had come to cherish. The socioeconomic gains enjoyed by lower-income Ecuadorians under Correa were being dismantled, and as a result Moreno's support dropped below 30 percent (the lowest Correa's approval rating had ever dropped was about 51 percent). Through his neoliberal economic policies and austerity measures Moreno had essentially broken the state-society pact of the Citizens' Revolution. All of this opened a door that had been closed for over a decade, and Indigenous leaders walked through it. They believed that they would be supported by a majority of Ecuadorians, and those we spoke to confirmed that the protests were made possible by a high degree of solidarity between Indigenous and non-Indigenous working-class sectors who were affected by the austerity measures. "We arrived in Quito on October 8," said one of our participants. "The people came out to support us, they applauded, gave us food. There was racism from the upper class, some of this was in the press. But they are a small group. Among the working class, Indigenous and mestizos, there was solidarity." His colleague agreed "The people rose up, not just Indigenous sectors." (anonymous interviews with the author and Chiriboga, December 17, 2019). Another interviewee described how leaders of non-Indigenous social and labor organizations called to ask how they could help, and how his organization received overwhelmingly supportive messages on social media (anonymous interview with the author and Chiriboga, December 19, 2019).

October 2019 was the first nationwide Indigenous uprising of the social media age. As such, the protests provide valuable insight for Indigenous leaders into how these tools can be used to support—and to attack—CSOs during a crisis. According to those we interviewed, the use of ICTs was the greatest distinguishing factor between the protests of 2019 and those of the 1990s and the impact was primarily positive.

First, ICTs were used extensively to support mobilization, especially among younger people. They were used to coordinate protests across large distances and dispersed populations. Many participants explained that due to internal migration, the physical proximity and tightly knit communities that used to favor mobilization efforts thirty years ago no longer reflect reality in rural regions. But communities are connected through apps such as WhatsApp which can be easily used to create virtual discussion groups to plan marches and other activities. A leader from a community near Otavalo described how social media were used to plan a march from Imbabura to Quito. Messages were sent back and forth over WhatsApp and Facebook and, as a result, leaders managed to mobilize far more people than expected. Within hours, hundreds of people were marching to join Indigenous groups in the capital (anonymous interview with the author, December 18, 2019). He and others identified rapid communication afforded by social media with leaders all over the country as a key ingredient in their success.

Second, Indigenous organizations used social media to inform themselves about what was going on around the country and to disseminate their version of events to domestic and international audiences. Ecuadorians, particularly young people, increasingly get their news through social media, and Indigenous organizations understand that this means they must have a presence if their voices are to be heard. A local community radio director told me that while his local audience is small, the station can reach people nationally and internationally through the Internet. His station has over 124,000 followers on social media (a number that far exceeds the population of the station's village), but he believes that he was able to reach many more during the protests through Facebook and other platforms. Social media are used to counter the messages of traditional media outlets. Another representative of the radio station argued that public media are used to disseminate state propaganda, while private outlets serve their owners' economic interests, which, in October 2019, involved defending the governments' neoliberal policies. "Traditional media has the power to inform and to misinform, and they often use their power to misinform. Community media has the power to inform," he argued. "Public and private media were focusing only on vandalism and violence to paint us as terrorists. This is manipulation and it comes from economic elites. With social media, we can correct this. The population is more conscious of this; media lacks credibility, they turn to us" (anonymous interview with the author and Chiriboga, December 17, 2019).

Finally, Indigenous activists used social media to make state aggression visible. I observed this first-hand during the second week of October, and millions of Ecuadorians and citizens across the globe were also watching. By October 10, dozens of protesters, including prominent Indigenous leaders such as CONAIE president Jamie Vargas, took refuge in Quito's Casa de la Cultura. This resulted in a state of siege; protesters refused to emerge from the national museum, which was surrounded by state forces. The Twitter accounts of organizations such as CONAIE and ECUARUNARI, which have hundreds of thousands of followers, were constantly sending out messages to the world. Some of the tweets reiterated Indigenous demands, while others disseminated images of injured protesters. The pictures of bloody and battered individuals were accompanied by text denouncing Moreno and Romo as the perpetrators of this violence and calling for them to face legal consequences. Participants also countered government claims that protestors initiated the violence by posting videos showing that state forces attacked demonstrators without provocation. The ability to make state aggression visible in this way would have been unthinkable only a decade ago and, according to participants, ensured that the government knew the world was watching.

Content analysis of social media during these weeks reveals a sharp contrast between the narratives deployed by Indigenous CSOs, on the one hand, and state agencies/media outlets, on the other. CONAIE and its partners portrayed protesters as peaceful, and they focused on the diversity of the communities protesting, with particular emphasis on the fact that many protesters brought their families, including children, to the marches. Importantly, the message was one of shared responsibility for pursuing social justice; their demands were not only beneficial to Indigenous peoples but to all Ecuadorians. Increasingly, they disseminated messages and images about state violence. The most frequently used hashtags were #DaysOfResistance and #WeAreCONAIE. State agencies focused on the efforts of the government to restore order and end the chaos. Moreno's and Romo's tweets thanked the military and the police for their work and expressed concern over their safety. They and various ministers also posted extensively about their openness to dialogue and their reasonable attempts to reach a consensus. They also urged people not to listen to "false" information disseminated by some CSOs. The most frequently used hashtags were #Government-ForAll and #Peace.

Finally, mainstream media outlets, with few exceptions, focused consistently on damage to property and disruption of business, attributing them to the "excesses" of protesters. Television stations and newspapers tended to downplay the violence and repression of the police. Teleamazonas, the country's largest television network, was unsympathetic and even hostile toward Indigenous protesters, with some reports framing them as subversive groups akin to leftist guerrillas. With other news outlets it also tended to portray those involved as irrational mobs manipulated by CONAIE. They completely ignored the organizational structure of CONAIE and its members, their close relationship with the communities, and the personal stakes at play for thousands of individuals who marched to Quito and other cities. With the single exception of *El Universo* newspaper, there was virtually no attempt to engage with the underlying socioeconomic context behind the uprisings, such as rural poverty or systematic racism. The CSOs certainly responded to this narrative via their own social media platforms, but these messages were generally ignored by mainstream media. They were, however, picked up by alternative media outlets, as well as by other CSOs and some opposition politicians.

Even those Indigenous leaders who see the benefits of using ICTs acknowledge that social media can be used against them. While Indigenous organizations used social media to denounce state violence, other actors used these platforms to exaggerate the death toll. The individuals we spoke to were not sure who was behind these efforts, but information was disseminated via social media that suggested hundreds of fatalities in Quito (there were in fact eleven deaths). They claimed this had a "demoralizing" effect on Indigenous people in the provinces, and that the intention was to keep them from joining the protests. A FICI representative stressed that this is why "we have official social media accounts and make it known so that people won't believe false accounts trying to trick them" (anonymous interview with the author and Chiriboga, December 17, 2019). Another negative impact of social media according to interviewees was the potential for surveillance. While those we spoke to had no proof that they had been monitored online, they recognized that state security agencies have the capacity to do so and that this may jeopardize mobilization efforts in the future.

But the negotiations that took place between Indigenous leaders and government ministers over the weekend of October 12–13, 2019, illustrate the evolving role that ICTs are playing in the tactical repertoire of CSOs. The proceedings were open to anyone who wanted to watch. While the government hoped to conduct the negotiations behind closed doors, Indigenous leaders from CONAIE and other organizations insisted that they be live streamed over social media. During the talks, Indigenous leaders drew on the constitution of 2008, a document which many of these same leaders (and some members of the governing party) had helped to draft a decade earlier. They referenced the social and economic rights that they had insisted on during the 2008 constituent assembly. Ecuadorians followed the proceedings closely on social media, as Indigenous leaders had anticipated. Some segments went viral. One of the observations most frequently made was about the extent to which the Indigenous participants, most of whom had little formal education, outmaneuvered Moreno's negotiating team of ministers with their degrees from foreign universities.

Indigenous Civil Society in Ecuador: Evolution and Future Prospects

While Indigenous civil society was less visible from 2005 to 2019, it had not experienced a decline, unless one focuses only on large-scale mobilizations and disruptive action. These tactics served CONAIE and its allies well in the 1990s, but they are not indefinitely sustainable. By the end of the first decade of the twenty-first century, Indigenous leaders had successfully influenced the drafting of the new constitution, created new state-society mechanisms, and developed considerable experience in navigating their country's political landscape. This is not a sign of co-optation, but rather a new, long-term strategy for pursuing their goals.

The Citizens' Revolution established a paradoxical citizenship regime that promised to improve the lot of Indigenous peoples through socioeconomic equality and recognition of cultural rights, while simultaneously distinguishing between legitimate and illegitimate expressions of citizenship. Despite its limitations, it did create new channels and opportunities for engaging in politics, but a number of contextual factors also made protest a less useful tactic. It made perfect sense that Indigenous CSOs would take advantage of the wider variety of tactics and mechanisms available to them to pursue their goals. This meant less protest (and therefore less visibility) but it did not mean that work stopped; it morphed into the type of ongoing, sustained action that is less about performances and more about long-term civic action.

But when the multifaceted approach does not work, Indigenous civil society in Ecuador is able to turn to mass mobilization, as Lenín Moreno and María Romo discovered in October 2019 (Romo was dismissed in November, in large part based on pressure from civil society due to her role in acts of violence committed against protesters.) The Citizens' Revolution challenged the neoliberal model by promoting socioeconomic rights and shifting the discourse (if not the practice) around political rights. The focus on social rights was backed up with significant wealth redistribution, which had a tangible effect on quality of life for poor and middle-class Ecuadorians. But while the Correa government created an unprecedented framework of legislation and mechanisms to improve political rights through direct democracy, the outcomes of these efforts are contradictory and ambiguous. Citizen participation initiatives seem to have promoted controlled inclusion and there was little tolerance for opposition, leading many to argue that political and civil rights either remained unchanged or were reversed. In contrast, Moreno's government expanded civil rights but withdrew the social rights that had been granted over the previous decade. But the Citizens' Revolution raised the expectations of Ecuadorians, particularly the poor and traditionally marginalized, and Moreno was elected on a promise to maintain its achievements. The expansion of social rights lifted many Ecuadorians out of poverty and provided them with access to health care, education, and higher incomes. The participatory democracy initiatives, while never fully realized in practice, nevertheless served to politicize a segment of the population long excluded from the public sphere. The complex sociopolitical context that emerged generated both opportunities and barriers for Indigenous civil society, and CSOs have striven to adapt.

Of course, there is considerable variation between different organizations' capacity to deploy a successful multiscalar positioning strategy. These differences are based primarily on size and resource mobilization capacity, as well as on the strength of alliances. The largest organizations are able to hire lawyers and other professionals; CONAIE has its own full-time university-trained communications specialist. Political opportunities are another variable that affects organizations' ability to pursue their goals. The Indigenous population in the Amazon region is much smaller, more dispersed, and more diverse than the large Andean Kichwa population. But, as their territories overlap with Ecuador's oilfields, they represent a significant threat to state and private economic interests. This explains why leaders of Amazonian organizations have experienced higher levels of repression and are more fearful of confrontation with the state.

There are two important factors that distinguish Indigenous civil society in Ecuador from its counterparts in other Latin American countries, including Bolivia and Chile. One is the structure of civil society: a strong, democratic umbrella organization at the top of the pyramid, with three large and integrated organizations that represent the country's regions (Andes, Amazon, and the coast), each of which works with provincial organizations within its region. These in turn network with local bodies. This structure, which is unique in Latin America, allows for a level of coordination not available to Indigenous civil society in other countries. This does not mean that organizations function according to a top-down approach. Almost all of the individuals we interviewed stressed the democratic nature of the Indigenous governance system, and the ability to participate in local assemblies that "feed up" all the way to CONAIE's leadership.

Closely related to this structure, the second factor is the remarkable ability of disparate Indigenous actors to form a united front in times of crisis and to work under the auspices of CONAIE. This is not to say that Indigenous organizations in Ecuador are homogeneous or that they speak with a single voice. To the contrary, there have been intense and public disagreements between leaders and organizations over the decades. But most put these differences aside when confronted with mutual threats. My friend María explained this to me over a decade earlier: "Not all Indigenous groups agree with CONAIE, and the different groups often disagree on points. But when it comes to important goals like the constitution, it is remarkable how we are able to come together" (María Maya, interview with the author December 5, 2009). Ten years later, Salomé Quishpe echoed María in a quote I provide at the beginning of this chapter.

The neoliberal economic measures introduced by the Moreno government in October 2019 threatened the social citizenship regime introduced by the previous administration. This created a political opportunity for Indigenous leaders who felt that they were no longer able to achieve their goals by working through the authorized system. They led the largest protests in a generation and ultimately forced the government to back down. This result is of interest for a number of reasons. First, it demonstrates the ongoing strength of Indigenous civil society in Ecuador. CONAIE and its allies would not have been able to coordinate such a large-scale effort if they had in fact been significantly weakened after 2005. The nationwide uprising could not have happened so quickly and so decisively without Indigenous organizations' robust mobilizing networks, resource mobilization and public communications capacity, strong alliances, and their increasing skill with using ICTs. Second, these events require that we reengage with questions about why people mobilize. Moreno increased civil rights but diminished social and economic rights. The outcome suggests that people are more likely to mobilize over economic and social rights than civil and political rights.

Third, the uprising calls into question the importance of identity for mobilizing Indigenous peoples, especially youth. All of the individuals we spoke to in December 2019 described the October uprisings as more of a class struggle than one that pitted Indigenous peoples against mestizos. Leaders compared what they called a change-seeking social uprising to the protests of the 1990s. Back then, "people were motivated by common goals: land, identity. Now it is more for economic reasons. Then we were fighting for rights we didn't have. Now we have many of those rights on paper; it is now about how the country and its resources are governed" (anonymous interview with the author and Chiriboga, December 17, 2019). This is a significant shift; in the last few decades of the twentieth century, prominent Indigenous leaders sought to bring identity to the forefront. In so doing, they hoped to wrestle control away from religious and leftist actors who had mobilized their communities in the past and to emphasize Indigenous-specific decolonialization. Do recent developments indicate a move back to class-based politics among Ecuadorian Indigenous organizations? This is unlikely; long-term strategies involve a continued commitment to pursuing traditional Indigenous claims and decolonization. Rights related to land, natural resources, and culture will continue to guide organizations' ongoing, multiscalar positioning approach. But when it comes to short-term goals, such as forcing the government to withdraw Decree 883, Indigenous strategists see the benefit in engaging with other sectors of the population to pursue a common goal. But this is likely a temporary shift in their tactical repertoire. Indigenous organizations now have a more diverse and complex range of strategies and tactics to build on, and more experience with using them.

Fourth, solidarity with other (primarily working-class) sectors, such as transportation workers and public university students, provided Indigenous

CSOs with moral support, legitimacy, and made the use of repression more costly for the state. Finally, the strategic use of ICTs, and social media in particular, made this the first major protest of the Internet age for Indigenous civil society in Ecuador. They skillfully used these tools both to mobilize supporters and to take control of the narrative around the protest.

3 Bolivia

Democratic Participation or Controlled Inclusion?

On October 26, 2019, a faction of Bolivia's National Council of Ayllus and Markas of Qullasuyu (Consejo Nacional de Ayllus y Markas del Qullasuyu, CONAMAQ), a confederation of traditional Indigenous governing bodies, encouraged its members to reject the electoral victory of President Evo Morales and his MAS party. Once a MAS ally, the CONAMAQ had split into two camps due to the government's increasingly authoritarian practices and its support for development projects in ancestral territories. Bolivia's first Indigenous president had been elected in 2005 and the MAS had dominated the country's political scene for nearly fifteen years. On October 25, 2019, the Electoral Tribunal declared that the leftist incumbent had narrowly achieved the level of support required to avoid a runoff with his centrist rival. But while there was little doubt about the legitimacy of his three previous election victories (2005, 2009, 2014), the results of the 2019 campaign were heavily contested. By the first week in November, tens of thousands of mostly non-Indigenous urban supporters of the opposition took over the streets of Santa Cruz, Cochabamba, Sucre, and La Paz. Shouting "Bolivia is not Cuba or Venezuela," they called for fresh elections.

On November 10, Morales, his vice-president, and several other MAS officials stepped down under pressure from the country's top military officer. The next day, ultraconservative opposition figure Jeanine Áñez declared herself president. The next official in the line of succession following the resignations, Áñez was sworn in at the Palacio Quemado (the official residence of the Bolivian president) in La Paz surrounded by high-ranking military officers. A right-wing Christian, her disdain for the country's Indigenous population was no secret; she had previously used Twitter to denounce their "Satanic practices" and to say that they were not welcomed in the country's urban areas.

On November 15, tens of thousands of protesters once again took to the streets of Bolivian cities and blocked rural roads throughout the country.

But these were not the same people who had been protesting weeks earlier. Led by pro-MAS Indigenous CSOs and peasant unions, they demanded that Morales be allowed to return to the Palacio Quemado. Áñez deployed the military and declared that she would grant immunity to soldiers for any acts of violence committed against pro-Morales protesters, a statement which she later walked back under pressure from the international community.

The contrast between the two presidents was striking. Morales, an Aymara coca grower from rural Cochabamba, consistently emphasized his Indigenous heritage and portrayed himself as a simple farmer and activist. Áñez is from Beni in the so-called Media Luna (eastern lowlands). That region prides itself on its unique—and distinctly non-Indigenous—*camba* identity and has been a stronghold of opposition to Indigenous participation in national politics (Fabricant and Postero 2013). Áñez presents as a Westernized woman who would not look out of place on the streets of Madrid's fashionable Salamanca neighborhood. The ministers she appointed also look very different from those who served under the MAS; there was not a single Indigenous face in the interim cabinet.

The contested election and its aftermath laid bare the deep divisions within Indigenous civil society in Bolivia. Once united behind Morales, CSOs were now on opposite sides of a growing political chasm. Indigenous peoples are never a homogeneous bloc. As noted in the previous chapter, Ecuadorian Indigenous organizations do not always agree and were divided, among other things, over support for former president Correa. But most CSOs were willing and able to close ranks under the leadership of CONAIE when confronted with a common threat. A similar pattern had developed in Bolivia in the early and mid-2000s, but this unity had fallen apart by 2011, when CONAMAQ and, two years later, CIDOB split into two blocs. The antigovernment factions of each CSO withdrew from the progovernment Pact for Unity and labeled themselves as "organic" organizations (Canessa 2014; Paige 2020). Tensions between pro- and anti-Morales Indigenous CSOs remained high throughout the 2010s and manifested themselves again following the 2019 election. In the days following Áñez's swearing in, the anti-Morales CONAMAQ faction declared on Facebook that its members had not experienced repression at the hands of the new government, because they were "busy working rather than causing trouble like the *masistas*." While these CSOs quickly lost any enthusiasm they may have had for the increasingly repressive interim government, this type of reaction would have been unthinkable in the mid-2000s. It demonstrates the level of animosity that developed within Indigenous civil society.

Despite the split, Morales enjoyed strong and consistent support from vast sectors of Indigenous civil society, particularly in the highlands and the temperate central valleys. The MAS fostered active participation in decision making (Canessa 2012, 2014; Gustafson 2017; Paige 2020). This helped to deepen democracy and produced positive results for Indigenous communities across Bolivia. But many would argue that it also led to co-optation of important sectors of civil society, resulting in controlled inclusion (Castañeda and Morales 2008; De la Torre 2016; Laserna 2011).

This chapter demonstrates that Indigenous CSOs in Bolivia found themselves maneuvering a very different political landscape in the MAS era. An indigenized social citizenship regime and a system of participatory democracy mechanisms provided unprecedented access to the state while it sought to limit associational space outside of this new participatory system. Bolivian organizations in 2010s recentered their tactical repertoires around the MAS's new participatory architecture and focused on civic political action. For a time at least, Bolivia was calmer than it had been in decades. Some Indigenous sectors, particularly those in resource rich regions of the eastern tropical lowlands, contested the MAS's extractive policies, but the social and political gains achieved under the Indigenous-led government limited political opportunities for opposing Morales. Because the government retained the support of a majority of Indigenous Bolivians, this resulted in a split rather than the nationwide protests that had marked the earlier neoliberal period.

Indigenous CSOs and their leaders have developed a remarkable level of political experience and impressive mobilizing capacity. When their social and political gains were threatened by the unelected interim administration of 2019–20, they drew on these skills to lead a series of large-scale uprisings. But the political opportunities had shifted in favor of their opponents, and their mobilizing structures had been weakened by years of integration with MAS and by the growing rift between Indigenous CSOs. This made it more difficult to foster a united movement against the right-wing caretaker government. The MAS, led by Morales's former economy minister, Luis Arce, regained power in November 2020 through a landslide electoral victory. It is not clear whether the channels created by the MAS will remain viable in the future, but the rift between Indigenous CSOs may allow the government to strategically play different factions against each other.

Mobilizing Structures, Political Opportunities, and Citizenship: From Neoliberal Multiculturalism to *Plurinacionalidad* to Controlled Inclusion?

Like Ecuador, Bolivia in the 1990s and early 2000s experienced a period of almost constant political instability. Following the establishment of electoral democracy in 1982, civilian governments enacted a system of pacted democracy, in which political coalitions agreed to share power in order to promote stability and growth (Assies 2004; Muñoz-Pogossian 2008). This pact ensured the implementation of neoliberal policies favorable to the country's economic elites and foreign investors. Power passed back and forth between the Revolutionary Nationalist Movement (Movimiento Nacionalista Revolucionario, MNR), which by the 1980s had abandoned the party's original revolutionary ideals and moved to the center-right, and the hard-right Nationalist Democratic Action (Acción Democrática Nacionalista, ADN). In the early 1990s, this elite neoliberal consensus was challenged by Indigenous actors, who rejected the traditional parties and sought a genuinely leftist political option. New political opportunities made possible by the return to liberal democracy allowed the left, which had been suppressed under the military dictatorships of the 1960s and 1970s, to play an increasingly active role in Bolivian politics. The progressive forces that emerged in the 1990s, however, were distinct from those that had led the 1952 Bolivian National Revolution. These movements drew on Indigenous history and identity, and the mobilizing networks they built emerged as the country's most powerful civil society actors (Paige 2020; Rice 2012; Yashar 2005). A series of notable victories in the 1990s and early 2000s suggested that the tide had turned in Bolivia; the right and its neoliberal agenda were clearly in retreat.

The election of Morales, a leftist Aymara coca grower, in 2005 launched a new era in Bolivian politics. Social and political rights were extended to Indigenous peoples to an extent never before experienced in the country's history, although the political rights were granted with conditions attached. The government's program, which included nationalization of natural resources, land reform, and a new indigenized social citizenship regime, represented a sharp break with the preceding neoliberal era (Canessa 2012; Do Alto 2011; Fabricant and Gustafson 2011; Rice 2016). Improvements in living standards and a reduction in poverty were achieved through extensive social investments made possible through a strong demand for resources such as natural gas and lithium.

The MAS grew out of Indigenous civil society and its leaders were determined to govern in collaboration with these allies. Indigenous CSOs were welcomed in the national policymaking process. The MAS government created new state-sanctioned mechanisms based on its commitment to grassroots participatory democracy and continued to engage with the movements on which the party's foundations were built (Canessa 2007, 2012; Rice 2016). These arrangements provided new political opportunities for peoples long excluded from decision making. But in exchange for influence and access to decision making, CSOs were expected to support the MAS and refrain from rocking the boat. From 2006 to about 2011, this produced a relatively stable political environment with the government enjoying support and participation from most of the country's largest Indigenous organizations, as well as from working-class sectors of civil society. But these new political rights remained conditional and could be withdrawn from uncooperative CSOs. And as in other Pink Tide countries, the expansion of political and social rights was accompanied by the gradual curbing of civil rights (De la Torre 2016). In this context, some Indigenous CSOs thrived by aligning their strategies and tactics with the state, while others were left behind, eventually leading to the fracturing of Indigenous civil society and opening the door for actors who would seek to reverse the MAS's experiment.

Conflict between disparate Indigenous peoples, and between local communities and Indigenous leaders, is not unique to the MAS era. Thomson (2002) proposes an alternative reading of the Andean uprisings of the late eighteenth century, arguing that the base was as dissatisfied with its own caciques (Indigenous chiefs) as it was with colonial officials. Peasants mobilized against unresponsive caciques, who were gradually replaced by grassroots movements. These shifts had a profound impact on the social and political structures that developed in the Bolivian altiplano, leading to the emergence of communal forms of democratic governance rooted in local autonomy and the common good (Thomson 2002). Over the next two centuries, these structures continued to coexist with non-Indigenous state institutions.

Bolivian sociologist René Zavaleta uses the term sociedad abigarrada (motley society) to capture the multisocietal condition that characterizes his country. Western/capitalist and Andean/precapitalist social structures, modes of production, and worldviews coexist uneasily within a territory over which the Bolivian nation-state claims full autonomy. The superposition of different civilizational logics produces a disjointed, variegated social formation that complicates efforts of Bolivian state actors to develop national projects (Zavaleta 1986, 1990). One consequence of this *sociedad abigarrada* has been the sustained challenge to the hegemonic project of liberal democracy. From the latter half of the twentieth century onward, Indigenous communities continue to express themselves through structures of self-organization and communal governance. The MAS claimed to embrace and to support this alternative political project. As we will see in this chapter, it has recognized at least some of the structures, practices, and worldviews that were ignored by the neoliberal state. But ultimately, the MAS has also promoted a universalizing project, constructing a generic Indigenous identity that fails to grapple with the particularities of Bolivia's diverse social logics. This has created a complex, shifting political opportunity structure and citizenship regime that affects how different sets of Indigenous actors engage in the public sphere. It has also shaped their multiscalar positioning practices, providing some actors with unprecedented access to the state while reinforcing traditional mobilizing structures in a way that has ultimately led to divisions within Indigenous civil society.

Political Opportunities

As in Ecuador, the development of powerful mobilizing networks allowed Indigenous actors to force the state to open political spaces. As part of its package of reforms, the neoliberal Sánchez de Lozada government (1993–97 and 2002–3) introduced the Popular Participation Law (Ley de Participación Popular, LPP) in 1994. The LPP delegated resources to local levels of government, created 300 new rural municipalities (most of which were majority-Indigenous), and directed 20 percent of state revenue to these mechanisms, to be distributed according to population (Oxhorn 2017). The centerpiece of the LPP was the recognition of territorial base organizations (OTBs). These included already existing traditional and popular forms of organization and allowed them to be governed according to the local practices. The OTBs have the power to request funds, develop local projects, represent their communities in dealings with municipalities and other OTBs, and lead collective work projects (Postero 2007; Tapia 2007). The law also created local governance roles for Indigenous communities through oversight committees. The institutional design of the mechanisms was developed by the state with little input from civil society, however, and sought to incorporate existing organizations into the state, thus diminishing their autonomy (Postero 2007). But while many Indigenous communities participated in OTBs, organizations remained autonomous and critical. The activists

I spoke to in 2009 were unenthusiastic about the LPP and maintained a deep animosity toward Sánchez de Lozada and his allies.

The election of the MAS was nothing short of a revolution with respect to the political opportunities afforded to Indigenous CSOs in Bolivia. The party, founded as a political vehicle for social movements, integrated Indigenous and rural organizations into its structure (Zegada et al. 2011). When the MAS came to power, its governance structure included founding members such as the CSUTCB, the Syndicalist Confederation of Intercultural Communities of Bolivia (Confederación Sindical de Comunidades Interculturales de Bolivia, CSCB, a union of rural farmers from the lowlands), and the Bartolina Sisa Federation, the country's largest Indigenous women's organization (Paige 2020). Various other CSOs joined in the following years. The party's National Leadership Council included representatives from constituent organizations, and most were elected by members of the latter. This governance model provided Indigenous organizations with unprecedented access to decision making. Particularly in the early years of the Morales administration, they became key players in Bolivian politics. This was not only reflected at the executive level; by 2016, two-thirds of the elected members of the Legislative Assembly were from CSOs. In the early years of Morales's administration, the inclusion of participatory democracy practices and the creation of mechanisms to ensure ongoing dialogue between civil society and the government ensured the support of key Indigenous organizations (Rice 2016).

In March 2006, the MAS government responded to the demands of CIDOB, CSUTCB, and others by officially convening a Constituent Assembly in the colonial city of Sucre. The new constitution was promulgated in February 2009, having been approved by 61.4 percent of voters two weeks earlier. But the refounding of the Bolivian state also presents a paradox. Morales's governance innovations went much further than Correa's; there is little question that they transformed Bolivian democracy and institutions at all levels of the state (Lupien 2011). But the MAS revolution simultaneously concentrated power in the hands of the president while extending citizen participation to the previously excluded sectors of the population. The constitution, for example, requires that Indigenous communities be consulted with respect to resource extraction yet nationalizes natural resources, giving the central government the final word on development projects. The tensions inherent in these arrangements bubbled to the surface in a dramatic fashion during the 2011 TIPNIS crisis, which ultimately led to the rift between Indigenous CSOs (Sánchez-López 2015).

Another important and related consideration is the scope of participation that is "available" to citizens. A number of respondents I spoke to pointed out that the new model of democracy was supposed to provide citizens with both a greater role in everyday decisions that affect their lives and to expand political participation, yet there is consensus that while the former has been achieved, the latter goal lags behind (Lupien 2017). Many of these individuals were concerned about extending participatory democracy to higher-level policy areas, something which the local bodies do not adequately address. A leader from a CIDOB faction that broke with the MAS reflected this concern:

> It is important that our communities' self-governance practices are recognized, but many of the most important decisions that affect our lives are not local, they are made at the state level. Decisions about resource extraction and so-called development, for example. Well, we must be consulted about such things but it is the central government that decides. There are mechanisms for that and we can participate and voice our opinions but these things are still in the hands of legislators, of representatives, and at the end of the day the president. If we are really to decolonize the state, we have to find ways to change this. (Anonymous interview with the author, May 10, 2018)

The tension between expanding democracy and concentrating power affects the political opportunity structure for civil society in other ways, including with respect to information and ICTs. In Bolivia, control over the circulation of ideas has long been dominated by colonial elites and their descendants; major television networks and newspapers are owned by the country's wealthiest families, who have strong connections with the traditional political parties (Villanueva 2008). Most of the country's major networks and newspapers have ties to one of the neoliberal political parties that governed Bolivia from the mid-twentieth century to 2005 and their owners tend to be large landowners or industrialists (Becerra and Mastrini 2009). The traditional corporate media in Bolivia have a history of negatively constructing and misrepresenting Indigenous peoples and their collective action (Lupien 2013). Not surprisingly then, communication became a contested space of political struggle between the Morales government, Indigenous CSOs, and Bolivia's traditional elite.

The 2009 constitution directly addresses the democratization of media and technologies. On the positive side, it grants all Bolivians freedom of thought and expression, and the right to information. This includes "equitable access to telecommunications" as one of a series of universal rights. The constitution grants specific sets of rights to Indigenous peoples, including to create and administer their own media platforms and networks. The state is charged with implementing strategies to support the use of ICTs in Indigenous communities, including promoting community media and incorporating Indigenous knowledge into the online world. At the same time, however, the constitution gives the government considerable control over the regulation of media and ICTs (Lupien, Chiriboga, and Machaca 2021). This includes the power to dismantle media monopolies and to award (or cancel) broadcast licenses. Following the "social responsibility" provisions in the Venezuelan Magna Carta promulgated by Morales's ally Hugo Chávez in 1999, the Bolivian constitution requires that publicly disseminated information "respect the principles of truth and responsibility." The MAS government claimed these regulations ensure voice equalization by taking this power out of elite hands, although critics worry about who determines what constitutes truthful information.

The most significant shift in Bolivia's information landscape comes in the form of two pieces of legislation. The Law Against Racism and Any Form of Discrimination, promulgated in 2010, contains a number of articles aimed at the media and other instruments of information, essentially banning the dissemination of racist ideas and language. The General Telecommunication, Information and Communication Technologies Law (August 2011) promotes information pluralism through supporting universal access to communication technologies and the equitable distribution of broadcasting licenses, including giving 17 percent of media licenses to Indigenous and Afro-Bolivian communities. The Bolivian Indigenous Peoples' Audiovisual Council (Coordinadora Audiovisual Indígena Originaria de Bolivia, CAIB) argued that these measures would ensure equality and equity in the dissemination of information. All thirty-six organizations in Bolivia supported the spirit of the laws, although about a third (those that had developed a tense relationship with the MAS) worried about the power they gave to the government.

Like other countries in the region, Bolivia's Penal Code contains *desacato* provisions. Article 162 previously stated that an individual who "slanders, offends, or defames" a public official may face up to two years in prison. This article was declared unconstitutional in 2012, but articles 282 and 283, which impose similar sanctions for damaging the reputation of particular individuals or groups, remain on the books. Bolivia has also specifically written ICTs into its *desacato* laws. These laws were used by Morales infrequently compared to Correa in Ecuador, but in November 2019 the right-wing interim government warned that it would "go after" and incarcerate people who committed "sedition"—a crime that is vaguely defined and carries up to three years in prison under Bolivian law. In my follow-up communications with participants in early 2020, leaders of pro-MAS organizations told me that they believed these comments were directed against them, and that they have advised friends to censor what they post on social media.

Bolivia's criminal code penalizes "terrorism" (defined as violent acts against public security and human life) with up to twenty years in prison and "sedition" (defined vaguely as rising against government authority) with up to three years. In 2011 and 2012, the Morales administration passed additional laws that sought to regulate the financing of terrorism and "separatism." While this was primarily intended to address the actions of right-wing opposition movements in the Media Luna, the Morales administration used such laws against Indigenous leaders. CIDOB leader Adolfo Chávez was charged with "damage to the state" for his role in protests against the construction of a highway through the Isiboro Sécure National Park and Indigenous Territory (Territorio Indígena y Parque Nacional Isiboro Sécure, TIPNIS) in 2011 (Roncken 2019). This incident and others generated the split between pro- and anti-MAS Indigenous organizations, with representatives from latter telling me they were wary of using social media.

Morales's administration expanded political rights to Indigenous Bolivians to an extent not seen elsewhere in Latin America. Bolivia's governance structure under the MAS incorporated direct participation of supportive CSOs. Popular sectors allied with the MAS enjoyed the capacity to pressure the Morales government from below and to hold it accountable to their demands. This made the MAS more responsive that leftist governments in other Latin American states, which ensures that it has continuing—if sometimes hesitant—support in many of Bolivia's most heavily Indigenous departments. The danger is that design of these institutions creates relationships with the state that may simultaneously promote more inclusive decision making while establishing parameters around democratic participation. Civil society organizations (as well as individuals) may effectively exercise this newfound agency only through state-sanctioned channels.

The seizure of power by ultraconservative forces in November 2019 signaled a dramatic shift in political opportunities for Bolivia's Indigenous peoples. Interior Minister Arturo Murillo quickly announced that the interim government had no qualms about using the legal tools at its disposal to silence Indigenous protesters who continued to support the MAS. At least two Indigenous leaders we interviewed in 2018 had in fact been charged under these laws by the right-wing Áñez administration in early 2020. They were accused of sedition and of "digital terrorism" for social media posts opposing the unelected government. We will meet these individuals later in this chapter when I recount what they told me from exile in Argentina.

In December, Murillo announced the creation of a new "antiterrorism" police unit to fight against "foreign threats" to national security (presumably emanating from Cuba and Venezuela). The minister provided no evidence to demonstrate the existence of foreign terrorist activities on Bolivian soil, but several Indigenous leaders told me during online follow-up conversations in July 2020 that the unit was being used against pro-MAS Indigenous organizations.

While the political opportunity structure shifted yet again in late 2020 when Luis Arce was elected president, the interim period demonstrates that Indigenous civil society can be weakened through political fragmentation and reliance on the MAS's structures. It remains to be seen whether the MAS under Arce—who is not Indigenous—will be able to rebuild its relationship with Indigenous civil society in the post-Morales Bolivia.

Citizenship Regime

As Tapia (2006) observes, citizenship is a historical process that includes rights but also the design of institutions that support the exercise of those rights. The nature of Bolivian citizenship has shifted dramatically and frequently from the mid-twentieth century onward. Indigenous peoples were essentially disenfranchised until the 1952 revolution. The MNR government created a corporatist regime which, for the first time, recognized Indigenous peoples as citizens. It implemented universal suffrage and provided limited social rights, and it (unintentionally) created spaces for local political and economic autonomy. This allowed Indigenous leaders and activists to build the extensive mobilizing networks discussed above. But the MNR sought to incorporate Indigenous peoples into the state as peasants and to erase ethnic identity, a project which clearly failed as communities increasingly mobilized around their indigeneity (Rivera Cusicanqui 2012).

In 1994, the Sánchez de Lozada government modified the constitution to include recognition of Bolivia's cultural diversity. This was indicative of the growing influence of Indigenous civil society and demonstrated a significant change in policy (De la Peña 2005). But the new constitutional provisions, and the LPP which institutionalized the changes, did not transform the citizenship regime in the way that Indigenous leaders had hoped. The 1994 reforms added words like "pluricultural" and "multiethnic" to article 1 of the constitution but retained the notion of a single Bolivian nation. The reforms also decentralized the state, bringing decision making closer to communities, but focused on individual rather than collective rights. At the same time, neoliberal policies withdrew the limited social rights and access points provided by the previous corporatist citizenship regime and challenged local autonomy by incorporating preexisting community governance mechanisms (such as the OTBs) into the state (Tapia 2007). This broke the corporatist pact that had sustained the country's political system in the aftermath of the National Revolution (Postero 2007).

The MAS transformed Bolivia's citizenship regime to an extent that remains unmatched in Latin America. The new regime focused on decolonization and encouraged Indigenous Bolivians to take pride in their heritage. Ultimately, decolonization in the Bolivian context is about recognizing that while the country has been an independent republic since 1825, its institutions and culture have continued to reflect the interests of a small light-skinned ruling class in the Media Luna. The process has various dimensions, including recognition of Indigenous nations within the state, land and cultural rights rooted in preconquest history, and changes to the structure of the state. To support these efforts, Morales created the Vice-Ministry of Decolonization, a unique institution whose mandate is to work with CSOs and all organs of the state to achieve decolonization (Rice 2016).

The new regime recognizes the concept of plurinationality. Article 1 defines Bolivia as being founded on political, economic, legal, cultural, and linguistic pluralism. But the MAS went further than this, rejecting *mestizaje* as an ideology and creating a homogeneous national citizenship according to which the nation is reimagined as Indigenous. Canessa (2014) argues, however, that these efforts in fact construct a narrative that favors a Quechua and Aymara majority while dispossessing others. State discourse promotes a universal, even globalized Indigenous identity; the MAS's citizenship regime may in fact represent the Andeanization of the state at the expense of lowland groups with very distinct cultural practices and political grievances. Canessa also points out that lowland Indigenous communities are more likely to seek protection of difference rather than incorporation into a national indigenized citizenship regime.

The decolonized, indigenized citizenship regime affects various sets of rights related to traditional Indigenous claims. The 2009 new constitution enshrines the right of Indigenous peoples to legal titles to their territories, which has been a central demand of CIDOB and other lowland groups. Political rights of autonomy and self-determination are granted to Indigenous nations, giving them control over the ancestral territories. The new constitution states that cultural diversity is at the heart of the plurinational state, which has the responsibility to protect and respect all cultures (Lupien 2011). These provisions have led to a shift in hiring practices for the civil service, which requires many public-sector workers to have a working knowledge of an Indigenous language. Ximena, a Quechua communications specialist who worked for three ministries under the MAS, spoke of how this has transformed the face of the civil service. "I used to be ashamed to wear my traditional clothing to go to work. Now, in every government department, our sisters and brothers are visible and are proud to show their indigeneity. This is an important aspect of citizenship: people from our communities being represented at all levels of the state" (Ximena, interview with the author, May 5, 2018).

As in Ecuador, social citizenship was extended through an unprecedented level of social spending. The 2009 constitution states that Bolivia will adopt a pluralistic economic model that will include and promote communitarian, public, cooperative, and private forms of production and organization. The MAS has put these rights into practice with concrete measures to extend social citizenship to the traditionally marginalized. By 2018, real GDP per capita had increased by 50 percent above its 2005 level and it has grown at double the rate for Latin America since 2006. Unemployment was nearly halved by 2008 and remained at just over 4 percent by 2018 (Arauz et al. 2019). Strong economic growth has led to a 42 percent reduction in poverty and a 60 percent decline in extreme poverty since Morales took power. At the same time, the Gini coefficient, an index used to measure inequality, declined from 0.60 in 2000 to 0.46 in 2016 (Vargas and Garriga 2015). Much of this has been accomplished through the MAS's extensive social programs, including support for families with children, the elderly, and pregnant women. Redistributive policies and social investment earned Morales widespread and sustained popularity. While the results have been positive, these improvements to standard of living have also undercut support for protest.

Shortly after arriving in Bolivia in May 2018, Soledad and I traveled to El Alto to meet with six Indigenous leaders who had agreed to serve as an advisory council. Four were from the altiplano while two had traveled from the lowland Santa Cruz and Beni departments to participate in a meeting with a government ministry. I wanted to ensure I captured a representative sample of CSOs in my fieldwork. The leaders looked at my tentative list and deemed it incomplete. They stressed the diversity of Indigenous CSOs in Bolivia not only in terms of ethnicity and geography but also function, historical model of governance, and orientation. By the end of the meeting, I had a significantly longer list in my hands with the largest number of CSOs among the three countries.

In contrast to Ecuador, where Indigenous civil society has adopted Westernized forms of governance (such as the state-sanctioned "commune"), Bolivian communities are more likely use a mix of Western and pre-Colombian organizational models (Lucero 2008). Bolivia's strong corporatist tradition has resulted in the development of powerful Indigenous-dominated unions and syndicates in both urban and rural areas, such as the CSTUCB and its affiliates, as well as the coca growers' union, in which Morales cut his political teeth. But this did not eliminate competing "traditional" models; both *ayllus* and *sindicatos* continue to exist, although the latter often function like a communal form of government similar to the former. In the final decade of the twentieth century, there has been a revival of the more "authentic" *ayllu* movement, as evidenced by the emergence of the CONAMAQ.

Bolivia does not have a national umbrella network that can claim to represent the majority of Indigenous peoples. But Indigenous Bolivians built a complex and effective network of mobilizing structures during the latter half of the twentieth century, including two prominent regional CSOs, a number of issue-specific organizations, and a civil society–based political party that transformed the country's political opportunity structure and citizenship regime. Indigenous CSOs in Bolivia essentially filled a vacuum left by the traditional leftist parties, which had abandoned their principles in support of the neoliberal project. They became the primary vehicles for political participation (Laruta 2008; Moscoso 2008). By the 1990s, it was clear that Bolivian political leaders ignored the demands of these networks at their own peril. But Indigenous civil society never quite developed the cohesive structure of its Ecuadorian equivalent.

The CSUTCB, representing Bolivia's largest Indigenous groups (the Quechua and Aymara-speaking peoples), became Bolivia's most important CSO based in the Andes. It continues to work closely with it affiliated rural unions, many of which built on preexisting rural unions but integrated Indigenous governance practices (García Linera 2008). It has also created strong ties with coca-growers' unions, including the confederation they established to fight attempts to eradicate coca. In El Alto, the country's largest Aymara city, with a population nearly as large as that of adjacent La Paz, neighborhood councils organized into an umbrella organization, the Federation of Neighborhood Councils of El Alto (Federación de Juntas Vecinales de El Alto, FEJUVE El Alto), and would eventually collaborate with the CSUTCB to organize national protests. The CSUTCB has not established formal hierarchical mechanisms for engaging with its allied organizations, but it coordinates strategies and action through informal processes and assemblies. CIDOB plays a similar role in the eastern lowlands and would become the country's second largest Indigenous organization. It supports and coordinates political action with provincial and local CSOs in the provinces of the Media Luna, where Indigenous communities are smaller but more ethnically diverse.

Meanwhile, CONAMAQ seeks to act as a high-level governing body for the Andean region. Its structure resembles an Indigenous parliament with leaders representing the various *suyus* (regions) and various formal governance institutions such as the Jach'a Tantachawi, or Congress. But there is little coordination with peoples of the eastern lowlands.

Indigenous civil society has continued to evolve since 2005, with CSOs seeking to retain traditional practices and values while at the same time adapting to the changing political climate and to the accelerating pace of globalization. Indigenous Bolivians are widely recognized as trailblazers in the use of ICTs. Radio has long been (and remains) the most important tool for the creation and dissemination of local content. Bolivian miners' radio stations, first launched in the 1940s, are considered pioneers in the Americas and perhaps in the world (Pilco 2000). While often overlooked as an "old" technology by Westerners or wealthier Latin Americans, community radio involves a high level of citizen participation. Television, commercial radio, and print media in Bolivia are characterized by the dissemination of unidirectional messages that flow from elites in the urban centers (and increasingly by transnational interests located outside of the country) to "the masses." In contrast, Indigenous radio focuses on local content and over the decades has produced counterhegemonic messages that represent a challenge to the dominant domestic and transnational media outlets (Lupien 2017). For these reasons, these stations can be considered an early manifestation of alternative communication. The miners' radio stations also served as a source of opposition to various right-wing military dictatorships (Lozada and Kúncar 2004). The history of *La Voz del Minero* (The voice of the miner) illustrates the history of this medium. One of the oldest programs, it originated in 1946 in the Potosí department. The program allowed locals to have a voice in the public sphere for the first time since colonization and soon became a cornerstone of the community transmitting news, music and political positions of the miners' unions (O'Connor 1990).

But Bolivian Indigenous CSOs have limited capacity when it comes to twenty-first-century Internet and digital technologies. While most organizations have at least basic equipment and Internet access in their offices, many smaller ones, particularly in isolated rural areas, do not. Leaders of larger organizations are often tech-savvy, and some hire administrative support personnel with computers skills. But according to interviewees, many Indigenous activists and community members still lack the skills required to use ICTs effectively and organizations do not have resources to train citizens or to hire technical experts. We therefore see a digital divide emerge even within Indigenous communities; CSOs may have computers, Internet access, and smartphones in their offices but do not have the resources to bring these skills to the people they represent.

The election of the Indigenous-dominated MAS set Bolivian organizations on a different course in comparison to their peers in other South American countries. I discuss the MAS's governance model later in this chapter, but the impact on Indigenous civil society mobilization networks is complex and multifaceted. The MAS provided CSOs with direct access to the policymaking process, but it also incorporated large segments of civil society into the state to an extent not seen in Ecuador or in other Latin American countries. These developments opened the halls of power to Indigenous voices but may have ultimately weakened the mobilizing structures that brought them there in the first place. Many CSOs and leaders became so closely integrated into the MAS state apparatus that their ability to engage in multiscalar positioning—particularly political action from the "outside"—may have been circumscribed.

Furthermore, and perhaps more importantly in the long term, this integration created deep divisions between those on the inside and the growing number of CSOs on the outside of this system. The Morales government's support of extractive and development projects damaged its relationship with some sectors of Indigenous civil society, particularly in the eastern Media Luna region. This means that it may no longer be possible to unite Indigenous mobilizing networks into a single movement, even in the face of a large-scale crisis. The aftermath of the 2019 elections makes this clear. As one Indigenous academic observer lamented, "The differences between pro and anti-MAS Indigenous organizations have become as pronounced as those between Indigenous sectors and the right-wing opposition, and this in the end weakens all of our organizations" (Macusaya, interview with Machaca, August 22, 2020).

Whether or not Indigenous organizations can unite again to pursue common goals will depend on how the country's new president chooses to engage with Indigenous civil society. If Luis Arce continues the pattern of incorporating supportive CSOs and excluding contesting actors, the internal rift will likely continue to divide Indigenous civil society.

Indigenous Civil Society in Twenty-First-Century Bolivia: Participation, Incorporation, and Rupture

My first interview with an Indigenous leader in 2018 took place at the Ministry of Communication in La Paz. As I sat in the waiting room watched over by a life-sized cardboard figure of Evo Morales, I thought about the implications of a CSO leader being employed by a state ministry. Over the next few months, I would visit several government offices. This is not because I set out to interview more state officials in Bolivia than in the other countries. As I discovered early on in the interview recruitment process, quite a few Indigenous leaders worked in the civil service. They had taken up full- or part-time employment in a department or ministry while they also juggled their duties in a CSO leadership role. The interviews focused on the latter, but it soon became clear that for some leaders, the two roles were closely intertwined. But I also spoke to Indigenous leaders who were deeply critical of Morales and would never consider working for his government, even as some continued to engage in state-society mechanisms.

Starting in 2005, most Indigenous organizations in Bolivia adjusted their strategies and tactics. They moved away from disruptive protest and engaged in the policy process to extent never seen in the region. They promoted political participation both within their communities and between civil society and the state. They continued to refine their strategies around resource mobilization, communication and public relations, and identity promotion, frequently aided by new government programs and mechanisms. Some began exploring the use of ICTs to support these tasks, although a number of barriers have prevented most Indigenous communities in Bolivia from taking full advantage of these tools.

The Indigenous leaders I spoke to helped to identify five reasons that disruptive tactics were replaced with alternative forms of engagement. First, the MAS government enjoyed an extended honeymoon with Indigenous CSOs following its election in 2005. Of course, this is not to say that all Indigenous Bolivians uncritically supported Morales. But the importance of having elected an Indigenous-led government for the first time in the country's history cannot be overstated. After centuries of colonialism (and neocolonialism) and decades of harmful neoliberal policies, Bolivians finally had an administration that was determined to expand social and political rights and forge a more inclusive Bolivia. No other political party proposed a similar agenda and the opposition parties continued to be dominated by a Media Luna–based (and often openly racist) elite. It therefore made more sense for Indigenous CSOs, even those who were not pleased with certain policies, to work with the MAS rather than to destabilize the government and risk the return of the right.

Second, the first few years of the Morales administration were dominated by the drafting of a new constitution that ultimately responded to many of the demands of Indigenous CSOs from both the altiplano and the lowlands. While not everyone was pleased with the process, participation in the Constituent Assembly was seen by most Indigenous citizens as a means of reshaping their country's future.

Third, the MAS not only expanded political and social rights, it created a new set of political institutions and state-society mechanisms intentionally designed to engage Indigenous CSOs in the policymaking process (and, some would argue, to incorporate them into the state). This participatory architecture provided leaders and activists with many options for pursuing their interests. Most felt that they were more likely to achieve their desired outcomes by participating in this system than by working against it.

Fourth, the MAS government's redistributive social policies improved the living standards of a significant proportion of Indigenous Bolivians. These individuals, like anyone else, want a better life for themselves and for their families. Reducing human insecurity directly addresses these concerns, and while many still remained poor, they understood that the opposition parties would likely reverse the gains they had achieved.

Finally, many Indigenous CSOs, particularly in the altiplano and central valleys, became so closely aligned with the MAS that the costs of withdrawing from this pact would have been extremely high. It would have cost them resources and access to the policy process but would have also forced them to readjust their tactical repertoire once again, without any guarantee that they would be more successful by working from the outside. As we will see, however, this does not imply a unidirectional top-down relationship between the MAS and allied CSOs. Most continued to operate as independent entities even when their representatives were working closely with state agencies. They remained able and willing to exert pressure on the government and many would argue that they were in a better position to do so. For this reason, I argue that they continued to deploy a multiscalar positioning strategy as opposed to having been co-opted by the MAS.

Following the TIPNIS crisis in 2011, this pattern changed. Some CSOs continued to work through the MAS's political architecture, others broke away and engaged in political action from the outside, while two of the largest organizations split into factions. The most symbolic manifestation of this change occurred within the Pact for Unity, a mechanism designed to bring together CSO leaders with Morales. CONAMAQ and CIDOB withdrew from the alliance in 2011, although the pro-MAS factions of each organization rejoined later. But even the CSOs that withdrew from direct participation did not turn to disruptive action alone but continued to develop a multiscalar positioning approach.

Political Participation and Influencing Policy

The MAS government's commitment to decolonialization and democratic diversification was part of a broader trend across Latin America that resulted in an explosion of participatory democracy initiatives. The Bolivian experiment was arguably the most ambitious and certainly the most indigenized. The MAS, founded by CSOs, created multiple state-society interface mechanisms that injected a healthy dose of demo-diversity into the public sphere. Indigenous civil society, formerly based on disruptive action and extrainstitutional tactics, or the "politics of the street" in the words of many of those I spoke to, was profoundly transformed during Morales's first two mandates. Under the MAS, they had many more choices as to how to engage in politics, including a myriad of participatory mechanisms at their disposal. Most took advantage of these options at one time or another.

Bolivian intellectuals have argued that a monocultural state limits democratization and that decolonializing citizenship means recognizing forms of associational life and governance beyond the traditional parameters of liberal representative democracy (Rivera Cusicanqui 2012; Tapia 2006). This requires the state accepting the right to cogovernance and reforming state institutions to include communitarian forms of decision making (Tapia 2007). The 2009 constitution establishes a new model for the state (Exeni Rodríguez 2012). First, it recognizes the existence of and bestows rights on nations and groups. This is in contrast to the dominant liberal model, which recognizes only individuals as rights holders. In keeping with this vision, the constitution places participatory and communitarian democracy on equal footing with representative democracy.

Second, the constitution paves the way for innovative structural and institutional changes that go well beyond the limited reforms of the LPP. Alternative and participatory governance practices are recognized in article 2, which states that "given the pre-colonial existence of Indigenous peoples and nations," these groups are entitled to autonomy, self-government, and recognition of traditional institutions. This legitimizes Indigenous self-government and recognizes that it can be practiced through traditional norms, practices, and forms of organization. Municipalities can also, by popular vote, convert to autonomous Indigenous territory status. These local governance mechanisms have a number of important powers under their jurisdiction, including the ability to define models of economic, social, political, and cultural development, the capacity to administer renewable natural resources, the management of protected areas, and the administration of justice to resolve conflicts and create agreements with other Indigenous peoples and local governments.

Four new mechanisms for direct citizen participation were created: referendums, local citizens' councils, citizen-led legislative initiatives, and prior consultation for Indigenous communities (see Rice 2016). Morales also reorganized the state at the highest level by creating new institutional interfaces to provide spaces for Indigenous participation in the policymaking process, including sectoral commissions and new vice-ministries such as Indigenous Justice, Traditional Health, Intercultural Education, Indigenous Autonomy, and Social Movement Coordination.

Indigenous leaders explained how some of these participatory mechanisms worked in practice. They discussed, for example, their experiences participating in the new vice-ministries or the sectoral commissions set up to channel civil society participation in areas such as social economy, culture, education, and state restructuring. Both the vice-ministries and the commissions have officers and mechanisms dedicated to interacting with

CSOs. They organize public forums, receive proposals, and transmit these to relevant authorities. Staff are charged with bidirectional communication with social organizations. In some cases, staff from the ministries and commissions travel directly to communities to hold meetings (*audiencias*) with CSOs and local Indigenous governments. Most Indigenous organizations, including the CSUTCB, CIDOB, and others, regularly submit proposals directly though these state-society interfaces. The CSUTCB, for example, has put forward hundreds of proposals since 2009, based on extensive consultations with its base, on everything from land tenure to bilingualism in the public service (Gómez, interview with the author and Machaca, June 25, 2018).

Indigenous actors, particularly in rural areas, participated in these consultation processes in large numbers, to the extent that some argued that the opinions of urban and non-Indigenous citizens would not be heard. Given the structure and origins of the MAS, this is not surprising. However, urban Aymara community organizers Manuel and Maria Choquechambi repeated to me in 2018 what they asserted the first time I visited them in 2009. They contend that the new participatory architecture is accessible to all Bolivians and that they, as urban dwellers, have participated in various processes instigated by vice-ministries such as Traditional Health, Intercultural Education, and Decolonization. They claim that many non-Indigenous citizens reject the participatory processes put in place by the MAS because they refuse to accept an Indigenous-led government. Maria stated firmly: "Indigenous people have had more political influence in the new Bolivia and because they [whites/mestizos] are hostile to the process, they refuse to participate or when they do, they only try to block progress" (Choquechambi, interview with the author, May 18, 2018).

In many rural areas, the community development work that CSOs do has changed little over the decades. This *trabajo en territorio* includes assisting with development projects, engaging communities through traditional decision-making practices, and brining feedback up to the state-society mechanisms they work with. Members of the Chichas Nation in the isolated Potosí department govern by holding *tantachachais* (traditional community governance meetings) and *jatun tantachachais*, which are meetings between various *ayllus* (communities) who belong to a particular nation. During these deliberative meetings, members make known their demands, identify problems such as encroachments on the nation's territories, propose projects, and provide input on possible solutions (Oropeza, interview with Machaca, July 4, 2018). The *tantachachais* fall outside of the state's participatory architecture, but they interact with state institutions. *Mallkus* (community leaders, or Elders), many of whom have local leadership roles in the devolved architecture of the Bolivian state, are expected to bring decisions made in the *tantachachais* into the state-society mechanisms discussed above. Understanding that many community members are unable to travel to attend *tantachachais*, Indigenous organizations regularly deploy agents throughout the territories they represent to take the pulse of the community.

A representative of the Moxeño people (Beni department) explained the challenges. "Our territory is vast, roads are poor and conditions make travel difficult, especially during the rainy season. So we have to go out to the communities to strengthen our relationships, to hear their needs, to listen" (Adhemar, interview with Machaca, August 29, 2018). Sonia, also from Beni, explained that they visit communities, collect feedback, and document the concerns raised so that they can bring these from the villages to the political arena (Ave, interview with Machaca, August 29, 2018). The CSOs also use the time they spend in the territories to support or provide technical assistance to local development projects, to provide workshops on Indigenous rights and how to claim them, and to offer various types of services that isolated communities would otherwise not have access to. This dimension of *trabajo en territorio* helps to shore up support for CSOs.

While Indigenous communities participate actively in both state-sanctioned participatory mechanisms and traditional local governance practices, many also continue to engage with liberal state institutions, drawing on the provisions of the new 2009 constitution, which sets quotas to ensure that Indigenous peoples are represented in the Plurinational Legislative Assembly, as well as in departmental and municipal governments. The Assembly of the Guaraní People, for example, develops a strong working relationship with designated elected Guaraní members at all levels of government, holding regular meetings with them to relay their communities' needs (Guzmán, interview with Machaca, August 9, 2018). Other organizations develop internal mechanisms charged with maintaining relations with (and exerting pressure on) particular state departments. The Plurinational Youth Council of Bolivia, for example, has established an "interministerial committee," whose members have knowledge of different policy areas and bring their concerns directly to the appropriate ministry. This task is facilitated by the creation of the new vice-ministries that are specifically dedicated to Indigenous concerns.

When all else fails, Indigenous civil society (or at least some segments of it) still engages in pressure campaigns, protests, marches, and roadblocks.

Here again, there is a clear divide between pro- and anti-MAS organizations. The former tend to be more likely to persist in engaging through the various channels discussed above (and to see no need for disruptive action). Many of the organizations opposed to the Morales government did in fact participate in the state's new participatory architecture but they were more likely to express disappointment with the processes and to turn to extrainstitutional tactics. As a member of an anti-MAS faction of CIDOB told me: "Because of who we are, our demands are rarely listed to in these state-sanctioned institutions. Doors are closed. We begin with dialogue but when that doesn't work, we contact the various peoples associated with our organization and we block roads" (anonymous interview with the author, May 10, 2018). Others claimed that before taking to the streets, they would first hold a press conference to present their concerns to the public, hoping that this would put pressure on uncooperative government officials.

Forming alliances with other Indigenous organizations and with allied domestic sectors remains a cornerstone of Bolivian Indigenous organizations' tactical repertoire. Within Bolivia, communities will often organize *tantachachais* between CSOs with similar interests or for the purpose of promoting understanding. These intergroup *tantachachais*, which are built around established procedures that require deliberation and listening, can serve to smooth out differences that would otherwise prevent collaboration. Leaders also understand that when pressure is applied by multiple allied organizations, demands are harder to ignore.

The Internet and social media are increasingly used by parties and candidates to promote their platforms and criticize their opponents. As Edgar Pomar, the director of the Social Communication program at Universidad Mayor de San Andrés (La Paz) noted: "Social media are now a fundamental part of political campaigns, this is very recent in Bolivia, just in the past few years. This is why the government created the Social Media Directorate within the Ministry of Communication" (Pomar, interview with the author and Machaca, May 14, 2018). Bolivian researchers have noted the same trend. The difference between the 2009 and 2014 general elections is striking. Unlike in 2009, much of the 2014 campaign played out online. Rocha (2015) demonstrates that every party had a website and all major parties used Facebook and Twitter, and there was a notable surge in the number of tweets and political memes. Communications specialists from both the MAS and opposition party, Unidad Nacional (UN), confirmed this trend to me, saying that a growing percentage of their budgets are dedicated to hiring full-time web and social media specialists. A UN representative affirmed,

"Today, any political project, any political message we want to deliver, it has to go through social media. But it isn't just a matter of putting content on social media; it requires a careful, planned communications strategy" (Kay, interview with Machaca, June 2, 2018).

Indigenous leaders I spoke to recognize the growing importance of social media in Bolivian politics. But while the state, political parties, and many private firms now have departments staffed by social media and communications experts, the vast majority of Indigenous organizations do not. Of the thirty-six organizations I worked with, only three had a staff member dedicated to social media and only two had a fully developed communications strategy. Just about everyone I spoke to recognized this as a disadvantage. Bolivian Indigenous leaders were more likely than their counterparts in the other two countries to view ICTs and social media as an obstacle to political participation and policy influence. They cited a number of reasons for this. First, despite efforts of the MAS government to extend infrastructure and coverage to rural areas (and a constitutional obligation to do so), Internet access in rural Bolivia remains expensive and slow, and coverage is uneven. Second, rural populations have no access to training, and few individuals are adept at using technologies. I noticed quite a bit of variation, however, even within a given rural region. This seems to be a result of the MAS's genuine but somewhat sluggish efforts to connect rural Bolivia to the Internet; infrastructure has been created in some localities while others are still waiting. In some cases, such as in the department of Potosí, I was struck by differences between communities a few kilometers apart; one village had a satellite tower installed, allowing relatively stable Internet access, while another down the road was unable to access the Web.

Of course, connecting a relatively large country with hundreds of isolated communities is no simple task and these efforts are a work in progress. But in the meantime, most rural communities continue to lack the necessary infrastructure. This makes it difficult for them to compete in online campaigns. As one leader stated: "The political sphere seems to be moving more and more online. But what this means for us is that we cannot participate in a growing area of the political sphere" (Herrera, interview with Machaca, July 31, 2018). Another added, "The government is online, is on social media. Political parties are there. Big companies that want to exploit our resources are there. They are using these technologies to promote, discuss. So if we are not there, what does that mean? It means our voices are absent from the public sphere, no?" (Ave, interview with Machaca, August 29, 2018).

As in Ecuador, a frequently recurring theme involved the use of social media to spread false information or defamatory comments against leaders and organizations. At least half of the participants we spoke to brought this up, and for many this is the most dangerous aspect of the social media age. Many others worried that social media were being used to present Indigenous civil society as backward, dangerous, or threatening and to defame their leaders. One leader told me that he had been the victim of an online smear campaign by individuals he believed to be associated with the La Paz municipal government. He argued that while defamation laws exist in Bolivia, it is difficult for one to defend one's honor when the attacker hides behind a keyboard (anonymous interview with the author, May 8, 2018). Another showed me a Facebook page that used his name and picture, and claimed to be his official Facebook account, but the posts appeared to incite political violence and suggest that the account holder was an alcoholic. Anti-MAS organizations believed that the central government was behind some of the online defamation campaigns against them, while pro-Morales leaders blame the right-wing opposition.

Overall, while many leaders agreed that ICTs—in particular cellphones and apps such as WhatsApp—were useful for communicating with partners, scheduling meetings and *tantachachais*, and sending documents to government agencies, there was a general consensus that technologies hurt rather than supported their political activities. This extends to mobilization. When I spoke in 2018 to Edgar Pomar, who chairs the country's primary academic department dedicated to social media studies, he was unable to identify a single major Indigenous protest event spurred by social media. During my fieldwork in 2018 and 2020, Indigenous leaders agreed.

Resource Mobilization

Indigenous communities have always had limited access to their country's resources and wealth, which for centuries remained concentrated in the hands of a small, primarily white and mestizo economic elite in the Media Luna. CSOs have developed creative ways of mobilizing the financial, human, information, and—more recently—ICT resources they need to engage in the public sphere. More so than in Ecuador, however, in the 2010s these strategies have depended on organizations' relationship with the governing party. Indigenous organizations in Bolivia are more likely to receive state funding than their Ecuadorian counterparts. Over half of the thirty-six organizations I worked with received public funding. Organizations can request funding from various ministries, as well as local OTBs, many of which are organized into Indigenous governments. These funds are usually directed at specific development projects and must be spent accordingly, although money can sometimes be used to support the organization or its political activities. Furthermore, the politicized nature of government funding practices enforces the concerns surrounding clientelist and patronage practices under the MAS.

A representative of Indigenous communities in the Pando department explained that they have been far more generously funded under Morales than by previous administrations: "Today it is very different, the government and the municipalities are required to take care of our needs, this is mandated by the president. So, when we want to hold an assembly, for example, we ask the municipality for support to help organize the assembly and pay for people's travel. We write a letter and a budget and present it to the appropriate officials" (Limpias, interview with Machaca, August 8, 2018). CIDOB representatives explained that they often present funding requests for specific projects directly to central government agencies. For example, an initiative to create an Indigenous language program for adults may be presented, with a budget, to the Vice-Ministry of Intercultural Education.

The MAS created the multimillion-dollar Indigenous Fund to finance development projects led by Indigenous and rural organizations. Many of the leaders I visited had benefited from the fund and used the money not only for projects in their communities but to enhance the capacity of their organizations. Some bought equipment such as computers, smartphones, and printers, some paid for Internet access, and others used the funds for traveling to meetings and workshops. Unfortunately—but not surprisingly given the prominence of clientelist and patronage practices in Latin America—decisions regarding access to the funding were highly politicized. Based on our interviews, it appears that money from the Indigenous Fund was almost exclusively distributed to pro-MAS organizations and denied to those that were known to oppose the government. This, according to leaders, became far more pronounced after the 2011 rift that occurred following the TIPNIS crisis.

In 2015, the fund was at the center of the largest corruption scandal since Evo Morales took office in 2006. The attorney general's office began investigating forty-nine projects based on evidence that over US$20 million intended for CSOs had been transferred to private bank accounts. More than 200 people have been arrested on embezzlement and other charges, including Julia Ramos, Morales's former minister of Justice and Rural Development, representatives of various Indigenous CSOs, and several MAS senators. The minister of Institutional Transparency and the Fight against Corruption accused those responsible of "mismanagement" but insisted that the government would not exonerate MAS-affiliated individuals. The government subsequently liquidated the fund in 2015, cutting of this important resource. Needless to say, the scandal deepened the tensions between pro- and anti-MAS Indigenous organizations, the latter accusing the former of having been co-opted and corrupted.

Support from NGOs and religious organizations also appears to have dried up since 2005. Most of the leaders we spoke to were uncertain as to why this happened, although some had their own theories. Pro-MAS community leaders argued that the new government created a variety of funding programs for social organizations, eliminating the need for external financial support which, according to them, was often guided by private interests. The president of the Center of Indigenous Peoples of La Paz said that the Indigenous Fund was an important resource-mobilization initiative that supported organizations and communities along with NGO donations, but he linked the decline in support from external sources with the elimination of the Fund. According to him, the corruption scandal generated by the misdeeds of a few may have shaken the confidence NGOs had placed in Bolivian Indigenous organizations (Johnson Jiménez, CPILAP, La Paz, June 18, 2018).

A representative of the youth wing of an anti-MAS faction of CIDOB provided a different perspective: "Nobody wants to give us support because we are known as being opposed to the government. So, NGOs and foundations in Bolivia are afraid to support us because they could suffer consequences, foreign NGOs don't want to fund us because they may also face problems" (Tomás, interview with the author and Machaca, May 30, 2018).

Whatever the reasons, many NGOs that funded Bolivian CSOs during the neoliberal period have withdrawn or limited their engagement. For those that do not receive state funding, and even for some that do, *autogestión* (self-management) remains a key resource mobilization strategy. Bolivian organizations have developed a wide range of practices. In contrast to the other two countries studied in this book, Bolivian Indigenous communities are able to claim income from activities related to resources located on their territories. The Guaraní receive regular income from local governments through the Direct Tax on Hydrocarbons (Impuesto Directo a los Hidrocarburos, IDH). The rural municipalities collect this tax from companies involved in natural gas extraction and distribute a percentage of it to the Assembly of the Guaraní People, which serves as the representative of local Guaraní communities. The Assembly then presents an Annual Operational Plan and distributes the economic resources accordingly (Alfonso Guzmán, interview with Machaca, August 9, 2018). The Center of Guarayo Native Peoples' Organizations (Central de Organizaciones de Pueblos Nativos Guarayos, COPNAG) in Santa Cruz department boasts that it is autonomous in the management of its resources. The law requires companies involved in resource extraction to pays a percentage to the Guarayo people directly because, according to the body's president, "this land, these resources belong to us." The COPNAG has enlisted the support of seven local governments to support its tax collection efforts, a strategy that was approved in a Great Assembly (Yubanore, interview with Machaca, October 1, 2018).

Indigenous peoples who do not live on territories that are rich in natural resources develop alternative *autogestión* strategies. As in Ecuador, many organizations raise revenue through commercialization of various products. Many of the leaders I spoke to are seeking ICT-related solutions to sell their products and to compete with commercial producers. Some felt that technologies could help them to export their products internationally to consumers in Western countries who are interested in purchasing Indigenous handicrafts and clothing online. As a seamstress from El Alto, Bolivia, explained: "Here, in Bolivia, whites and mestizos won't buy my clothes. They say, 'We don't want to dress like Indigenous people, we don't want others to think we are Indigenous.' Who buys my clothes? Foreigners. But we can only sell so much in the tourist markets; the Internet lets us reach potential buyers all over the world" (Rona, interview with the author, May 18, 2018).

Other organizations rely on traditional Quechua and Aymara communitarian practices such as the *mink'a*, or *minqua* (voluntary collective labor for community improvement projects) and the *ayni* (reciprocal exchange of goods and services). The *mink'a* is a traditional Andean collective labor system that has existed since the time of the Inca empire. The Inca required people to participate in "community service" as a means of building their vast empire, but the tradition continues to be used voluntarily by Indigenous peoples in Bolivia, Ecuador, and among Quechua and Aymara peoples in northern Chile. The most basic definition is "a peasant tradition that involves neighbors and friends working together on a common goal to improve their community" (Copa, interview with Machaca, July 4, 2018). The common goal depends on the needs of the community, but can involve harvesting goods, building or improving homes, or repairing local infrastructure. These practices can also serve to support political activities, although according to an altiplano Elder, "before it was easier because people were used to it, they only spread the word and communicated by word of mouth and people came. Now, people are more individualistic, it is harder to mobilize for the *mink'a* and the *ayni*" (García, interview with Machaca, July 4, 2018).

Communication and Public Relations

Despite having demonstrated innovation with film and radio in the twentieth century, Indigenous CSOs in Bolivia face challenges when it comes to twenty-first-century technologies such as social media. Bolivia is the least developed of the three countries studied in the book and, despite recent advances, remains the poorest nation in South America. Communications and IT infrastructure are limited, particularly outside of the largest cities. Bolivia is one of the least connected countries in South America; less than half the population has Internet access, and even less in the rural areas, while 95 percent of Bolivians who do access the Internet do so from their cellphones (Rocha Fuentes 2015). Bolivia has a vast and rugged terrain, and many Indigenous communities are located in isolated regions accessed by poor roads. For all of these reasons, communication is a challenge. It is also essential; all types of organizations need to communicate with various stakeholders, including government, allies, and their own communities.

Indigenous Bolivians have demonstrated creativity over the years. In the 2010s and 2020s, they use a variety of tactics to reach their supporters, from ancient relay systems to new technologies—where infrastructure permits. While the larger organizations now have Facebook and Twitter accounts, these are primarily used to promote local culture, post photographs, and advertise events. A handful of leaders said that they had used social media to make international audiences aware of Indigenous rights violations or condemn state actions (such as during the TIPNIS crisis), but these uses were relatively rare.

Until very recently, communication between leaders and rural communities looked much as it did centuries ago. This is slowly starting to change. At the time of my first visit in 2009, some communities in the altiplano still communicated through the *chasqui*, a messenger who would walk from village to village to deliver messages directly to people's homes, a practice which dates back to the Inca empire.[1] In 2018, most *chasquis* had been replaced by cellphones, WhatsApp, and—when these are not available—radio, as these obviously allow for more rapid communication. Even now some *ayllus* continue to rely on in-person delivery systems. The Chichas Nation, for example, has replaced the *chasqui* with the *kamachi* (a sort of right-hand man to the community leader, or *Mallku*). Rather than going from door to door, the *kamachi* delivers a written announcement (such as invitations to an assembly) to a village official, who in turn disseminates the message to members of his community. The *Mallku* explained that few people have cellphones in some communities due to geographic isolation, and that sometimes even radio cannot reach the more remote locations (Oropeza, interview with Machaca, July 4, 2018).

The MAS government has supported the development of community media. The state has financed the creation of a network of over forty local community stations in Indigenous villages known as the National Network of Indigenous Peoples' Radio. Most stations are independent of the state. The 2011 Telecommunications Law has facilitated the acquisition of the necessary license and frequencies for individuals and groups previously not able to afford them in a market-based framework. Several of the communities I visited credit the law with allowing them to establish new stations and to obtain the necessary licenses due to the provision that reserves a certain percentage of frequencies for Indigenous groups.

Representatives of opposition parties and a number of journalists I spoke to charged that many government-supported community media outlets have been co-opted by the MAS. They claim that the 17 percent of licenses reserved for civil society and Indigenous communities simply means more airtime for government propaganda. But the CSOs that have established community media outlets take their independence from the government very seriously. Leaders also point out that they are not associated with government-controlled community radio stations but seek to foster a community-run network of organizations dedicated to generating debate, inter- and intracultural communication, and dialogue, goals they define as closely related to information pluralism and democratization.

While many in the communities they represent do not have Internet access, Indigenous leaders see the value of having an online presence beyond their communities to enhance visibility. Leaders noted that ICTs can help to strengthen ties between organizations or government agencies (particularly local government) in that they allow for faster and more efficient communication, which helps to coordinate efforts. Pointing out that even in isolated communities there is at least one individual with a cellphone, a communications director for a Guaraní organization explained: "Within minutes we can send a message to most communities, it could sometimes take days before" (Alfonso Guzmán, interview with Machaca, August 9, 2018).

Use of technologies for communication with the general (non-Indigenous) public, whether at the domestic or international level, remains limited, yet this is arguably the most important potential use of social media. Indigenous organizations seek to increase their capacity to communicate with the public by allowing Indigenous actors to deliver their messages without an intermediary. As we will see later in this chapter, this turned out to be a weakness during the pro-MAS Indigenous protests in late 2019 and 2020, during which opposition forces were able to dominate the online narrative.

The content analysis of the social media platforms of Bolivian Indigenous CSOs reveals that Twitter, Facebook, and other platforms are used infrequently, even by the larger organizations such as CIDOB, although their social media presence has increased over the past few years. For example, the largest Indigenous CSOs in Bolivia produced only a handful of tweets regarding the TIPNIS crisis in the early 2010s.

Identity Promotion and Socialization

Indigenous community members I have spoken to over a ten-year period have agreed that identity is a primary motivating factor with respect to civil society engagement because it provides people with a sense of pride and purpose. When I asked about how they promote their culture in 2018, most participants said that they continue to do so as they always have, through traditional dress, music, dance, food, ceremony, and the practice of ancestral customs (such as traditional medicine) in everyday life. CSO leaders said that they keep these traditions alive by organizing festivals, performances, and events such as "culture nights." But many are concerned that the political and mobilizing power of cultural identity is being lost through globalization. Elders stress the importance of the "home-family-community" relationship in ensuring the intergenerational transmission of language and identity, and they believe that this process largely depends on territorial concentration and relations of proximity, which are threatened by both outmigration and technology.

If the cultural and technological dimensions of globalization took longer to penetrate the continent's least developed country, they had clearly arrived by the 2010s. Information and entertainment disseminated by mass media are targeted at an audience assumed to be increasingly homogeneous in the context of globalization, with little room for alternative cultures, participatory content development, or local voices. To some extent, Indigenous Bolivians are sheltered from this due the lack of access in many communities, as well as by the continuing popularity of local radio. The community stations offer a wide variety of programing from news to music to culturally sensitive information on health, politics, and local issues. They broadcast in Indigenous languages such as Quechua, Aymara, and Guaraní, in addition to Spanish and promote language teaching and revitalization. The stations are also credited with providing women in rural communities with access to the means of communication. In many cases, women with little formal education and no experience in broadcasting have the opportunity to engage in dialogue with and raise awareness about issues that would otherwise not be discussed in their villages. One particularly popular program, *Wakichikuy wasiyuj allin kawsayta tarinapaj* (Prepare to live well), is broadcast in Quechua by a grandmother, her two daughters, and a granddaughter. The aim of the program is to stimulate women's participation in the public sphere, and it is credited with teaching women about their political rights and empowering them to demand respect in the public and private spheres. Aymara women have also used radio to encourage the production and distribution of Indigenous culture, including organizing fairs where women entrepreneurs can sell their products (Lupien 2017).

The Internet and social media, although less accessible in Bolivia than in most Latin American countries, play an increasingly important role in the lives of young people and this has divided Indigenous leaders. According to cyberoptimists, digital technologies should facilitate the efforts of marginalized groups to promote identity and a sense of belonging by allowing them to reach a geographically dispersed audience. But there were relatively few cyberoptimists among the leaders I spoke to. Most perceived digital technologies and the Internet as a potentially fatal threat to Indigenous identity, especially among youth. Concerns ranged from the dominance of English and Spanish on the Internet and the impact of this on the vitality of Indigenous languages to the pull of Western cultural products, which are more easily disseminated online. *Mallku* Carlos expressed this sentiment forcefully, but he echoed what the majority of his counterparts told us: "This social media has been a massive attack on our culture, in part because we do not yet understand how to manage these technologies. The subjugation of our culture is more easily coming from outside with foreign music, movies, with different harmful messages on Facebook, clothing even, young people see foreign clothes on the Internet and they want to dress like that. So we have to try to control this by valorizing our own culture and parents have to watch what their children do online" (Oropeza, interview with Machaca, July 4, 2018).

Another lamented that "young people go on Facebook, YouTube, and it changes them. It makes them ashamed of their culture" (Sánchez, interview with Machaca, October 1, 2018). But leaders also fear the impact that this will have on political solidarity and their ability to mobilize young people. The Elder continued: "these technologies do much harm because young people do not understand what an Indigenous movement is anymore because on their social networks they are immersed in current, ephemeral things, it's all about the moment, they forget about ancestral practices, but also about what their parents and their grandparents did, what they fought for."

Wilma Mendoza, leader of the National Confederation of Indigenous Women, expressed a similar concern: "These tools are good when used well, but most of the time they are not used well by young people. Much depends on how they use the networks, because sometimes as much as you instill their values as children . . . many of these things teach people to give up identity, to change their ideologies" (Mendoza, interview with the author and Machaca, May 31, 2018). Even the leader of one of Bolivia's largest Indigenous youth organizations agrees. Jeaneth said of social media, "In some ways they [ICTs] do harm; many young people no longer identify with who they are, their thinking is changing" (Torrez, interview with Machaca, July 7, 2018).

The ideological and cultural changes that these leaders perceive make it more difficult, they believe, to maintain strong collective action efforts. And if identity was a key tool in creating Indigenous civil society during the peak of the protest cycle, they are worried about the long-term impact of the globalizing effect that the Internet is bringing into rural Bolivia. They ask: How can we maintain strong political collective action in the face of weakening identity, and what are the political consequences if we are not able to do so? This was unclear when I conducted the bulk of my fieldwork in Bolivia in 2018. A year later, questions of Indigenous political solidarity would become even more urgent in the face of a new threat.

The October 2019 Elections: Indigenous Civil Society Divided

The official results of the October 2019 election gave former president Carlos Mesa (2003–5) 36.5 percent of the vote to Morales's 47 percent. This represented a significant decline in support for the MAS leader, although it provided him (by 0.05 percent) with the 10 percent lead he needed to avoid a run-off with Mesa. The numbers were contested by the opposition and by some foreign observers. Claims of fraud were based on a suspension of the preliminary vote count and the subsequent publication of the official numbers, which showed Morales winning by just over 10 percent. The will of the Bolivian people remains unclear. An audit by the Organization of American States (OAS) found "significant irregularities" and encouraged the government to hold new elections, a suggestion that Morales accepted prior to being deposed by the military. In contrast to the OAS's findings, an independent academic study found no evidence of electoral fraud (Curiel and Williams 2020).

Divided opinions regarding the results were reflected in the series of follow-up interviews Soledad and I conducted from June to August of 2020. Pro-MAS CSOs insisted that claims of fraud were fabricated by the right-wing opposition, in collaboration with their U.S. allies. Those that had broken with Morales believed that fraud had taken place and looked forward to fresh elections. In any case, anti-Morales protests began the day after the elections, on October 21, 2019, and turned increasingly violent over the next two weeks. There were peaceful marches and demonstrations across the country but protestors also attacked MAS officials and their homes (including kidnapping a mayor), burned down local Electoral Tribunal offices, and committed other acts of vandalism. Confrontations broke out between pro- and anti-MAS demonstrators, leading to several fatalities. Local police were mobilized to restore order, although by the first week in November, the Armed Forces declared that they would not use force to keep Morales in power. Even if Indigenous Bolivians were in the minority among those seeking to oust Morales, prominent CSOs did not shy away from making their perspective known. The self-described "organic" factions of CONAMAQ and CIDOB took to social media to denounce Morales and call for new elections.

On November 10, armed forces general Williams Kaliman advised Morales to resign. The president complied and left the country to seek asylum in Mexico. He was later invited to Argentina by that country's newly elected leftist president Alberto Fernández. Morales's vice-president and the MAS first president of the Senate also resigned, leaving ultraconservative senator Jeanine Áñez the next official in the line of succession. The transfer of power was welcomed by celebrations in the streets of Bolivia's cities. But this was not the end of the 2019 protests.

On the day Morales left for Mexico, the nature and the composition of the nationwide protests abruptly shifted. In La Paz, tens of thousands of pro-Morales protesters clashed with police, military, and opposition forces on November 12. Carrying wiphala flags (the multicolored flag used by Andean Indigenous groups and adopted by the MAS) and banners supporting "Evo," they made their way to the city center to demand that Morales be restored to the presidency. In El Alto, demonstrators blocked roads to the La Paz international airport, while in rural areas, protestors set up roadblocks to prevent the delivery of goods to the cities.

On November 13, as Áñez was sworn in carrying an oversized Bible and surrounded by military officers, thousands of Morales supporters forced their way to the National Assembly building waving wiphala flags and calling the transfer of power a U.S.-backed coup. While the army and some local police forces refused to intervene during the earlier (anti-MAS) stage of the protests, their reluctance to use force against fellow Bolivians seems to have diminished once Áñez and her cabinet were in power. Pro-Morales protests were met with considerable force, from tear gas to beatings. Citizens attempting to march from El Alto to the center of La Paz were prevented from doing so, while in rural Bolivia Indigenous farmers were violently dispersed when trying to enter the city of Cochabamba. Dozens of Indigenous protesters were killed by security forces. Meanwhile, interior minister Murillo threatened to arrest for "subversion" MAS legislators who refused to recognize Áñez's legitimacy and threatened to charge pro-MAS journalists with "sedition."

As in Ecuador, Bolivia experienced a decline in the use of disruptive protest following the election of a leftist Pink Tide president, although not entirely for the same reasons. Under the Correa administration, the majority of politically oriented organizations had experienced some degree of repression, including legal prosecution and violence. Fear of repression was not entirely absent in Bolivia, particularly in parts of the eastern lowlands, where memories of the TIPNIS crisis were still fresh, but while some leaders were certainly unhappy with the MAS government, I rarely came across expressions of fear in Bolivia in 2009 and 2018 as I did in Ecuador and Chile. Despite a growing rift between pro- and anti-Morales Indigenous organizations, the MAS was keenly aware of the fact that it drew its support from sectors of Indigenous civil society, and its votes from Indigenous citizens. This left the MAS with less room to maneuver than in Ecuador, whose government relied far less on Indigenous support, or Chile, where the governing party received none at all.

So why did Indigenous CSOs return to large-scale protest following the 2019 elections? The response depends on which CSOs we are talking about. Those that had developed a hostile relationship with the Morales regime (and the anti-MAS factions of those that split in two), believed that the communities they serve had not benefited from the extension of political rights offered to supportive actors, and argued that their civil rights had not been respected. Some communities in resource-rich territories felt that the new citizenship regime did not fully apply to them. But they were in the minority among Indigenous CSOs and therefore the political opportunities available to them were limited. The anti-Morales demonstrations in October 2019 changed the political opportunity structure and at least some of the leaders I spoke to felt that it was strategically useful to align themselves with the self-described "pro-democracy" forces. They hoped that this would provide them with new allies and political opportunities once the MAS was out of power. My follow-up discussions in 2020 revealed a different tone. While the anti-Morales factions did not want the ex-president to return, they were far less enthusiastic about the forces that had engineered his downfall. Still, they recognized that their political positions spared them from the political persecution and state violence that pro-MAS CSOs were subjected to under the interim government.

Far more Indigenous Bolivians participated in the uprisings that sought to restore Morales to power, and their reasons for doing so were clearly different. These people were compelled to occupy public spaces, cut off roads and supply lines, and clash with security forces for a number of reasons. They felt that the social citizenship regime they had fought for would be threatened under a new right-wing government, that their newfound political rights would be withdrawn, and that the closing off of political spaces they had become accustomed to left them with few options.

In Bolivia, the right did not return to power in the 2010s through elections (Chile) or due to a rightward policy shift by a president elected on a left-leaning platform (Ecuador). The 2014 and 2019 elections demonstrated a clear shift in Bolivian politics. The MAS recentered the political spectrum on a program of social citizenship. Parties that openly embraced neoliberalism limited their appeal to middle-class and elite sectors, primarily in the Media Luna. Parties and candidates that hoped to compete with the MAS found themselves in the position of having to accept much of that party's agenda, while attempting to differentiate themselves based on promises of "restoring" democracy. Perhaps the most telling feature of Bolivia's 2019 election is that Mesa, Morales's main opponent, was not allied with the

Media Luna–based right, but rather positioned himself as a moderate reformer on the center-left of the political spectrum.

When Áñez took power, she originally claimed that she would lead a caretaker government whose only purpose would be to oversee fresh elections. But she immediately began making important policy changes, which signaled a desire to reverse much of the MAS's legacy. Many Indigenous leaders interpreted this as a move to revert to a neoliberal citizenship regime and withdraw their hard-won social and political gains. By appointing a cabinet with no Indigenous ministers, Áñez signaled that they would have no place in government. Indeed, the many state-society mechanisms that Indigenous CSOs had engaged in for fifteen years were now closed to them. Disruptive action became the only tactic available to them, and for tens of thousands of Indigenous Bolivians, the threats to their social and political citizenship were serious enough to act despite the threats to their physical safety posed by state repression. But unlike the early 2000s, they were not supported by all sectors of Indigenous civil society.

In the summer of 2020, Soledad and I spoke with eight Indigenous leaders and activists to solicit their perspectives on the largest nationwide uprisings since the early 2000s. We also spoke to six opposition journalists and activists who welcomed Morales's resignation. Interviewing MAS supporters was not an easy task, as a majority of our participants did not want to talk openly about their participation in the events of 2019 for fear of reprisals. Most Indigenous leaders, but particularly those who had supported the MAS, were genuinely frightened of the interim regime. Two spoke to us from exile in Argentina (where they had joined Evo Morales). Several CIDOB and CONAMAQ officials we had spoken to the previous year were no longer in their positions and their whereabouts were unclear. Some of those that did consent to speak to us insisted on complete anonymity in the reporting of their perspectives. Some would agree to respond anonymously only in writing. These individuals sent their responses to our questions from unidentified email accounts (without their real names attached). Many of the organizations I worked with in 2018 closed their social media accounts in November 2019, or at the very least deleted tweets and Facebook posts. Many reported receiving anonymous threats via email or social media, warning them to stay out of politics or face serious consequences. Given the threats made by the interim government against opponents, this is hardly surprising, but I had never encountered this level of fear under the MAS, even among those groups who openly opposed Morales.

I will introduce the two leaders who spoke to me from exile in Argentina. They described, among other things, the communications and ICT-related strategies used by both sides during the upheaval that took place in October and November 2019. Eduardo is a youth activist and community journalist. For several years, he hosted a radio program called *Resistencia Radio*, which was supportive (through not uncritical) of the MAS, as well as a Facebook page La Resistencia Bolivia, where he posted news-related texts, editorials, and videos. In the days that followed Morales's departure, Eduardo's radio program and Facebook page focused on exposing repression against Indigenous protesters. An arrest warrant was issued following his coverage of events at Senkata, a district in the Aymara city of El Alto. On November 19, 2020, eight citizens who were protesting to demand the restoration of Morales were killed by security forces and many more were injured in what activists now call the Senkata Massacre. The Áñez regime charged Eduardo with sedition and terrorism for reporting on the state violence.

Eduardo continued to disseminate these messages and images from his new home in Argentina throughout 2020. Speaking about what he and his friends experienced in November 2019, he related that "the supporters of the coup began to enter the community radio stations and beat the program hosts, the radio operators, the technicians, and they began to close the stations one by one, and they did that with all the community networks. It became dangerous to even film or record because, if someone recorded what was happing on the ground and they were not from the private right-wing media, they were silenced and some were imprisoned."

Eduardo insisted on the importance of community and independent media, because mainstream private outlets ignored what he refers to as the massacres committed by the Áñez regime and sought to criminalize the "popular movement" by labeling them as terrorists. "They lied that [pro-MAS Indigenous protesters] were associated with the FARC [Revolutionary Armed Forces of Colombia]. Many of my colleagues began to close their Facebook accounts out of fear."

Eduardo believed that had it not been for the ability of his friends to disseminate their version of events through social media, the de facto government would have been able to cover up acts of state violence against Indigenous protesters. "Social media was key, we used Facebook because they silenced all the alternative media: newspapers, community networks, so we use our digital media which is La Resistencia Bolivia [Facebook]. We could report on the massacres because we received videos from everywhere, from people who were there, photos. For example, what happened in Senkata. Private media were showing one thing, but we were showing what was happening on the street. That is why they issued arrest warrants."

José, a self-described digital activist, also considered himself a political refugee in Argentina when I spoke with him again in the summer of 2020. He had been charged in absentia with sedition, attacks on the state and "digital terrorism," apparently for his opposition to what he labelled a right-wing, U.S.-backed coup. Both he and Eduardo described an elaborate social media strategy designed to delegitimize the results of the 2019 elections and to turn Bolivians against the MAS. Returning to a theme that had come up in my fieldwork the previous year, José argued that elite-backed opposition forces benefited from their extensive human, technical, and financial resources to develop more sophisticated cyber strategies. He argued that the MAS and Indigenous organizations always demonstrated a "deficiency in terms of mastering social media." As I had previously discovered, it wasn't until 2016 that the MAS government created a department responsible for developing social media strategies. In the meantime, opposition parties and right-wing business and civil society groups had been creating an extensive network of pages and online groups.

According to José, they put these online networks into action following the October elections. "They began locating people in the middle-class neighborhoods and they added them as friends (on the social media accounts), they sent them false news of so-called electoral fraud and people began to believe these stories they received on WhatsApp. They went to Facebook to corroborate the information and found the same fake news. This was a planned and coordinated effort."

He added that the communications experts behind these efforts received technical and financial support from well-trained foreign actors. In my separate interview with Eduardo, he also confirmed the existence of organized anti-MAS campaigns over social media. He argued that he and his colleagues have identified more than 80,000 accounts that were created in late 2019 to "bombard people with fake news about the elections" and felt that this campaign effectively allowed the "coup plotters" to dominate the Bolivian social media landscape.

And yet, like Eduardo, he also pointed out the benefits of social media. Comparing the Áñez government to the neoliberal administration of Sánchez de Lozada in the early 2000s, he pointed out that images of the violence committed by the state in 2020 traveled around the world within hours, whereas Sánchez de Lozada was able to repress dissent with little international attention. He believed that Indigenous organizations have taken time to catch up with those who would seek to exclude them but insists that they are learning how to appropriate these tools. In early 2021, the elected Arce administration dropped the charges against individuals accused by the Áñez regime of sedition and other crimes.

Most of the interviewees I spoke to in 2020, on both sides of the divide, identify two camps in the 2019 protests with distinct forms of protest. The *pititas* (the name was adopted by the antigovernment protesters themselves following a disparaging remark made by Morales regarding their use of ropes to block the streets) mobilized in response to the Electoral Tribunal's announcement of what they believed to be fraudulent elections results. The *wiphalas* (those carrying the wiphala flag) were the primarily Indigenous protesters who took to the streets following Morales's resignation.

But most observers made another important distinction. Indigenous writers and academics Carlos Macusaya and Wilmer Machaca argued that the *pitita* mobilization was carried out by middle-class urban groups. This is perhaps an oversimplification. As I wrote at the beginning of this chapter, there were Indigenous organizations and protesters who supported Morales's ouster, although they expected fresh elections sooner rather than later. But Indigenous protesters were in the minority among *pititas,* and there is no question that the October 2019 uprising was different from any that Bolivia had witnessed in modern history. For decades, disruptive action in Bolivia was carried out by Indigenous civil society, sometimes supported by labor unions. The "Pitita Revolution" was perhaps the first time in Bolivian history that the urban middle classes mobilized on such a scale.

There were other differences between the two camps, including mobilization strategies. The *pititas'* demands and grievances were distinct from those that Indigenous CSOs had been fighting for since the 1990s. There was no talk of social rights, of redistribution, or identity. Rather, the discourse that emerged from these protests revolved around a hegemonic Western construction of representative democracy. This narrative was intended to appeal to audiences in the Global North, by aligning frames around "democracy" with the "correct" liberal (but not participatory) model preferred by the United States and its allies. There was no acknowledgment of the participatory communitarian forms of democracy practiced under the MAS. Nor did these protesters view social rights as an important ingredient of a healthy democracy; their discourse focused on liberal civil and political rights. Given the Áñez regime's determination to privatize everything that

Morales had nationalized during his mandate, there is also a strong link made between democracy and private property. Eduardo put it this way: "The *pititas* were not on the streets because of an empty refrigerator, it is not that they were starving. What they had was an ideological discourse around democracy when in reality we lived in a very democratic country." What became clear from speaking to people on both sides of the divide is that the pro and anti-MAS actors hold very contrasting—and possibly incompatible—conceptions of democracy.

The middle-class mestizo youth who dominated the *pitita* demonstrations had little experience with protest. They blocked streets in central La Paz and the affluent South Zone, and equivalent districts in other cities. In short, they occupied their own spaces, but this had minimal effect on supply lines or transportation. The *wiphala* protests that emerged later were actually far more disruptive. Uprisings in El Alto shut down the country's largest gas plant and the capital's international airport. Blockades of roads across the country cut off food and supply lines to the major cities. Unlike the *pititas*, the primarily Indigenous protesters who took to the streets following Morales's departure had plenty of experience with shutting down the country. They knew how and where to strike. The middle-class groups did not have the ability to paralyze the economy. This suggests that the Pitita Revolution did not overthrow Evo Morales. Rather, the president resigned due to pressure from the military and the national police, whose leaders were in turn influenced by Bolivian elites and foreign (primarily American) actors. This is further supported by the fact that the military refused to "pacify" the *pitita* demonstrations, but were quick to suppress Morales's supporters, as they did at Senkata.

Ultimately, the frames deployed by the right-wing opposition ensured the support of the U.S., Canadian, and most Western European governments. These protesters were defending the "correct" (Western) conception of democracy (and by extension private property) against a "flawed" form of communitarian governance based on a "backward" (Indigenous) worldview. This frame alignment, which generated a narrative around freedom versus barbarism, appealed not only to Western leaders but also to Latin American elites and middle classes. It ultimately ensured the *pitita* movement's success, because their tactics alone were not disruptive enough to destabilize the government. It also clearly convinced military authorities, who in Latin America are notoriously conservative and supportive of elite interests. And of course, race is certainly a factor. The military was concerned about the optics of using violence against lighter-skinned urban citizens, while demonstrating little hesitation in attacking darker-skinned, working-class Indigenous protesters only days later.

Indigenous interviewees distinguished between the 2019 uprisings and the movements of the 1990s and early 2000s. According to Wilmer Machaca, an Aymara writer and intellectual, the earlier movements "were led by the working class, by Indigenous peoples who had been oppressed, by those who did not have privileges, those who had no access to anything. In those demonstrations there were dreams of a utopia, a political project, for example, the nationalization of hydrocarbons, the Constituent Assembly. It was about taking back the country by and for Indigenous peoples." In contrast, he describes the 2019 *pitita* demonstrations as being immersed in the "culture of feelings, anger, and misinformation" that social media have created. Those demonstrations, he believes, were not inspired by a utopian progressive project but were guided by emotion and a single goal: to expel the MAS government regardless of the results of the election in order to restore the neoliberal project.

But Wilma Mendoza, leader of the National Confederation of Indigenous Women of Bolivia, was more critical of Indigenous civil society itself:

> In the nineties the calls to action were legitimate and organic and they were felt deeply because they were aimed at recovering territory and land and that is why the people mobilized. The social organizations that led the Water War and the Gas War had clear goals, too; they wanted to prevent privatization of these resources. The Indigenous movement was clear about what it was looking for. But last year, when the MAS has been in power for so long and there was a lack of transparency in the elections, the calls to action had no direction, even those made by my Confederation. That is why the calls made by the leaders did not have the same weight because it doesn't seem like we are fighting for a conviction, for something you need and that is the difference between the 90s and last year. (Mendoza, interview with the author and Machaca, June 18, 2020)

Another obvious difference between the past protest cycle and 2019 is the use of social media. Those leading the mobilizations in the 1990s and early 2000s used pamphlets, in-person assemblies, and community radio to launch calls to action, as the Internet was available to only a handful of Bolivians at the time. But a clear contrast also emerged with respect to the social media strategies used by the *pititas* and the *wiphalas*. The former used social media extensively to mobilize supporters, to develop the aforementioned frames around a Western conception of liberal democracy, and to construct a narrative according to which they had been suppressed by the authoritarian MAS. According to anti-MAS journalists and students I spoke to, this was a coherent social media campaign organized by middle-class Bolivians.

Yhoryet, a young anti-Morales communications specialist who was hired to work in the Vice-Ministry of Communications under the Áñez administration, explained to me how this developed. In the days following the election, there was a sustained and coordinated effort among young people to use their Twitter accounts to report incidents of voter fraud. She indicated that many people who did not have Twitter accounts created one in October for that purpose. #Soypitita (#IAmPitita) became the most widely trending hashtag in Bolivia that month. A campaign was also organized over WhatsApp, the most commonly used app in Bolivia. La Resistencia Juvenil (RJ), an anti-MAS youth group that claims to support a "return" to democracy, coordinated an effort to create large groups on the app in order to disseminate calls for demonstrations in the days following the election. According to Yhoryet and some of the anti-MAS students we interviewed, within days thousands of Bolivians had joined these WhatsApp groups and knew when and where the next demonstration would take place. RJ and similar organizations used their social media platforms to connect with like-minded actors in Latin America and the Global North, ensuring that their framing of the events would dominate international headlines. These efforts were led by people like Yhoryet: young, educated Bolivians who use ICTs in their daily lives. They have smartphones and regular access to the Internet. They are technologically savvy and know how to use social media to their advantage.

Eduardo and José agreed that this campaign was effective, confirming that the opposition's articulation of the situation was facilitated by technology. But they added that there was an imbalance between pro and anti-MAS campaigns, because the latter were more likely to comprise well-off individuals with more sophisticated ICTs and better Internet access.

In contrast, the *wiphalas* who mobilized in late November were more likely to be Indigenous, rural, and poor, had limited access to ICTs, and few were tech-savvy. This is reflected in their relatively limited use of ICTs and social media. For the most part, Facebook and WhatsApp were used to disseminate images and accounts of violence by the Áñez regime after the fact. These tools were rarely used to call for mobilization and there is no evidence of a coordinated campaign to develop, align, and deploy frames or to organize a coherent civil society. A student who participated in the *wiphala* demonstrations said: "I believe that social networks, rather than helping us to mobilize, were used to discredit our marches, to minimize them by portraying us as mindless puppets [of the MAS]. They were used to construct a narrative around the 'good, civil, prodemocracy' Bolivians and the 'bad, backward' people like us" (anonymous interview with the author, June 10, 2020). She went on to explain that in her working-class neighborhood, social media were not used to mobilize. Because many people in her district do not have cellphones or regular Internet access, they used other means to communicate and summon each other, including beating drums or pots. But of course, it is not possible to construct a narrative and disseminate it to the world using these types of instruments.

In short, the middle classes who organized the anti-Morales protests used ICTs and social media extensively for offensive purposes: mobilization and the construction of a narrative and a set of frames to articulate their demands. The use of these tools by those who took to the streets once the former group achieved their goal was limited and primarily defensive. They used social media for denouncing violence after the fact, to seek information beyond the mainstream media, and, eventually, to tell the world their version of events. But according to Eduardo and José, it is difficult for them to compete with the well-resourced, tech-savvy, U.S.-supported campaign of their opponents. They argue that Indigenous organizations must focus on acquiring these skills and on developing coherent and collaborative social media and communications strategies in 2020s.

The social media content analysis I conducted in 2020 supports these findings. Relatively few Indigenous CSOs were using social media, leaving the online space to be disputed by government agencies and mainstream media. Those pro-MAS CSOs that did use Twitter and Facebook in late October 2019 tended to portray Indigenous protesters as peaceful and just, while opposition forces (who became the government as of mid-November) were framed as racist. This was the framing used by the Bartolinas women's organization, for example, although they and other pro-MAS CSOs stopped posting content once the new government took power due to fear of reprisals. Common hashtags include #EvoWeAreWithYou, #HandsOffBolivia, and #NoToTheCoup. Morales himself took to Twitter to accuse his opponents of being racists, terrorists, and coup plotters. The anti-Morales Indigenous CSOs tended to be critical of the election results in October but mostly remained silent in November.

Of course, once Áñez took power, the official state social media accounts changed hands and the messages shifted abruptly. The interim president's messages, often with religious overtones, focused on democracy and freedom, as well as the bravery of the citizens (who stood up to Morales) in the face of the violent *masistas*. The new government's favorite hashtags were more likely to be #ChristHasReturned and #FreeBolivia. Private media outlets tended to strongly support the right-wing opposition (and later interim government). Red UNO, one of Bolivia's major television networks, focused its reporting on the anti-MAS protests, which it implicitly depicted as heroic, and framed the whole process as a national sacrifice. Pro-MAS protesters are shown alongside images of violence and property damage. The language used in mainstream media reporting reflects this pattern: the middle-class, anti-Morales collective action is labeled as "citizen protests," while the word "citizen" is never used to describe MAS supporters. Here again, then, the dominant narrative is clearly controlled by the right-wing forces that have long aligned themselves against Indigenous interests.

Indigenous Civil Society in Bolivia: Evolution and Future Prospects

Zavaleta's (1986) *sociedad abigarrada* continues to characterize Bolivia's sociopolitical landscape, and Indigenous civil society reflects the variegated context in which it has developed. Indigenous actors engage on multiple scales and across the spectrum of state and "traditional" institutions and practices. The MAS has incorporated some elements of this homogeneous society while rejecting others. This has produced an uneasy and disjointed relationship between recognition of local particularities and the universalizing pretensions of the government's postneoliberal project. It has led to the development of a unique configuration of multiscalar positioning. On the one hand, new political opportunities and an indigenized citizenship regime have provided access points to the state. Actors aligned with the project have options that were denied to them in pre-Morales Bolivia (and during the interim regime). But the exclusion of other voices has exacerbated tensions within Indigenous civil society and leaves in place a social structure that acknowledges some logics while withholding recognition from others, leading these actors to develop a very different type of positioning.

Indigenous CSOs in Bolivia have accomplished something that has eluded their counterparts in the rest of Latin America. They managed to take control of their country's political institutions, draft a new constitution based on an Indigenous citizenship, launch a far-reaching project aimed at decolonizing the state, and create new state-society mechanisms that provided channels for the country's most marginalized citizens to influence policy. These are extraordinary accomplishments in their own right. CSOs also maintained pressure on the government to follow a post- (or anti-) neoliberal agenda. While the majority of Bolivians remain poor, there is plenty of evidence that demonstrates an improvement in living standards under the MAS. The Indigenous-led government was able to balance improving human development indicators with maintaining a strong overall economy. Bolivia closed 2018 with one of the highest economic growth rates in Latin America (a growth of 4.7 percent in gross domestic product). In 2019, the growth rate was predicted to close at 4.3 percent, compared to 1.3 percent for the region as a whole. Investment also remained strong, averaging 21.8 percent of GDP annually from 2014 to 2018 (Arauz et al., 2019). The country was praised for its success at achieving "strong growth and poverty reduction" by the IMF, which is generally not a strong proponent of left-wing governments.

Redistributive policies, a postneoliberal indigenized citizenship regime, and participatory democracy initiatives earned Morales widespread and sustained popularity. While the results have been positive, these improvements may have also undercut support for protest, mobilization, and ultimately for Indigenous CSOs. During our interviews in 2018, many leaders lamented that it was more difficult to mobilize people then than in the 1990s. This is always a dilemma for CSOs that represent marginalized population groups. The more concessions they secure from the state, the more likely their supporters are to be satisfied with perceived gains and the less likely they are to risk these by opposing the government. CSOs obviously cannot stop pursuing the interests of their constituents and securing gains in return for cooperation should not be read as uncritical co-optation. And as in Ecuador, it is important not to assume that a decline in the protest cycle suggests that Indigenous civil society has been weakened or has become less active.

Indigenous CSOs have become masters of multiscalar positioning since the 2000s. They have succeeded in broadening the democratic process, pursuing their goals through institutional means by engaging in the new participatory architecture that they themselves helped to build. Some argue that the MAS experiment led to co-optation and controlled inclusion. But inclusion is preferable to exclusion, and it is both condescending and inaccurate to assume that Indigenous CSOs that participate in governance through state-society mechanisms have been passively co-opted. In fact, under the MAS, Indigenous CSOs used these mechanisms to consistently and continually pressure the government, as opposed to being manipulated by it. The relationship that developed between pro-MAS sectors of civil society and the government was far more equal and "push and pull" than many observers were willing to admit. But it was a complex relationship that ended up linking the work of many CSOs too closely to the MAS-dominated state and maintaining solidarity among disparate CSOs became increasingly arduous for all parties involved.

Indigenous civil society banded together in the face of harmful neoliberal policies and state repression in the 1990s and early 2000s. That unity was more difficult to maintain in the context of a system that welcomed some as participants and excluded others. Fragmentation produced a certain fragility, and in November 2019 Indigenous Bolivians and the organizations that represent them found themselves on the outside looking in once again. Under Áñez, political opportunities were less favorable to Indigenous CSOs than they had been since the military dictatorships of the 1970s. The interim regime could not dismantle the large, developed mobilizing structures that Indigenous activists had built over the past century, although it did narrow the tactical repertoire available to Indigenous actors. When state-society mechanisms are closed, CSOs have few options other than direct, disruptive action.

Unlike in the 1990s and early 2000s, Indigenous civil society actors in 2019 appeared unable to put their differences aside even in the face of a common threat. But this did not signal a collapse of Indigenous civil society. The experience and political skills CSOs gained in the 2010s had not been lost. The Áñez regime's decision to reschedule the elections, for example, led to mass mobilizations across the country involving Indigenous civil society but also the country's largest labor union. They essentially shut down much of the country for weeks, demonstrating that Indigenous civil society is still able to use direct action effectively. And while they temporarily lost access to the state and its inclusion mechanisms, pro-MAS CSOs did manage to mobilize a majority of Indigenous citizens to restore the MAS to power at the end of 2020, even if led by someone other than Evo Morales. They did this by deploying "traditional" tactics, through established mobilizing structures and with a strong focus on contesting and occupying physical spaces.

The use of ICTs was extremely limited among Indigenous CSOs. Rather than contributing to their efforts, social media in particular were weaponized against segments of Indigenous civil society during the 2019 uprisings. This suggests that the virtual sphere remains peripheral to multiscalar positioning for Indigenous actors in Bolivia. But it also demonstrates that Indigenous civil society is able to operate outside of the networked society, delinking from a hostile online world entirely while continuing to pursue their goals in the "real" world. The lessons Indigenous CSOs have learned, and the partnerships they have built at home and abroad, will support their efforts to contest any efforts to reverse they gains they have made. It remains to be seen how Indigenous Bolivians will rebuild their unique civil society in the face of an uncertain future.

4 Chile (Wallmapu)

Continuing Resistance, Emerging Renaissance

. . . .

On November 14, 2018, twenty-four-year-old Camilo Catrillanca was shot dead by agents of a special police unit near the Mapuche community of Temucuicui, in the Araucanía region. Members of the Jungle Command, a tactical reaction force of the Carabineros (Chilean National Police) established in 2018 to fight "terrorism," would later claim that they were pursuing Catrillanca because they believed that he was involved in a series of car thefts. The officers insisted that they shot the Mapuche activist because he was brandishing a weapon.

In the not-so-distant past, this may have been the end of the matter. There would have been an investigation, but the Carabineros's version of events would have been accepted by the relevant authorities and the case would have been closed. Catrillanca would have become yet another Indigenous victim of the Chilean state. Dozens of Mapuche have been killed by security forces over the decades, while many more have been arbitrarily charged with terrorism and sedition (Antileo Baeza et al. 2015; Cayuqueo 2018). But the Carabineros neglected to consider the widespread use of social media in 2018. Two videos of the incident emerged and were disseminated widely on Facebook and other platforms. They showed that Catrillanca was unarmed and that he was fleeing from police on a tractor when he was shot in the back of the neck.

Social media exploded with images and messages denouncing the extrajudicial killing and calling for justice. President Sebastián Piñera (2018–22) was forced to apologize and to ask for the resignation of the chief of the Carabineros and several other high-ranking officials. The officers involved were arrested and charged, and the man who pulled the trigger claimed that he was forced by the head of the Jungle Command to lie about what had transpired. Mass demonstrations in the Araucanía, but also in Santiago, called for the unit to be dismantled and demanded the resignation of Interior Minister Andrés Chadwick, Piñera's cousin and once a supporter of military dictator Augusto Pinochet (1973–90). Chile, which prides itself on being a model liberal democracy in an otherwise unstable region, faced embarrassment as it was condemned by international human rights organizations.

When Alberto, my Mapuche research assistant, and I began our fieldwork in November 2018, the pain caused by these events was still raw. Representatives from both "civic" and more militant CSOs were angry, but as the videos were widely shared over the next few weeks, they expressed a sense of consolation that Chileans—and the world—would see what had really happened in Temucuicui. They celebrated the resignation of senior police officials and the arrest of officers responsible for the killing. They were pleased that Chadwick was subjected to the humiliation of being grilled by a congressional human rights committee, although they expressed disappointment that he was not forced from office (this did happen the following year, but more on that later).

A year after Catrillanca's death, Chile erupted into the largest antigovernment protests since the end of the Pinochet dictatorship in 1990. Unlike the events in Ecuador and Bolivia, the Chilean protests were not led by Indigenous organizations, nor were Mapuche protesters the primary protagonists. But they did have a significant impact and their participation demonstrated the evolution of Mapuche civil society. Both Mapuche and non-Indigenous protestors carried signs with Catrillanca's likeness and antipolice slogans throughout the nationwide 2019 uprisings. The young activist had become a symbol of resistance to the state.

In this chapter, I argue that Mapuche CSOs have less political experience to build on when compared with their regional counterparts, as the country's repressive military regime left little space for the development of mobilizing structures. At the same time, the rigid political opportunity structure and static citizenship regime that have characterized Chile since 1990 provide few options for Mapuche CSOs. The citizenship regime remains staunchly (neo)liberal, and there are few political participation opportunities beyond the voting booth. This has led some activists to opt for disruptive, even violent, action as the only path available to them, while others have chosen to concentrate their efforts on Mapuche nation building.

In the past few years, we have witnessed the birth of dynamic new CSOs that use ICTs to promote and revitalize Mapuche identity. In terms of both scope and innovation, Mapuche use of ICTs for cultural, social, and political development exceeds what I witnessed in the other two countries. The increasing militarization of Mapuche territories in the Araucanía makes their task difficult, however. Mapuche civil society remains fractured along various fault lines, and there are tensions between those who support and oppose violent, confrontational tactics.

Recent events, however, may serve to shift political opportunities in favor of Mapuche civil society and expand opportunities for multiscalar positioning. Chileans have increasingly demanded that their state expand social rights and draft a new constitution. These are two goals that both civic and "uncivic" actors within Mapuche civil society have been struggling for since the return to democracy. In the aftermath of the 2019 protests, CSOs willing to engage with "civic" tactics may have an unprecedented opportunity to forge alliances with like-minded Mapuche organizations and with non-Indigenous sectors of Chilean civil society.

Mobilizing Structures, Political Opportunities, and Citizenship: Repression, Resistance, and Negotiation

There are at least nine distinct Indigenous peoples in Chile. The Mapuche are by far the largest, comprising about 84 percent of the country's Indigenous population. My research was conducted primarily in the Araucanía, the region with the largest concentration of Mapuche. The Mapuche are unique in Latin America in that a significant part of their homeland of Wallmapu south of the Biobío River remained independent during Spanish colonial rule. It was conquered by Chile in the 1880s following a campaign known as the "pacification" of the Araucanía (Crow 2013; Richards 2010, 2013). Mapuche sovereignty was in fact recognized by the Spanish crown, although some sectors of colonial society portrayed them as uncivilized barbarians. This narrative became dominant under the Chilean republic founded in 1818 in order to justify the "pacification" campaign (Bastías Rebolledo 2009; Pichinao Huenchuleo 2012). The Mapuche were conquered in 1883, much of their land was expropriated by the Chilean state and offered to (mostly European) settlers, and Mapuche communities were forcibly relocated to small land reserves called *reducciones*. But Crow (2013) invites us to resist binary readings of the past that divide actors into oppressors and helpless victims of state violence. Her historical research demonstrates a complex tradition of negotiation between the Chilean and Mapuche nations. She also elucidates the variegated approach Mapuche actors have adopted toward the Chilean state, oscillating between confrontation and dialogue (and sometimes both simultaneously), resisting some aspects of the state's nation-building project while consenting to others. We will see that these practices continue to shape Mapuche CSO's multiscalar positioning to the present day.

Unlike Bolivia and Ecuador, Chile has enjoyed political and economic stability since the return to electoral democracy in 1990 (Richards 2013). From 1990 to 2010, the country was governed by the Concertación, a coalition of nominally center-left parties. Pinochet and the military willingly ceded power to a civilian government, but they put various safeguards in place to ensure their continuing influence, including maintaining the military regime's 1980 constitution. When significant changes were finally made to remove the most undemocratic elements of the constitution in 2005, observers generally agreed that Chile had become a consolidated democracy. Freedom House rates Chile as the most democratic country in Latin America.[1]

Mapuche communities tell a very different story. The establishment of liberal democracy certainly changed the political opportunity structure for Indigenous activists, who faced severe restrictions and state violence under the dictatorship. From 1990 onward, they were free to form and participate in CSOs. Dozens of new organizations were created both in the Araucanía and in Santiago, although they had few mobilizing structures on which to build. But despite the opening of associational space, Chilean institutions continued to discourage citizen participation in politics beyond the ballot box (Richards 2013). Chile was minimally affected by the wave of participatory democracy inspired by the Pink Tide that swept across the continent in the 2000s. The few new state-society mechanisms created through a 2011 Citizen Participation Law were limited in scope and primarily consultative (Lupien 2018a). This left Indigenous leaders with few points of access to the state. Chilean elites—including those of the Concertación—formed a strong consensus around the neoliberal model, affording significant rights to capital and business while demonstrating reluctance to recognize collective Indigenous grievances (Antileo Baeza et al. 2015). Essentially, the post-Pinochet state offered limited civil and political rights, omitting social rights or recognition of Indigenous identity. Given the importance to Chile's economy of forestry and other resource industries, and the strong concentration of these activities in Wallmapu, CSOs found themselves in an uphill battle against the state and powerful private interests (Pairicán 2013; Pichinao Huenchuleo 2012; Richards 2010).

Indigenous CSOs therefore faced numerous obstacles from 1990 onward: limited mobilizing capacity, restricted political opportunities, and a neoliberal citizenship regime that failed to recognize collective rights (Marimán 2012). Mapuche CSO's points of access to the state are relatively limited when compared to their counterparts in Ecuador and Bolivia. As a result, their multiscalar positioning approach has evolved differently. The lack of options means that the use of disruptive (even violent) tactics is more common here than in the other two countries, and this trend intensified in the 2010s (Antileo Baeza et al. 2015; Pairicán 2013). This dimension is what media attention—and much of the academic literature—has focused on, but it is only part of the story. In the 2010s, a new crop of CSOs is leading a Mapuche cultural revival focused on nation building, and adopting a more diverse tactical repertoire supported by ICTs.

At the same time, Chilean civil society has become less docile. In 2019, over a million Chileans took to the streets of Santiago and other cities to protest not only the Piñera government, but long-festering issues such as inequality and demands for a new, more democratic constitution. While Mapuche CSOs were not the primary protagonists, their presence was increasingly visible in the final months of 2019 and into 2020. They could certainly benefit from any changes that may result from the uprisings or they may be left out of the discussions yet again. It remains to be seen whether Mapuche CSOs can find ways of working with each other and with allied sectors of Chilean civil society to advance common interests.

Political Opportunities

Touted as the model Latin American representative democracy by Western liberals, Chile arguably has the worst record of the three countries when it comes to Indigenous peoples (Castellaro 2015; Marimán 2012; Pichinao Huenchuleo 2012; Richards 2013). This is due to a number of factors: the lingering institutionalized authoritarianism of the Pinochet era (including a constitution in desperate need of reform and heavy-handed "antiterrorism" laws), a dearth of state-society interface mechanisms, a lack of public support for Mapuche activism, an enduring security state mentality among political elites and segments of the middle class, and strong support for the "model" Chilean state by foreign powers and international organizations.

The Chilean Magna Carta has been modified several times since it was adopted under the military dictatorship, yet many of the most notorious provisions remained in place for fifteen years following the return to civilian government (Heiss 2017). These articles limited political opportunities for civil society—and particularly for Indigenous organizations—until the reforms of 2005 that finally removed many (but not all) of the undemocratic remnants of the Pinochet's constitution. Perhaps the one right that the constitution does fully protect is private property, which also represents a challenge to Mapuche collective land claims.

Chile's lingering authoritarian legal framework restricts political opportunities (Marimán 2012; Pairicán 2013). The country retained a series of punitive *desacato* articles in both the criminal code and the State Security Law. The latter punished "contempt" for public authorities as a crime against national security until a 2001 Freedom of Expression law eliminated the crime of *desacato*, although libel and defamation laws can still be used to file civil suits. Section 264 of the criminal code prohibits "threats" against public figures, although the Inter-American Court of Human Rights has argued that the wording is ambiguous and leaves what constitutes a threat open to a broad interpretation. The majority of Indigenous leaders and activists we spoke to were aware of recent instances of these laws being used against members of their communities and argue that calls for the resignation of public officials have been interpreted as "threats" by those same authorities. All but two of the Indigenous participants Alberto and I interviewed claimed that they or their colleagues have engaged in self-censorship out of fear that they could be accused of threatening certain political figures. One activist explained: "We speak of struggle, of centuries of struggle against the state to reclaim our land. And yes, even saying something like this will make some politicians in Santiago claim that we are threatening violence. So we have to be a bit careful about how we word things on social media" (anonymous interview with Lagos, February 2, 2019).

The elected governments that emerged after 1990 found Pinochet's 1984 Anti-Terrorism Act to be an efficient tool for suppressing dissent. It allows prosecutors to detain suspects without a trial for months, to call anonymous witnesses, and to request severe sentences. The use of the act has enabled Chile to convict dozens of Mapuche for crimes that would not be considered terrorism in other jurisdictions. A special rapporteurs' report on Indigenous rights urged the Chilean government to "refrain from using the anti-terrorism law to deal with events that occurred in the context of social protests by Mapuche peoples seeking to claim their rights."[2] Former interior minister Chadwick was particularly enthusiastic about charging Mapuche leaders as terrorists. In particular, his department's frequent use of the 1984 act provoked condemnation from the Inter-American Court and the

United Nations due to concerns that the laws were being used specifically against members of the Mapuche community.[3]

Accusations of terrorism and subversion have been leveled based on data collected from ITCs, in some cases based on false evidence. The most infamous example is Operation Hurricane, an undercover investigation by the Carabineros that led to the arrest of several Mapuche activists for "terrorism" in late 2017. In January 2018, Chile's public prosecutor's office concluded that evidence presented by the Carabineros, including social media conversations and cellphone data, had been fabricated. The prosecutor's office declared Operation Hurricane fraudulent and opened an investigation against the police force. The charges against the Mapuche individuals were dropped, but two of the interviewees who had been investigated believed that the Carabineros were victorious despite this outcome. "They got what they really wanted" said one man. "They wanted to scare us, they wanted us to know they are watching us on social media, to be fearful of using ICTs as a tool in our fight" (anonymous interview with Lagos, January 7, 2019).

Chilean security agencies have purchased Hacking Team's RCS software and have used drone-like surveillance balloons to spy on communities. Law requires that intercepting communications be authorized by a judge, who must receive this request from the public prosecutor's office, and that such surveillance can be conducted on only a limited basis. Yet a 2018 study conducted by the independent Center for Investigative Journalism (Centro de Investigación Periodistica, CIPER) in Santiago found that Chilean police intercepted calls and social media messages between journalists and their sources regarding the activities of Mapuche activists on a regular basis (Sepúlveda 2018). Mapuche community media journalists were specifically targeted, but there is no evidence that proper legal procedures were followed or that the officers involved in the investigation had reasonable grounds to conduct the surveillance. In any case, the Santiago-based NGO Derechos Digitales notes that judicial review is insufficient to safeguard privacy as the types of software available to governments today are far more invasive than simply intercepting communications; they allow security agencies to access everything from webcams to documents on a hard drive (Pérez De Acha 2016).

Unlike the new Bolivian and Ecuadorian constitutions, Chile's Magna Carta does not contain articles related to communication and ICTs. It does grant Chileans the right to both freedom of speech and access to information. But in sharp contrast to the other two countries, it contains no provisions related to information pluralism, community media, or limiting the power of private interests. Rather, it prohibits the state from establishing a monopoly over information outlets. The 1982 Telecommunications Law also dates from the Pinochet era. It has been updated to guarantee free expression but does not account for twenty-first-century technologies. Unlike the more recent Bolivian and Ecuadorian laws, it does not create any state-sanctioned information regulation bodies but it imposes sanctions for operating a radio or broadcast media outlet without a license. Participants told us that the law has been used on various occasions against Indigenous community radio stations in the Araucanía in order to silence their opposition to forestry or hydroelectric projects. The 2001 Freedom of Expression in Journalism Law provides media outlets with the right to disseminate information and express opinions without fear of reprisals. In theory, this allows Indigenous actors to criticize the government and to disseminate information according to their own worldview, yet the law is primarily aimed at protecting traditional mass media outlets and does little to promote information pluralism.

Since Chile's return to democracy in 1990, the country has regularly been considered a model of representative democracy in the region but one of the political systems with the least participation (Cameron, Hershberg, and Sharpe 2012; Lupien 2018a). In other words, elections are free and fair, and power changes hands peacefully, but citizens have few opportunities to participate in politics outside of the ballot box. There was a marked shift in discourse beginning with the first administration of President Michelle Bachelet (2006–10). She declared increased citizen participation to be an important goal, although participation in the Chilean context tends to be framed as an instrument for effective governance and policymaking and not as an alternative to representative democracy (Aguilera 2007; Cleuren 2007; Lupien 2018a). Concrete changes include the adoption of a new Citizen Participation Law (drafted by the Bachelet administration in 2010 but adopted under Piñera in 2011) that recognizes citizen participation as a right and provides stronger legal recognition to institutions such as the *juntas de vecinos* (neighborhood councils). It also creates civil society councils through which individuals or groups can provide feedback to government departments and ministries. While some Mapuche CSO representatives had participated in these mechanisms, none of the participants I spoke to felt that the new law or the shift in discourse has had an impact on their ability to engage with the state.

Citizenship Regime

The Chilean citizenship regime remains a product of the neoliberal era of the 1980s. The focus on individual rather than collective rights makes it difficult for Indigenous peoples, whose claims are inherently communitarian in nature, to frame their demands in a way that aligns with their country's citizenship regime (Marimán 2012). The Chilean constitution does not establish citizen participation as a right, nor does the language used in the Citizen Participation Law suggest some kind of radical shift in the relationship between civil society and the state. Rather, it tends to frame citizen participation in practical and pragmatic terms, emphasizing more effective and efficient public policy, strengthening communication between citizens and the government, and increasing transparency and confidence in government institutions (Lupien 2018a). The law clearly establishes citizen participation as falling "within a framework of co-responsibility" between citizens and the state, and participation is primarily consultative; there is no sense that the people play a direct leading role in decision making.

At the time of this writing, Chile remains one of the few countries in Latin America that does not recognize Indigenous peoples in its constitution. An Indigenous Law (Ley Indígena 19.253) was adopted in 1993 to "promote recognition, respect, appreciation and protection of Indigenous cultures, including artistic and cultural expression; as well as architectural, archaeological, and historical heritage." The law also created the National Corporation for Indigenous Development (Corporación Nacional de Desarrollo Indígena, CONADI), a state institution responsible for the coordination and implementation of development plans related to Indigenous peoples. It does not guarantee rights to ancestral territories or natural resources.

Chile's liberal citizenship regime aligns with country's political and economic institutions; it emphasizes civil and (limited) political rights but neglects social citizenship. On paper, all Chilean citizens enjoy the same basic rights and are expected to limit their political participation to the ballot box. Under the neoliberal multiculturalism that gradually emerged in the 1990s, Indigenous peoples are provided with minimal recognition through state-supported (nonthreatening) forms of cultural expression but are expected to integrate as full citizens and to abandon collective claims over land and political autonomy (Richards 2013). This resembles the citizenship regime established by neoliberal governments in Bolivia prior to the election of Evo Morales, which that country's Indigenous peoples ultimately rejected. But the Chilean version of multicultural citizenship is even weaker in that it did not recognize Indigenous local governance mechanisms such as Bolivia's OTBs, or state-society interfaces to channel Indigenous political participation. Instead, Indigenous peoples, who are assumed to be equal under the liberal citizenship regime, are expected to participate through the same mechanisms as the rest of the population (Antileo Baeza et al. 2015). The few Indigenous-centered institutions, such as the CONADI, are mandated only to support forms of cultural and artistic expression.

Mobilizing Networks and Resources

In the twenty-first century, Mapuche collective action is most frequently associated with the "uncivic"—and often violent—actions of the Coordinadora Arauco-Malleco (CAM), an organization dedicated to the restoration of an autonomous Wallmapu. This focus overlooks a rich history of diverse mobilizing structures and practices developed and appropriated by the Mapuche over the centuries.

The advisory group of Mapuche leaders and thinkers I met with at a Temuco university in November 2018 was the most diverse I had worked with in the three countries. It consisted of a farmer and former CAM member who had participated in acts of sabotage against forestry companies, a journalist who had founded an online Mapuche news site, a teacher working on an Internet-based Mapudungun language course, and two artists who brought along slick promotional materials for cultural events they were organizing. Rather than simply telling me about the variety of CSOs they belonged to, two presented Power Point slides, one showed us a film, and another displayed a series of glossy promotional materials. By the end of the afternoon, it became clear that Mapuche civil society was far more diverse and dynamic than media representations account for.

As Mapuche intellectual Pedro Cayuqueo (2018) reminds us, until recently Mapuche collective action was focused on dialogue and politics rather than confrontation. This history includes mechanisms through which the independent Mapuche interacted and negotiated with the Spanish crown, such as a series of parliaments in which each was recognized as an independent nation (Bastías Rebolledo 2009; Pichinao Huenchuleo 2012). Abut thirty-five parliaments were held during the colonial period to mediate matters such as territorial autonomy and cultural issues. These and traditional local governance mechanisms were suppressed by the centralizing ambitions of the Chilean state. The surviving Mapuche parliament, which served to unite communities across the ancestral territories, was deemed illegal in 1907.

Throughout most of the twentieth century, the civic institutional road was preferred by most Mapuche actors, although they were also willing to engage in "uncivic" actions, generally in collaboration with non-Indigenous sectors of the left. Between 1924 and 1973 (when Pinochet seized power), the most important Mapuche organizations focused on electoral politics and participated in formal institutions of Chilean civil society (Cayuqueo 2018). They were heavily involved in the expansion of unions in the late 1960s and also participated in land occupations from 1967 to 1973, which became the most common form of protest (Redondo Cardeñoso 2017). But Mapuche leaders were also involved in efforts to create peasant councils during this time period. These Communal Peasant Councils (Consejos Comunales Campesinos, CCCs) were organic base organizations of direct democracy intended to integrate farmers into a cohesive movement. The CCCs also included workers' committees, unions, and small Mapuche landowners. These mechanisms were a new form of collective action within the established legal framework, although land seizures and occupations continued (Cárcamo Hernández 2016). Mapuche who had migrated to the cities also participated in urban associational spaces, such as bakers' syndicates, which became an important space of engagement in civil society. Urban Mapuche in particular learned to appropriate and adapt popular associational spaces and tools that allowed them to survive (Curivil Bravo 2012).

The military dictatorship (1973–90) left little room for associational space and these mechanisms were suppressed. The remaining traditional governance structures through which Mapuche communities engaged in local decision making were deemed illegal by the Pinochet regime. Most of the Mapuche organizations that exist today were therefore founded in the late 1990s or 2000s, decades behind modern Indigenous CSOs in neighboring countries. This, along with disagreements over the tactics used by some of the more radical organizations, is why Mapuche civil society remains segmented and fractured. A local Mapuche scholar described civil society as comprising a series of "micro" organizations that are primarily local or issue-focused, and insisted that none can really claim to represent even the Araucanía, much less anything resembling national leadership (Natalia Caniguán, personal communication, February 9, 2020).

By the mid-1990s, the most prominent Mapuche CSOs turned to extrainstitutional tactics following disappointing efforts to engage with successive Concertación governments. The organizations that perhaps best characterize the nature of the conflict are the CAM, Council of All Lands (Consejo de Todas las Tierras, CTT), and the Mapuche Territorial Alliance (Alianza Territorial Mapuche, ATM). These CSOs call for an autonomous Mapuche homeland and reject what they see as the Chilean occupation that began in the 1880s. The CAM was founded in 1998 (not uncoincidentally the same year that Pinochet final stepped down as commander of the armed forces) and includes a military wing whose members, according to some accounts, were trained in the jungles of Colombia by the Revolutionary Armed Forces of Colombia (Fuerzas Armadas Revolucionarias de Colombia, FARC) (Carrera, 2010).

In addition to meeting with activists from the organizations mentioned above, I spoke with representatives from a growing number of CSOs that have established less conflictual relationships with the state, and many of these do not support the tactics or sovereigntist project of the CAM and the CTT. Most are concentrated in the Araucanía. These include regional organizations, such as Identidad Territorial Lafquenche, which works to unite and represent common interests of costal Mapuche communities in central Chile. The Self-Convened Mapuche Women's Group (Agrupación de Mujeres Mapuche Autoconvocadas), founded in 2012, seeks the "promotion and development of the rights and dignity of the Mapuche, focusing on education, culture, training, work, health, housing, environment, community development, and human rights." There are also a growing number of urban organizations in other parts of the country. For example, the Meli Wixan Mapu is an organization located in Santiago, where a growing wave of internal migration had brought thousands of young Mapuche to pursue economic opportunities. It seeks to preserve the culture of urban Mapuche and fight for their political rights.

There is also a new crop of dynamic Mapuche organizations that seek to engage in the public sphere through promoting culture, identity, and a rejuvenated sense of Mapuche nationhood. Ficwallmapu, created in 2015, seeks to "Promote dialogue between Indigenous and non-Indigenous Peoples, to encourage respect for cultural diversity, through audiovisual production and offering the opportunity for Indigenous filmmakers disseminate their works on topics relevant to the Original Peoples." Mapuexpress, founded in 2000, is an "information collective" that, through social communication and activism, seeks the to defend collective rights, nature, and territories. They pursue these objectives primarily through the diffusion of historical memory in Mapuche communities, the arts, education, and the revival of the Mapudungun language. A member of the collective's editorial team explained the different organizational structure they—and a growing number of Mapuche organizations—have developed:

> Our way of influencing politics has always been low-key, and it is based on our traditional ways, since we have seen that many Mapuche organizations have adopted a Western structure. We try to be as authentic as possible, to integrate our own cultural normative elements into the organization and its practices. For example, we are guided by traditional figures: *Lonko, Machi* [Mapuche community leaders]. With the state, we are constituted under the law so that we can sign agreements and things like that, but we as an organization are members of the territories in a natural organic way, we have a commitment to those forms of organization. (Salamanca, interview with Lagos, February 10, 2018)

ICTs are an important resource for Mapuche civil society. Since the 1990s, independent, bilingual (Spanish and Mapudungun) radio has become a key tool in an evolving Mapuche social, cultural, and nation-building project. Autonomous from both the state and the corporate actors that dominate Chilean media, Mapuche radio serves to decolonize the airwaves, or to disrupt what Cárcamo-Huechante (2013) calls "acoustic colonialism" through self-representation. Radio celebrates cultural traditions, encourages the use of Mapudungun, and provides a space for the Mapuche to carry out their struggle for territorial rights and autonomy. More broadly, radio is part of an effort to build a Mapuche public sphere (Cárcamo-Huechante 2013). By broadcasting across Wallmapu (Chile and Argentina), radio defies colonial borders and unites Mapuche communities into a political project (Mingo 2014).

In the twenty-first century, Mapuche CSOs are also using the Internet and social media to construct a virtual public sphere, and they have made significant strides in comparison to the other two countries. As the most developed country in the region, Chile has a relatively advanced ICT infrastructure and its people are more likely to have Internet access than elsewhere on the continent. By 2018, 89 percent of urban Chileans and 77 percent of those in rural areas had Internet access at home (compared to 44 percent of Bolivians). The Araucanía has the second lowest rate of Internet penetration in the country, but it still sits at an impressive 81 percent.[4] All of the Indigenous organizations I worked with had Internet access and standard equipment and all but one had developed one or more social media profiles. Only two of the organizations mentioned Internet access issues in local communities.

Mapuche Civil Society in the Twenty-First Century: Conflict and National Renaissance

The Mapuche have relatively few channels through which they can claim rights, and few rights to claim. In contrast to the multiscalar positioning strategies I encountered in the other two countries, Mapuche CSOs I worked with believe that they have two choices. They can either dedicate their efforts to cultural expression and nation building—including promoting the Mapudungun language and reviving cultural traditions—or they can fight for land rights and political autonomy through confrontation with the state. The most prominent and visible Mapuche CSOs have chosen the latter option. Even for those organizations that have diversified their tactical repertoire, political participation and influence on policy remain challenges. But focusing on the low-intensity conflict in the Araucanía overshadows the work of the dynamic emerging organizations that are reviving traditional governance practices and developing new approaches to communication, resource mobilization, and identity promotion. Increasingly, we are witnessing a mix of disruptive tactics to challenge the Chilean central state with greater civic engagement at the local level, where more political opportunities exist.

These starkly different approaches have prevented the development of a movement capable of uniting Mapuche CSOs, and this fragmentation has weakened Mapuche civil society's bargaining power vis-à-vis the state. There have been no large-scale "turning point" uprisings like those that rocked Bolivia and Ecuador in the 1990s. But this does not mean that Mapuche civil society has not had an impact on life in Wallmapu, particularly if we take a broader view that considers the results of collective action beyond concrete policy outcomes (McVeigh, Welch, and Bjarnason 2003; Meyer and Whittier 1994). Mapuche civil society, though a growing number of innovative and tech-savvy CSOs, has been successful in creating a sense of nationhood, of instilling a sense of empowerment in growing segments of the population, and of leading a cultural renaissance in the Araucanía and beyond (Millalen Paillal 2012). It is also important to note that for many Mapuche, multiscalar positioning involves another layer of complexity: an imagined cross-border nation that stretches across Chile and

Argentina. As Warren (2013) explains, this Mapuche nation "has undefined borders and draws on the historic diversity and looseness of Mapuche political organization while also making use of modern technologies and ways of solidifying identities." For CSOs that share this nation-building project, multiscalar positioning involves within-state and cross-border action, and the increasing use of ICTs to foster a sense of national identity among communities and individuals across Wallmapu.

Influencing Policy and Political Participation

The struggle over citizenship is reflected in the types of Mapuche organizations that have emerged since 1990. The most high-profile networks, such as CTT, CAM, and ATM, reject Chile's liberal citizenship regime and challenge the legitimacy of the state. A sense of national identity distinct from the Chilean nation distinguishes many Mapuche from their peers elsewhere in the region. Two Mapuche youth leaders I met with reinforced this sentiment. "We are not Chileans," they responded in unison. "Aymara and Quechua brothers and sisters you may have spoken to in the Andes, they were incorporated into the colonial states in the 1500s. We were independent for centuries and only conquered by the Chilean state in the late nineteenth century. This is why we have maintained our spirit of independence and why we still fight for it" (anonymous interview with the author, November 18, 2018). Many others would express similar sentiments over the next few months. They consider their nation to be Wallmapu and view Chile as an invader. Because parts of their ancestral territories are located in neighboring Argentina, many dream of a united Wallmapu that would cross the settler-imposed border.

Even among those organizations that reject the legitimacy of the Chilean state, there are significant differences with respect to strategies and tactics. CAM has certainly garnered the most media attention (Kowalczyk 2013). Its leaders refuse to negotiate with a state that they view as an occupying force, while the government has labeled it as a terrorist organization and has used legislation to criminalize the movement and its members. CAM's tactics have included land occupations, vandalism (including burning of private homes and farms), and sabotage. Conflict with the state is low-intensity but ongoing, with periodic flare-ups. In 2009, CAM activists occupied a private estate in the Araucanía Region and were ejected in a violent confrontation with authorities. Another flare-up occurred in early 2013. A march to commemorate a Mapuche student killed by police turned violent and was followed by various acts of sabotage. Around the same time, CAM activists were linked to an arson attack that killed an agribusiness couple on their estate near the town of Vilcún. Local *Machi* (leader) Celestino Cordova was charged with the crime and sentenced to eighteen years in prison, although he claims to be a political prisoner and CAM argues that the evidence against him was fabricated. Not surprisingly, its supporters have frequently engaged in violent clashes with police and many have been charged under the country's antiterrorism laws. CAM itself was labeled as a terrorist group by President Piñera in 2017. At this point, the organization is so closely associated with violent disruptive tactics that the doors to state-civil society access points have been slammed shut by both parties. CAM activists continue to see disruptive action and civil disobedience as the only paths available to them.

The CAM activists I spoke with described the organization's structure in detail. It includes a political wing, which engages in typical social movement activities such as communication, resource mobilization, and identity politics. In contrast to the other organizations studied in this book, it also includes armed units known as the Territorial Resistance Organs (Órganos de Resistencia Territorial, ORT). The various local ORT cells use arson, sabotage, and roadblocks to pressure both the state and extractive industries. Destruction of agribusiness equipment and activities is seen as a legitimate response to what activists view as the occupation of their land, and they hope that these acts will allow Mapuche communities to recover their territories by driving the companies out of the area. Following Camilo Catrillanca's death, CAM and allied organizations intensified their activities. In January 2019, ORT cells conducted a series of attacks against machinery owned by forestry companies operating in the Araucanía. CAM subsequently released a communiqué taking responsibility for these acts. The communiqué ends with a call to "continue advancing toward national liberation."

Members of the organization insist that the rigid and closed architecture of state institutions leaves them no choice. A former ORT militant indicated that CAM remains active because of a "lack of response from a colonialist and neoliberal State that refuses to hear our demands about our land, and the damage caused by forestry, mining, and hydroelectric dams in Wallmapu. We tried other tactics in the 1990s, but they refused to listen. That is why the CAM and the ORTs were launched in the first place" (anonymous interview with the author, November 17, 2018).

CTT and ATM have engaged in disruptive activities and are sometimes sympathetic with the means adopted by CAM, but they have diversified their tactical repertoires. CTT, founded in 1990, demonstrated its commitment to autonomy by introducing a flag for the Mapuche nation in defiance of the new civilian government. It operates informally by facilitating discussions among the Mapuche on how to exercise their rights, but it has also created its own formal institutions. CTT launched the School for Mapuche Self-Government in Temuco in 2009 to "contribute, through education and training, to the formation of Mapuche leaders" and to "set the standard in the field of education for social leadership based on the principle of self-determination and self-government."[5] In contrast to CAM, they have started to develop a multiscalar positioning strategy, engaging in the public sphere at the national and international levels. CTT representatives contributed actively to the drafting of UNDRIP, adopted in 2007. UNDRIP has provided the organization (and others across the region) with new mechanisms to pursue its goals, including challenging the state in international courts for failing to respect the provisions which require it to recognize Indigenous self-determination. Over the past decade, CTT has focused on developing a self-government project plan according to the provisions of UNDRIP.

The CTT representative I spoke with was frustrated with the slow pace of change at the central state level, although she was quick to point out that their strategies and tactics have borne fruit. She pointed to the Bachelet government's adoption of the International Labor Organization (ILO) Convention 169 in 2008 as a significant victory for her organization. ILO Convention 169 requires governments to consult with Indigenous communities regarding development projects that may affect them. The CTT representative acknowledged, however, that community perspectives expressed through consultation processes are not binding and that projects have proceeded without local support and have even been backed by CONADI. She indicated that she and her allies will continue to draw on international law to pressure the state into respecting its obligations to the Mapuche people, but they will not rule out direct action if these tactics fail (anonymous interview with the author, November 21, 2018).

ATM originally pursued a more neutral relationship with the state and continues to enter into dialogue with local government representatives. But it has increasingly turned to disruptive tactics against the forestry industry, claiming that it is too often ignored by powerful interests and their state allies. When asked to describe his role, an ATM leader provided some insight into his organization's objectives and approach:

It is inspired by the way in which the Mapuche people resisted the invasion of the Chilean state between the seventeenth and eighteenth centuries and how the different strategies were articulated to defend that territory. The objectives are in the same line, we seek the reconstruction of a people that has been subjected to subordination and disarticulation by the process of "Chileanization." This reconstruction objective includes language, culture, self-knowledge, and, of course, an autonomous relationship with Chilean society. It is also about recovering our territories; without territory there is no Mapuche people. And this requires acts of resistance; they won't simply give concessions. (Miguel, interview with Lagos, January 22, 2019)

Smaller, regional organizations are more likely to engage in a multiscalar positioning strategy. Identidad Territorial Lafquenche, which is based in the Biobío Region, just north of the Araucanía, focuses on influencing local leaders, and has supported the election of an Indigenous mayor in Tirúa as well as municipal councilors throughout the territory. But as many interviewees argued, putting pressure on elected officials usually requires some form of direct action. A leader from Tirúa explained: "We influence based on pressure, we do not have many tools, the community has very little strength, no one will listen to you if a group of ten or twenty people goes to ask for something, so our strategy is to unite to the communities of the territories, to organize larger demonstrations, that is the only way we have to generate an impact around our needs, the bigger the demonstrations, the better" (Pichún, interview with the author and Lagos, December 5, 2018).

Another type of Mapuche organization, growing in numbers if less visible, is focused on advancing the interests of Indigenous peoples through a cultural renaissance and education. The individuals involved in these CSOs have tacitly (if sometimes reluctantly) accepted the authority of the Chilean state and have chosen to engage with, rather than reject, neoliberal multiculturalism. This does not mean that they are not politicized or that they do not seek land rights and greater political autonomy. But their tactics rarely involve disruptive action, and they believe that Mapuche liberation can be more effectively achieved through a renewal of language, culture, and identity. They engage in the production of films, music, and other forms of cultural expression (often with a political goal), and they support the revival of the Mapudungun language. They seek to create a sense of pride and empowerment, particularly among young people, but also to foster respect and recognition for their culture beyond Wallmapu.

The Mapuexpress Collective, founded in 2000, is an excellent example of an organization that takes a unique and innovative approach to political participation. Its members, who travel directly to communities, have established or revived participatory spaces that draw on traditional governance practices, such as the *trawün* (community meeting). The *trawüns* begin with ceremonies and music, led by *longkos* (community chiefs), followed by debates and discussions. These revolve around developing collective positions that communities will take regarding local or national issues. The Mapuexpress Collective also engages in the public sphere by writing editorials for newspapers, organizing information campaigns for Indigenous and non-Indigenous audiences, creating videos and documentaries, and making extensive use of ICTs and social media to engage in the public sphere. Recently, it has developed a media wing and an online news site which it refers to as "the Voice of Wallmapu." As an organization with a political focus and a highly developed communications strategy, Mapuexpress is able to counter the narrative on the Mapuche conflict that dominates the headlines of mainstream news organizations. Morín Ortiz, communications director for Ficwallmapu, a similar organization, explained his organization's approach to politics:

> It is true that there is a need for making demands and there are legitimate reasons for resistance. But that type of political action, and the kinds of tactics used, can end up creating a closed space where the "converted" speak only to each other. We want to break this up a little, create spaces where people can learn about their culture, where they can develop an awareness of Mapuche identity. In the long term, this may have more of an impact and it also allows us to reach out to others. (Ortiz, interview with the author and Lagos, December 6, 2018)

He added that in order to do this, it is important to maintain an online presence and to "occupy and dispute virtual spaces with care." I also encountered a third type of community-based organization that is primarily concerned with local development and *trabajo en territorio*. Despite operating at a smaller scale, they are often as politicized as the other two types discussed above. They may (or may not) be sympathetic with CAM and other sovereigntist CSOs but their leaders generally work with local municipal governments (*comunas*) to promote infrastructure projects or obtain funds for their communities. Alejandra Aillapán and Daniel Barrera coordinate the Trafkintuwe Villarrica, an organization committed to the "defense and strengthening of Wallmapu through the open and inclusive articulation of local needs in an independent and autonomous space." They seek to promote the exchange of local experiences and knowledge with other communities through dialogue (nutxankawün) and Mapuche education (*kimeluwun*), engaging in *trabajo en territorio*, and the development of comprehensive proposals for collective well-being.

In recent years, these organizations have started using live streaming to encourage participation among people dispersed over the large geographic area that makes up Wallmapu. On some occasions, these virtual meetings, which integrate traditional ceremonies and practices, have included Mapuche across the border in Argentina. This important development for those who dream of a unified Wallmapu is facilitated by ICTs. Live streaming has become even more important during the COVID-19 pandemic. While the follow-up telephone and virtual interviews we conducted in 2020 were primarily focused on the 2019 uprisings, many interviewees discussed how ICTs have allowed communities and organizations to pursue ongoing political projects while maintaining social distancing practices.

Across the different types of CSO, representatives and activists expressed a strong resistance to any form of incorporation into the Chilean state. They recognize that direct engagement in the few state-society mechanisms that exist in Chile may provide access points to channel their demands and potentially receive state resources to support their organizations. But more so than in the other two countries, Mapuche leaders believe that working with agencies of the state is futile. This sentiment was expressed by some participants with respect to Wallmapuwen, a Mapuche nationalist party that was finally recognized by the Electoral Tribunal in 2017 after more than a decade of existence. The party advocates for self-governance, but many who support the goals of the party expressed their opposition to its strategy. A representative from a Temuco-based CSO expressed a common sentiment:

No good can come out of creating a political party. Even if they get elected to municipal government, or even to Congress, what good will that do? These state institutions are rigid, they are instruments of colonialism. You cannot build a nation using tools that were meant to tear it down. (Anonymous interview with the author, November 20, 2018)

Some brought up the Pachakutik party in Ecuador, arguing that it split Indigenous civil society, while others pointed out that the demographic situation in Chile could not lead to a party such as Bolivia's MAS actually taking power. More militant interviewees claimed that even if it managed to elect some candidates, this would require Wallmapuwen to negotiate with the Chilean state, a tactic which they dismiss as both futile and unacceptable.

Much of this reluctance stems from past experience. In the late 1980s, some Mapuche organizations allied themselves with leftist parties, and many agreed to support the Concertación when it took power in 1990. The 1993 Indigenous Law originally seemed like a step in the right direction following a dictatorship that refused to recognize the existence of Indigenous peoples, but it soon became clear that the law and the institutions it created would support Indigenous claims only when they were compatible with the interests of capital (Kowalczyk 2013). CONADI, which was supposed to serve as a mechanism through which Indigenous communities could engage in dialogue with the state, ended up supporting the construction of hydroelectric dams on Mapuche territories against the will of local communities. This soured the relationship between Mapuche leaders and the government and refocused political action on autonomy. It also raised enduring suspicions about state-society mechanisms and convinced many Indigenous people that working through invited spaces was a waste of time at best and would lead to controlled inclusion in the worst-case scenario.

A self-identified Mapuche sovereigntist I spoke to recalled his reaction to CONADI's positions in the 1990s: "It became clear that it [CONADI] and the Indigenous Law were not about responding to our legitimate demands. The real intention was to control us, to incorporate us into the state and to manage the conflict, but in favor of the developers" (anonymous interview with the author, November 18, 2018).

In any case, Chile has not adopted the types of participatory initiatives that cropped up elsewhere on the continent during the 2000s. Surprisingly, Chile was actually one of the first countries in Latin America to establish a system of participatory mechanisms through national legislation. The *juntas de vecinos* (neighborhood councils) have a history rooted in a particular conception of participatory democracy. Created in 1968, the councils were the centerpiece of the Popular Promotion program of the government of President Eduardo Frei (1964–70), aimed at reducing marginality (Oxhorn 2010). The *juntas* lost much of their independence during the Pinochet dictatorship but regained some vitality in the 1990s. In the years following the return to democracy, the roles and activities of these institutions expanded and they demonstrated great potential, particularly with respect to neighborhood improvement and standard-of-living issues. Still, the concern of the successive Concertación governments (1990–2010) with containing popular mobilization meant that the capacity of these neighborhood councils as an agent of large-scale participation remained limited. In Chile, there are no provisions to allow for neighborhood councils to establish themselves as Indigenous territorial entities or to govern themselves according to traditional practices.

To improve the quality of life of socially vulnerable neighborhoods in Chile, the "Quiero mi Barrio" (I love my neighborhood) program was implemented in 2006 to engage local actors in projects aimed at improving the physical and social environments (Aguirre et al. 2008). Managed by the Ministry of Housing and Urban Development (Ministerio de Vivienda y Urbanismo, MINVU), the program's goals include recovering deteriorated public spaces, reinforcing social relations between residents, and including citizens in urban development. Given that Mapuche citizens tend to suffer from high levels of social vulnerability and those in urban areas are more likely to live in poorer neighborhoods, the program was well received by some Indigenous organizations when it was first established.

Two interviewees, one in the small city of Osorno (Los Lagos region) and another in Greater Santiago, had participated in "Quiero mi Barrio." The program is designed to ensure that the specificities of each neighborhood are considered in project design, although this does not extend to recognizing the Indigenous identity of districts with large Mapuche populations. Both participants described relatively robust participatory processes that fostered a healthy relationship with MINVU and municipal officials, yet they pointed out that tensions arose when they sought to bring Indigenous-specific issues into the process.

Marta, originally from the Araucanía, settled in La Pintana on the southern edge of Greater Santiago in the 1990s, where she helped to establish a Mapuche women's organization. La Pintana has one of Santiago's largest Mapuche populations and is the city's poorest district. Its diverse population includes mestizo, Mapuche, and immigrant residents, which makes its neighborhoods excellent candidates for a program that seeks to both improve quality of life and promote social solidarity. Marta described the process she and other Mapuche women experienced in the late 2000s as they engaged with "Quiero mi Barrio" to improve public transportation to and from the neighborhood. La Pintana lies beyond the furthest reaches of the Santiago metro system, and the area was not adequately covered by buses. Marta and most of her friends are domestic workers; they have to travel to residences in the more upscale areas of the capital six days a week to earn income. This used to take up to two hours each way, as their employers live in exclusive *comunas* such as Las Condes and Vitacura on the other side of the vast metropolitan area.

The situation had dramatically improved when I first spoke to Marta in 2013. Two new minibus lines served the area, beginning at 5:00 a.m., as requested by locals. How they achieved this outcome is an interesting example of how "Quiero mi Barrio" works. The issue of transportation was first brought up through local neighborhood councils, which can put forward priorities through the "Quiero mi Barrio" consultation mechanisms. A series of assemblies were convened by the council leaders, during which local residents discussed everything from service routes to schedules. Using this feedback, council leaders established a "sectorial roundtable" consisting of council members, other local associations (representing the elderly, environmental issues, etc.), and officials from La Pintana's municipal transportation department. Representatives from the roundtable then brought the aggregated concerns and solutions to the Neighborhood Development Council, the "Quiero mi Barrio" mechanism through which residents interact with government. This body works directly with municipal departments and with representatives of the Housing and Urban Development Service (Servicios de Vivienda y Urbanización Metropolitano, SERVIU), the technical support branch of MINVU, which provides the expertise required to develop the projects. Resident representatives, including Marta, met with the municipal director of transportation armed with evidence of this community support, and plans were soon drawn up by the transportation department to extend bus service to the neighborhood (Marta, interview with the author, April 4, 2013).

Overall, then, Marta and her friends were pleased with the process. But as a member of a local Mapuche women's group, she recalled that attempts to discuss issues such as discrimination or to propose projects recognizing the Indigenous identity of La Pintana were rebuffed by both fellow residents and government officials. One such proposal involved a relatively inexpensive statue, to be erected in a local park, that would have recognized the strong Mapuche presence in the district since the 1970s. Marta and her friends recalled that they were told not to be troublemakers and that the program was not about fostering ethnic grievances. Susana recounted a similar reaction when she sought to point out the higher levels of poverty among Indigenous women as a member of the Neighborhood Development Council in Osorno. According to her, some mestizo neighbors feared that talk of Mapuche identity would lead to collective land claims and threaten private property (Susana, interview with the author, November 25, 2018). In both cases, these reactions sullied the relatively positive experience Indigenous women enjoyed until then and discouraged them from bringing up their identity in further interactions with participatory mechanisms.

In contrast to the closed institutions of the Chilean state, leaders described a participatory, collaborative governance process within Mapuche civil society. Alejandra and Daniel of Trafkintuwe Villarrica explained the internal participatory processes used by the organization. "This isn't a structured, hierarchical organization in the classical Western sense. It has emerged as a continuity of what the traditional Mapuche organization is, that is, it did not emerge as a legal entity within the framework of the Chilean state or laws but based on the idea of organization that always existed here before" (Villarica, interview with Lagos, January 22, 2019). An ATM representative explained the different dimensions of political engagement in his territories:

> Public life for us has two levels. One is the endogenous political life of our communities and organizations, and the relationships that exist within the Mapuche nation. These interactions take place in traditional ways, for example through the *nguillatunes* [large ceremonies to which people throughout the territories are invited], invitations of the territories, different ancestral practices including traditional games. This is our public sphere. There is another level associated with social protest, and while that is linked to our internal public sphere, it is also exogenous, outward-facing, it is directed at Chilean national society and to those who have power those who ultimately control power and who have interests in Wallmapu. Communication in that world takes advantage of the different existing channels, especially television and mass media, and more recently social media. (Miguel, interview with Lagos, January 22, 2019)

Mapuche CSOs were relatively early adopters of ICTs and have arguably done more with them than their counterparts in other countries. But while there has been considerable innovation in using ICTs to promote culture and language, their use for political engagement has been relatively limited. Leaders and communications agents from the organizations we worked with had differing opinions with respect to the impact of digital technologies on their work. These perspectives tended to align with the nature of the organization, their goals, and their tactical repertoire. Not surprisingly, the more politically oriented organizations had mixed views, but generally agreed that ICTs alone have not leveled the playing field with well-resourced actors. The ATM representative expressed what many of his peers felt: "Access to ICTs is one thing, control of these networks is another. Neither the Mapuche nor the Chileans have control of these networks. I think it is an ongoing issue because it [social media] is a control mechanism" (Miguel, interview with Lagos, January 22, 2019).

He went on to raise the example of Operation Huracán, which involved the use of ICTs by police intelligence agencies to generate fabricated evidence from social media.

> That is an example of the instrumentalization of ICTs to criminalize the struggle of Indigenous peoples, of the Mapuche people in this case. The good thing about this is that it was made public, it was discovered and now there is an investigation. But we have to remember these networks are permanently monitored, therefore ICTs are viewed with distrust by Indigenous actors. (Miguel, interview with Lagos, January 22, 2019)

In contrast, the leader of a small community described a different experience with social media: "For us, ICTs and social media have supported our work, they allow us to make what we are doing known, to reach more people, and not only regionally, now it can be nationally or even internationally" (Colli, interview with Lagos, February 10, 2019). Mapuche organizations dedicated to promoting culture and identity have demonstrated innovative and sophisticated uses of ICTs, developing everything from interactive digital news platforms to online courses. While they share concerns about the Western-led globalization of cyberspace, most also believe that making their voices heard at home and abroad makes their communities stronger in the long run. And both culturally and politically oriented organizations have used ICTs extensively to build alliances with Indigenous communities in Chile and internationally. They use social media platforms and communications tools such as WhatsApp to stay in touch and share strategies with Indigenous actors as far away as Canada. They have progressively become more sophisticated in developing these alliances and have developed considerable expertise in frame alignment, for example, aligning claims to natural resources with the interests of transnational environmental movements in order to gain expertise, moral support, legal counsel, and financial resources.

And yet, they have not developed the types of networks that their Bolivian and Ecuadorian have created. About half of the organizations I worked with have little or no contact with other Indigenous actors, while those that do tend to meet occasionally through informal networks. This may be starting to change: a Mapuche parliament was in held in 2007, the first in a century, and the idea was revived once again in the context of the 2019–20 nationwide protests.

Resource Mobilization

Given the acrimonious relationship between Mapuche civil society and the state, most CSOs have never depended on government resources, and this did not change in the 2010s. *Autogestión* is therefore at the core of resource mobilization strategies. The means through which Mapuche organizations raise revenue are varied and reflect their experience with cultural promotion and skill with using ICTs.

As in the other two countries, this often involves selling local produce, agricultural products, or handicrafts produced in the communities. ATM generates income to fund its activities by selling cereals, vegetables, and seeds donated by its members. Other organizations discussed raising revenue through animal auctions, lotteries, or through selling food such as *sopaipillas* (a type of fried pastry) to local markets. But Mapuche organizations stand out for their ability to develop and promote workshops and courses as a means of both mobilizing resources and promoting their culture. Mapuche organizations are taking advantage of a growing demand for Mapudungun language instruction in the Araucanía and elsewhere. Trafkintuwe Villarrica charges a small fee for language courses which are delivered by volunteer teachers, while others are developing online Mapudungun workshops in collaboration with experts from local universities. They believe that these online courses are a means of securing revenue while also contributing to the revival of the language among Mapuche youth.

CSOs dedicated to cultural promotion, considered *permitidos* by the state, are able to apply for specific grants. Organizations such as Ficwallmapu have applied to the Heritage and Culture program of CONADI to fund arts festivals and the production of videos, which in turn can serve as sources of revenue. Communities may apply for neighborhood improvement funds through local councils or the "Quiero mi Barrio" program, although they must do so as Chileans and not as members of a distinct people. Chilean media and state actors accuse some Mapuche organizations of mobilizing resources through illegal activities. The connection between CAM and drug trafficking appears to be tenuous—the organization's former leader, Emilio Berkhoff, was arrested for trafficking in 2020—but Chilean media and the state were quick to point out the link between Berkhoff and CAM, insinuating that the ties go deeper. There have also been reports about Colombian *narcos* (drug traffickers) in the Araucanía, although organizations are wary of any such links, viewing these types of reports as an effort to justify cutting off their resource mobilization activities and to further criminalize their collective action.

Communication and Public Relations

Media concentration is high throughout Latin America, but especially so in Chile. Two media groups, El Mercurio and Copesa, account for more than 90 percent of newspaper readership and also dominate the digital media industry, while four groups account for 70 percent of the radio market. We have seen that the former leftist governments in Bolivia and Ecuador created state media outlets and passed legislation requiring a proportion of broadcast licenses to be distributed to community organizations. There have been no similar reforms in Chile.

There was a strong consensus among interviewees that media framing has worked to positively construct "civic" groups that accept the established order and to negatively construct challengers by reproducing a narrative that induces hostility toward the aspirations and activities of "uncivic" Mapuche actors. Coverage portrays groups that seek social change as irrational actors to be feared and eliminated. Interviewees insist that coverage of events in Mapuche territories contains racial overtones that construct Indigenous actors as particularly dangerous. In addition, many of the leaders I spoke to argued that governments or other powerful actors in the region, such as the forestry industry, are supporting the spread of "fake news." They claim that they have been targeted by such campaigns, and several showed me social media posts linking specific Mapuche CSOs or individuals with acts of sabotage, although no evidence is provided.

But the Mapuche have never been passive, and their proactive collective action extends to communication. They have been trailblazers among Indigenous peoples in Latin America when it comes to using film—and increasingly digital technologies—to tell their stories. Mapuche media question notion of citizenship and support claims to sovereignty and territorial unity. They offer counterrepresentations of past and present struggles, and of misrepresented issues (Córdova 2018; Salazar 2003). Mapuexpress serves as a counter public sphere for contesting official narratives and documenting alternate histories (Grillo 2006). Recent Mapuche media initiatives I encountered include online courses, YouTube videos, and extensive social media campaigns.

Overall, interviewees were split on whether the misinformation spread by ICTs outweighs the benefits of being able to disseminate information. One communications director summarized what many others expressed:

> Social media allows us to get our messages out without going through an intermediary. This is good, because private media often twist things to serve the agenda of their owners, they distort our messages. But with social media, there is so much disinformation, so many lies spread about Indigenous peoples, about who we are and what we want. And they [mining companies and their state allies] have a lot more money to design expensive campaigns . . . so whose voice to you think is heard? (Saavedra, interview with the author and Lagos, November 11, 2018)

Yet many spoke of the unfulfilled potential for democratization of the information landscape, particularly when it comes to young people. While social media are used against Mapuche organizations, their leaders and communications agents also understand that these technologies can allow them to have a voice, something that was impossible when corporate media monopolized the dissemination of information. But interviewees also insisted that ICTs must be used with extreme caution when communicating with other organizations regarding political issues (such as land claims) or when mobilizing protest. Many believed that state surveillance of both telephone conversations and communication via social media platforms reduces the potential advantages that ICTs could offer for building alliances. Two participants even mentioned that for this reason, they have brought back the traditional messenger (*werken*) who travels to different communities to deliver information in person, because these types of messages cannot be intercepted.

Some Mapuche leaders believe that ICTs provide yet another sphere for officials to engage in political persecution. As one leader stated: "Technologies have some benefits for us, but governments have the capacity to use them much more effectively than we do. ICTs make it easier to communicate with supporters, but they also make it easier for them [state and foreign agents] to monitor us, to know what we say and do" (Karen, interview with Lagos, March 4, 2019). Another was more blunt, claiming that he "does not trust social media, ICTs, because we know that it is now easier for them [state officials] to watch us than in the past" (anonymous interview with Lagos, January 23, 2019). These fears lead to self-censorship and severely limit the potential of ICTs to support Indigenous mobilization.

There was more enthusiasm over the growing number of Mapuche online news sites, which have "brought news back into local hands, tak[ing] some of that power away from big corporate media outlets, provid[ing] our own perspectives on what is happening in our territories and even allow[ing] us to experiment with our own journalistic practices" (Núñez, interview with the author and Lagos, December 18, 2018). But a representative of Ficwallmapu expressed concern that "we still don't have any control of the Internet. Those that do can erase everything we put on there, our history would be erased" (Morin, interview with the author and Lagos, December 5, 2018).

Some also discussed using social media to contest dominant narratives by denouncing human rights abuses. Referring to the killing of Camilo Catrillanca, a Mapuche activist stated: "They [the Carabineros] tried to use social media to say he was a terrorist, that he was shooting at them. But guess what? We used the same tools to show the world that they were lying. And this time, the world believed us" (anonymous interview with the author, December 4, 2018). Another said: "Social media played a key role which made this situation very different compared to other extrajudicial killings in the past. Within hours, what happened was all over the national and international news. They couldn't just cover it up as they used to do. It also allowed us to mobilize thousands of people, and this led to real consequences for those responsible" (anonymous interview with Lagos, December 12, 2018).

Overall, Mapuche CSOs believe that while ICTs can facilitate communication and public relations, there remains a divide that replicates (even if to a lesser extent) the "traditional" media landscape. Jimy, a Mapuche communications specialist, argued that "communication is all about what resources you control. When you have the economic means, when you can pay to buy the different means of disseminating information, you can manipulate them at will, you can deliver the information that you want. We do not have the means to do that, but the government, the state, and large companies can fully exploit these tools in ways that we cannot" (Pichún, interview with the author and Lagos, December 5, 2018). Yet speaking about Catrillanca, Jimy admitted that while traditional media was complicit in the attempted cover up, the truth was communicated to the word via social media.

My social media content analysis supports Jimy's insights regarding ICTs and the balance of power. Mapuche CSOs use social media to disseminate messages and audiovisual content according to their primary focus: politically oriented organizations generally criticize state repression and police violence while demanding autonomy and land rights. Their messages target politicians, Mapuche citizens and the international community. CSOs dedicated to cultural promotion and revival also post about land rights and militarization, but their content primarily revolves around language, culture, and pride. In the aftermath of the Catrillanca case, there was a flurry of activity consisting in calls to action, posts about other Mapuche victims of police violence, as well as more general commentary about systematic repression. My social media content analysis revealed that #Catrillanca was one of the most popular hashtags for Indigenous CSOs and non-Indigenous activists from late 2018 and throughout 2019.

Content produced by state agencies took on a very different tone with respect to the Catrillanca case, depicting the government as just and truthful, and Carabineros that killed the young man as "isolated cases." The content analysis shows that social media posts from the executive, the Interior Ministry, and the secretary of the government associate Mapuche collective action with delinquency, looting, and organized crime. There is a not so subtle narrative that opposes thugs who use violence against peaceful citizens versus the non-Indigenous victims of rural violence, but there is no acknowledgement of the roots of the conflict. Chile's mainstream media outlets adopt the same tone, focusing on the disruption of business activities and aggressions against Carabineros by Mapuche activists. With one exception, outlets defended the Carabineros, while painting the officers involved in Catrillanca incident as "bad apples." Taking the biased reporting of other mainstream media to a new level, Universidad Autónoma de Chile TV, based in Temuco (Araucanía) provided a platform to far-right politicians such as José Antonio Kast without soliciting the perspective of Mapuche leaders. True to his typical hostility towards Indigenous communities, Kast called the killing an accident and sympathized with victims of "rural violence" (white landowners) while questioning the video evidence once it surfaced. There is no indication that government agencies and media outlets have engaged with or acknowledged any dimension of narrative promoted by Mapuche CSOs, regardless of their tactics and orientation.

Mapuche leaders I spoke to place a great deal of importance on education as a vehicle for socialization and promoting identity. Like most Chilean institutions, the country's school system has until recently ignored Indigenous epistemologies and knowledge. This has evolved slowly through, for example, the inclusion in the national curriculum of a course on Indigenous history and culture, and the introduction in 2009 of Mapudungun language courses in schools where over 50 percent of students are Mapuche. The Araucanía Region has also seen the creation of "bicultural" schools aimed at reinforcing the language, culture, and identity of Mapuche children through teaching and "situated learning" practices designed to transmit traditional ways of knowing and doing (Luna, Telechea, and Caniguan 2018). But such schools are few and far between, and in most settings Indigenous content is compartmentalized into a single course rather than being integrated throughout the curriculum. Community leaders remain concerned about loss of identity and the impact this may have on the ability of CSOs to pursue their goals.

Lonko (elder) Ernesto Huenchulaf is president of the Mapuche Education Council, which seeks to expand and further indigenize education by playing a decision-making role in the ongoing development of the Ministry of Education's Intercultural Bilingual Education Program. His organization is responsible for the accreditation of traditional educators who work in schools implementing the program and provides guidance on the forms of knowledge that schools should be teaching, in collaboration with Lonkos. This important epistemological work is challenging the very nature of education in the Araucanía. Teaching and knowledge, according to Ernesto and his colleagues, is about more than sitting in a classroom. It is about lived experiences, and "being Mapuche" (Huenchulaf, interview with the author and Lagos, December 2, 2018). For many community members, this also means engaging in forms of resistance. The ATM and other politically oriented organizations have developed workshops which they deliver in high schools (when allowed to do so) and in community centers to reinforce the relationship between Mapuche identity and a long history of resistance to cultural integration.

Mapuche CSOs have been at the forefront of using ICTs for teaching and learning; they are pioneers among Indigenous peoples worldwide in this respect. Online education has become a priority; websites and videos are being used to promote culture, art, and music. For some, this serves to promote identity and culture by making Indigenous heritage available on the Internet, where Mapuche youth who have left the territories can access it and where the world can discover their rich heritage. For others, ICTs serve to unite Mapuche people in Chile and Argentina by proving tools to showcase forms of cultural expression across the border, thus enhancing awareness and generating solidarity (Núñez, interview with the author and Lagos, December 18, 2018).

More so than in the other two countries, interviewees placed a great deal of importance on the Mapudungun language and on its relationship with identity. Interviewees were pleased to see the dissemination of online videos and radio stations in Mapudungun, and social media allows these to have a greater reach. The number of online Mapudungun language courses has grown exponentially over the past decade, and the organizations involved claim that many people are registering for these courses because they wish to "reconnect" with their identity. The language classes, which are becoming increasingly sophisticated as organizations work with local universities to enhance their IT and course design capacity, integrate music and images that seek to create an online "virtual lived experience" to immerse students in Mapuche culture. One program is even looking at virtual reality technology so that Mapuche youth who have moved away from Wallmapu can learn about language and culture while virtually exploring traditional territories.

While less common than in the other two countries, some also worried that ICTs were chipping away at traditional practices and values. A representative from the Pu Weni Indigenous Association believes that "they diminish our Mapuche tradition of going to visit people, to see how they are, to talk to them in person" (Millañir, interview with Lagos, December 22, 2018). Those who expressed this concern feared the impact that a lack of in-person contact has had on solidarity across the territories. Others hope to use ICTs to contest frames and dominant discourse in online spaces. But some expressed concern about how social media are being used to reproduce a dominant narrative that paints Mapuche activism as "terrorism" regardless of whether violence is involved. Onésima, a spokeswoman for a Mapuche youth organization explained: "For many people, especially young people, if it doesn't happen on social media, it doesn't exist. That means that we have to view the online world, like our traditional territories, as a contested space. If we don't contest the powerful in these virtual spaces, their narrative about us will dominate. If we learn to use these tools properly, we can counter that narrative and create our own" (Lienqueo, interview with the author and Lagos, December 7, 2018).

The "Mapuche Conflict," #Catrillanca, and the 2019 Protests

The conflict between the state and certain Mapuche organizations intensified in the late 2010s. The government response to unrest in the Araucanía has focused on "pacification" through criminalization of Mapuche organizations such as CAM and the use of force against its members. The participants I spoke to, including those who belong to "civic," nonconfrontational CSOs, noted a growing police and military presence in their communities, including armored vehicles. These forces, they claim, are not there to provide security and justice to the region's inhabitants but rather to protect the interests of the agribusinesses and forestry industries. Piñera's administration has intensified this "occupation" through the creation of a "counterterrorism" unit of the Special Police Operations Group (Grupo de Operaciones Policiales Especiales, GOPE), the tactical operations branch of the Carabineros with a history of suppressing Mapuche dissent. The so-called Jungle Command unit lost what little legitimacy it may have had following its clumsy attempts to cover up the extrajudicial killing of Camilo Catrillanca. According to those I spoke to, the militarization of the Araucanía, now symbolized by the death of the young activist, has only exacerbated the already tense situation. Many peaceful activists told me that some of their friends or relatives felt compelled to engage in more direct action as a response to the presence of heavily armed agents in their communities. Most insisted that civilians not aligned with CAM—including Mapuche women and children—have been harassed and intimidated by GOPE agents. The Chilean government's approach to the Mapuche conflict is frequently criticized not only for the deployment of militarized special forces but also for the overzealous application of the Anti-Terrorism Law, which allows for longer prison sentences and the use of anonymous witness testimony if a case is defined as terrorist act.

Government actors also deploy a divide-and-conquer strategy according to which the state interacts with some Indigenous organizations while excluding others. Not surprisingly, authorities have been more willing to work with "civic" organizations focused on culture and identity. Several of these have received funds from CONADI for the development of arts and culture festivals, for example, although there is an expectation that these events will refrain from disseminating political messages. Authorities have shunned organizations that promote territorial autonomy as uncivic and have reproduced a binary narrative that divides activists into "good vs. bad" categories. But even those that have maintained a nonconflictual relationship with the state are wary; there is no equivalent of the types of government-aligned CSOs that we saw in Bolivia under the MAS and as a result, fewer instances of multiscalar positioning.

The 2019–20 protests were the largest in the country's postdictatorship history. The disturbances began in Santiago and were ignited by a fare increase in the city's subway system. Yet what began as a mass fare evasion protest quickly expanded into much more than that. Millions of Chileans took to the streets in October and November 2019 to tell the government that they were fed up with the rising cost of living, rigid social divisions, and persistent inequality. On October 10, Piñera declared a state of emergency and deployed the Armed Forces to restore order after over eighty subway stations were vandalized. The government also began using state security and antiterrorism laws against protesters and declared a curfew in Santiago, but the protests continued to spread to Concepción, Valparaíso, and other cities. By November, nearly thirty people had been killed by security forces and over 2,500 had been seriously injured. Interior minister Andrés Chadwick, who had come under fire the previous year for his handling of the Catrillanca case, was not able to hang on to his position this time round and was forced to resign. On November 15, Congress agreed to hold a national referendum to draft a new constitution, a long-time demand of nonelite sectors of Chilean civil society. This was an extraordinary development for a country with deeply conservative institutions. It must have been a difficult concession for a right-wing administration that counted numerous *pinochetistas* in cabinet, but the scale of the protests left Piñera with little choice. Originally scheduled for April 2020, the referendum was postponed due to COVID-19.

The Araucanía seemed to be unusually calm given the fact that the scenes playing out across the country were usually associated with that region more than any other. During follow-up telephone conservations in early 2020, many interviewees pointed out that the violence directed against white and mestizo protesters in the country's largest cities would give Chileans a taste of what the Mapuche have endured for decades. They hoped that Chileans would better understand their struggle following these events.

Despite their relatively limited visibility when compared with concurrent events in Bolivia and Ecuador, Indigenous peoples were not absent from the late 2019 uprisings that rocked Chile. On November 14, the first anniversary of Catrillanca's death, Mapuche organizations called for their communities to join the protests. Thousands did, carrying signs featuring the young man's picture and denouncing police repression. One of the most iconic images from the November 2019 protests is a photo of protesters standing on a military statue at Plaza Baquedano in Santiago's upscale Providencia district. At the top of the pyramid, a protester is seen waving a large Mapuche flag as the city burns in the background. The picture became a symbol of the protests and inspired the renaming of the square as Plaza Dignidad (Dignity Square). At around the same time, Indigenous protestors destroyed statues of colonial-era political figures in Temuco, the capital of the Araucanía.

Surprisingly given the widespread use of ICTs by Mapuche organizations, social media seems to have played a secondary role in the protests. Various CSOs did post messages encouraging their members to join the demonstrations, but social media were not used to organizing a coherent mobilization effort. This is in part due to concerns over state agencies monitoring the Internet and that any calls to action posted on social media would be intercepted by security forces. Individual activists did make extensive use of social media to record and disseminate acts of state violence, however. Videos of peaceful protestors hit in the face by rubber bullets and sustaining serious eye injuries went viral and the government was condemned by international NGOs. These images and the ensuing outrage are at least part of what led to the resignation of prominent cabinet ministers, including Chadwick, and forced Piñera to agree to constitutional reform.

My online content analysis reveals that the Chilean media focused on the violence and destruction caused by the protests, with little sympathy for the protesters. There were isolated calls for reconciliation and dialogue, but most of the editorials promoted a "law and order" approach to protests. In general, media did not cover Indigenous involvement in these nationwide protests; they ignored the links to the conflict in the Araucanía and the Catrillanca case, despite the presence of Mapuche flags and signs with the young man's likeness. The only exception appears to the TV Universidad de Concepción, which produced numerous reports on the protests from an Indigenous perspective and noted the conspicuous presence of the modern Mapuche flag.

Indeed, perhaps the most interesting development is that the Mapuche flag was increasingly visible at demonstrations across the country in late

2019 and, according to interviewees who participated in the protests, many of the flag bearers were not Indigenous. In a country where the majority of the population has consistently supported the actions of the state against Indigenous protest, some Mapuche activists dared to hope that this was a positive sign. Said one participant who traveled to Santiago from a small town in Biobío region, "I had never seen that before, mestizos carrying the Mapuche flag as a symbol of resistance. We hope that this will not fade, that it will give Chileans a new respect for our movement and what we are trying to accomplish" (Chani, interview with the author, April 21, 2020). She and others spoke of positive experiences of solidarity between Mapuche and non-Indigenous protesters during the protests, professing that this was the first time that they had ever walked side by side with (non-Indigenous) Chileans in a collective protest against the state.

Mapuche leaders I spoke to in 2020 viewed the events as an opportunity to build bridges with other sectors. The leader of an organization I had visited in 2018 said "the violence used by the state has shown Chileans how repressive their state is. It has shattered the illusions that many of them had about being a model democracy in South America. This kind of violence is usually used against our people, now it is used against everyone who fights the status quo" (anonymous interview with the author, February 14, 2020). If they are correct and the solidarity with other sectors endures, this may shift political opportunities in favor of Mapuche organizations. But alliances with non-Indigenous civil society tend to be short-lived, particularly given that people in the capital and other large cities can easily ignore what is happening in southern Chile. Still, there is a sense that their struggle is now linked to that of disaffected Chileans across the country.

One point of cross-sectorial agreement involves constitutional reform. When the referendum was finally held in October 2020, 78 percent of voters supported the drafting of a new constitution. The process itself, which took place from May 2021 to May 2022, was messy, with various competing interests seeking to make their mark. Among other issues, calls for decentralization and devolution of power have provoked divisions within Mapuche civil society and between Mapuche and non-Indigenous sectors.

The fragmentation of Mapuche civil society, both within Wallmapu and between Indigenous organizations and other sectors, has been an impediment to cohesive collective action. It is still difficult for Mapuche organizations themselves to agree on strategies and tactics. In addition to supporting constitutional reform, an alliance of Mapuche organizations calling itself Mapuche Territories for the Koyaqtun announced an attempt at building an alliance that would focus on autonomy and a revived Fütxa Koyaqtun (traditional parliament).

Many Mapuche CSOs in the Araucanía hope for a devolution of power that would create a special autonomous status. It is not difficult to anticipate that some of these demands will bring Mapuche leaders into conflict with the state and other powerful actors, but many ordinary Chileans may also be wary about demands for autonomy, particularly those in the Araucanía. Mapuche organizations themselves have not reached a consensus. Following the announcement of a constitutional convention, Mapuche CSOs were divided over whether or not to participate at all, with some of the more militant activists maintaining the objection to participating in state institutions. These actors believe that participation in the constitutional reform process legitimizes the sovereignty of the Chilean state over Wallmapu. Interviewees who share this perspective told us that they will not participate in the process.

But the scale of the protests has sent a message to the government and opened up space for Mapuche reformers to pursue their goals. Whether the newfound solidarity between the Mapuche and other alienated Chileans will last, it has opened up a window for politically oriented Mapuche organizations to seek new alliances and align their positions with the emerging master frame that demands greater equality and the deepening of democracy.

Mapuche Civil Society: Evolution and Future Prospects

Mapuche CSOs, like popular sectors of Chilean civil society, lack institutionalized channels of representation. The participatory architecture developed in Bolivia under Morales—and to a lesser extent in Correa's Ecuador—does not exist in Chile. The mechanisms that have been created are primarily consultative and limited in scope. They do not devolve decision-making power to citizens and do not provide spaces for identity-based or collective claims. The multiscalar positioning tactics that have emerged are therefore somewhat different from those that Indigenous actors in Bolivia and Ecuador have mastered. Post-1990 Mapuche activism has been divided between confrontation with the state and the construction of a cultural renaissance, but there is evidence of a shift toward a more diverse set of tactics. The Mapuche are far from being a homogeneous bloc of actors and a growing number of CSOs are exploring innovative ways of engaging in the public sphere through the promotion of culture, identity, and language. Thus far, though, these efforts have done little to move the needle with respect to land claims and demands for greater autonomy.

The state deploys a three-pronged strategy to contain dissent. First, the association of Mapuche activism with violence provides security agencies with a pretext for repression. They are able to do so with the support of the majority of Chileans and using legislative tools at their disposal (Antileo Baeza et al. 2015; Richards 2013). Second, the state seeks to work with selected "civic" Mapuche civil society organizations and exclude "uncivic" social movement activists from the public sphere by granting nonthreatening concessions (primarily around cultural expression) to the former while criminalizing the activities of more politically oriented organizations (Córdova 2018; Richards 2010). Third, the state, its private-sector allies whose economic interests are threatened by Mapuche claims, and the mainstream media work together to produce a narrative that frames Mapuche activists as illegitimate and as terrorists. This discourse in turn further helps to reinforce the argument in favor of the militarization of Mapuche territories (Cayuqueo 2018; Pairicán 2013). The liberal citizenship regime leaves little space for collective grievances and public opinion has not favored the Mapuche struggle. The consistent repression of protest in the Araucanía, the continuing fragmentation of Mapuche civil society, and (from 2018 to 2022) the return of a right-wing government with authoritarian sympathies, have further constrained political opportunities.

Mapuche civil society is distinct from Indigenous civil societies in the other two countries. It remains fragmented and dispersed. The lack of unifying CSOs has limited the type of large-scale organization that brought substantive policy outcomes to Indigenous civil society in Ecuador and Bolivia. But the differences are more profound than organizational structure, and the scale of collective action is not the only criterion by which civil society can be evaluated. For one thing, Mapuche civil society has developed a sense of nationhood that is practically absent in much of the region (Millalen Paillal 2012). One component of the Mapuche political program that has emerged emphasizes distinct ethnocultural traditions, while another focuses on a new political structure that would transform relations with Chile and the world (Marimán 2012; Pairicán 2013). Indigenous movements in Bolivia and Ecuador seek to reposition sovereignty from the central state to Indigenous civil society. They do not reject the state or seek to create independent states, but to pursue forms of governance outside of the liberal framework that has been imposed on them (Picq 2018; Tapia 2006).

This challenges state sovereignty from within. With a few exceptions, Indigenous peoples in these countries identify as Ecuadorian and Bolivian, although these identities may coexist with a sense of belonging to Kichwa, Aymara, Shuar, or Guaraní nations within the nation.

In contrast, the Mapuche have constructed a sense of national identity that is distinct from the Chilean state and grounded in their long history of independence. Many prominent CSOs seek full political autonomy; some promote the creation of an independent Wallmapu that encompasses communities in Chile and Argentina (Warren 2013). While support for this project is certainly not universal, this distinct sense of nationhood cuts across both "civic" and confrontational sectors of Mapuche civil society (Marimán 2012; Pairicán 2013). These goals are clearly far more difficult to achieve, as the independence project supported by some sectors challenges the very integrity of the Chilean nation state.

While Mapuche civil society has been less successful in achieving tangible policy outcomes, it has excelled when it comes to promoting identity, language, and culture. And more so than in the other two countries, Mapuche CSOs have used ICTs to develop and foster identity. Mapuche programmers, for example, are developing software for learning Mapudungun, while young activists I spoke to in Temuco discussed virtual-reality platforms that allow Mapuche migrants to immerse themselves in the landscapes of Wallmapu. As Cayuqueo (2018) notes, identity and culture are not relics; they evolve, but they remain Mapuche. The development of this nation-building project, and the role of ICTs as a mobilizing resource in promoting Mapuche identity, culture, and political aspirations, demonstrates that multiscalar positioning can look very different depending on political opportunities and resource mobilization capacity.

There is another development that may shift political opportunities in favor of the Mapuche. More and more Chileans are fed up with their country's rigid social structure, deep inequality, and unresponsive governments. The inclusion of Mapuche symbols and the solidarity demonstrated during the historic 2019 protests suggest that the political opportunity structure may be shifting even as Mapuche CSOs gain more political experience and skill. The drafting of a new constitution in 2022 opened another window of opportunity for Mapuche leaders to press their claims.

The draft constitution, revealed in May 2022, demonstrates the efforts of Mapuche organizations that have chosen to engage in a multiscalar positioning approach throughout the constitutional reform process. By working through state institutions such as the Constituent Assembly, drawing on international norms to ensure adherence to UNDRIP and ILO Convention 169, using ICTs to construct a favorable narrative, and collaborating with supportive sectors of Chilean civil society, Mapuche leaders have finally succeeded in gaining constitutional recognition for Indigenous peoples. The new supreme law recognizes Chile as a plurinational state and even includes a clause for the restitution of traditional territories. These are significant gains. But the draft constitution does not go as far as many Mapuche would have liked; it does not, for example, create a special status allowing for the devolution of power to the Araucanía and adjacent regions. These gains will therefore fail to satisfy segments of Mapuche civil society that will accept nothing less than increased autonomy or full political independence.

5 Indigenous Civil Society in Comparative Perspective

· ·

Indigenous movements in the late twentieth century emerged when a strong sense of collective identity and the withdrawal of social rights were combined with resource mobilization strategies and favorable political opportunity windows (Lupien 2011; Rice 2012; Yashar 2005). These factors encouraged Indigenous communities to mobilize around a set of demands rooted in their history as the original inhabitants of their lands (Albó 2004; Colloredo-Mansfeld 2009; Field 1994; Yashar 2007). Preexisting networks present in many Indigenous communities facilitated mobilization by providing them with structures on which to build, and the expansion of liberal democracy provided the associational space required to mobilize (Paige 2020; Yashar 1998, 2005). Attacks on social rights through neoliberal austerity provided the spark that lit the fire (Postero 2007; Yashar 2005). How do the different paths taken in Bolivia, Ecuador, and Chile matter when it comes to the ways in which CSOs engage in the public sphere in the twenty-first century?

Comparing Political Landscapes

Ecuador, Bolivia, and Chile were all electoral democracies during the period under study, although Bolivia experienced a period of democratic regression under an unelected authoritarian regime from November 2019 to November 2020. The three countries nominally provide all citizens with the right to vote and stand for office, the right to form and participate in civil society, the right to engage in protest, and freedom of expression. Beyond these minimal civil and political rights, the political opportunity structures, citizenship regimes, and mobilizing structures have evolved differently in the three countries, and this has had an impact on how CSOs pursue their goals. Bolivia and Ecuador underwent dramatic changes engineered by strong left-wing governments from the mid-2000s to late 2010s, while Chile did not. We should therefore expect to see differences in how CSOs have evolved in these countries. Table 5.1 provides a summary of the similarities and differences discussed in this chapter.

TABLE 5.1 Comparative summary, similarities and differences:
Indigenous civil society in Bolivia, Ecuador, and Chile

	Bolivia	Ecuador	Chile
Political opportunities	High levels of public support for government (2006–19), Indigenous and collective rights in new constitution, participatory democracy, some incorporation of civil society, robust local participation, fragmented civil society (2011–)	High levels of public support for government (2007–17), Indigenous and collective rights in new constitution, participatory democracy (limited in practice), increasing levels of repression, robust local participation, cohesive civil society	Limited public support for CSOs, Indigenous rights not in constitution, individual over collective rights, limited citizen participation, some local participation, fragmented civil society
Mobilizing structures	Two large regional CSOs, multiple local CSOs, state-society participatory mechanisms, OTBs, unions, traditional *ayllus*, service organizations	One national umbrella CSO, One alternative national CSO, three large regional CSOs, 24 provincial CSOs, multiple local CSOs, local communal councils, service organizations	Various regional CSOs, multiple local CSOs, specialized (media, education) and service organizations
Citizenship regime	Plurinational, social citizenship	Social citizenship, plurinational (not implemented in practice)	Liberal, neoliberal multiculturalism
Political participation	Extensive local participation, some incorporation into state, participatory mechanisms, disruptive action lowlands (2011–present), disruptive action highlands (2019–20)	Extensive local participation, some direct engagement with state, disruptive action (2019–20)	Disruptive action, local political participation, limited engagement with state, low-intensity conflict, autonomous Mapuche nation building
Resource Mobilization	Significant but segmented state funding, *autogestión* (products, some tax/royalties collection)	*Autogestión* (products, tourism), limited/segmented state funding	*Autogestión* (educational, products), very limited state funding

(*continued*)

TABLE 5.1 (*continued*)

	Bolivia	Ecuador	Chile
Communication and Public Relations	Primarily in-person, limited use of ICTs to communicate with other CSOs; state media sympathetic to, private media hostile to MAS-aligned CSOs	Primarily in-person, increasing use of ICTs to communicate with other CSOs; hostile private and state media	Extensive use of ICTs to communicate with Mapuche and Chilean public; hostile private media
Identity and Education	Identity diminishing among youth; limited use of ICTs to promote identity and socialization; traditional practices (festivals, music, etc.)	Identity diminishing among youth; limited use of ICTs to promote identity and socialization; traditional practices (festivals, music, etc.)	Online courses, language promotion, national (Mapuche) identity building
Mobilization	Mobilization capacity strong regionally (marches, roadblocks, etc.); limited by fragmentation at national level	Mobilization capacity strong regionally and at national level (marches, roadblocks, etc.)	Mobilization capacity limited regionally and at national level. Some local capacity. Localized acts of violence by some CSOs and state

Political Opportunities

The Pink Tide that swept through Bolivia and Ecuador in the latter half of the 2000s shifted political opportunities and citizenship regimes in complex ways, opening new avenues for Indigenous actors to engage in politics, granting a number of their traditional demands, and incorporating some sectors of Indigenous civil society while simultaneously creating new constraints (Cameron 2009; De la Torre 2016; Lupien 2018a; Spronk 2008; Trujillo 2010). The political opportunity structure and citizenship regime in Chile also present a paradox, although in a different way. Chileans enjoy liberal political and civil rights on paper, but in practice the state has little tolerance for dissent and seeks to demobilize the population (Cameron, Hershberg, and Sharpe 2012; Oxhorn 2010). These factors would have a different impact on how Indigenous CSOs and multiscalar positioning have evolved in the three countries.

Chile's political opportunity structure has evolved since 1990, but far more slowly and in a less radical direction. The discourse of popular partici- pation became fashionable for a time, although it was framed as a pragmatic means of improving governance rather than as an alternative model of demo- cratic politics and it does not bestow special rights on Indigenous peoples (Richards 2013; Aguilera 2007). In Bolivia and Ecuador, the political oppor- tunity structure during the Morales and Correa eras was characterized by high levels of public support for governments and their policies, socioeco- nomic gains that satisfied the majority of lower- and middle-income citizens, and new participatory architecture that provided access points to the state but also allowed popular governments to label those who continued deploy extrainstitutional means as enemies of the people (García-Guadilla 2008; Lupien 2018a; Ramírez and Welp 2011; Rice 2016). Both countries wrote so- cial rights into their constitutions and implemented extensive new programs to address poverty and inequality in the late 2000s. Both have embraced participatory democracy in theory if not always in practice. They promoted a conception of active, social, and collective citizenship that places primacy on direct participation in decision making (at the local level) in pursuit of communitarian goals. The new constitutions also recognized the existence of Indigenous nations and conferred on them a set of rights related to land, natural resources, culture, and self-government (Lupien 2011). But these re- gimes extended certain rights while withdrawing others.

So what does the political opportunity structure look like for Indigenous peoples heading into the 2020s, and what does it mean for the organizations that represent them? Despite the radical changes made by the Pink Tide gov- ernments, Indigenous organizations face similar challenges in all three countries with respect to political opportunities. These include ambiguous communications policies, restrictive libel laws, authoritarian national security legislation, and an increased government interest in intrusive technologies and surveillance.

Citizen participation and communication are key examples of this paradox. As the previous chapters have shown, in Bolivia and Ecuador participatory democracy reforms, nominally intended to deepen democracy and expand participation, create relationships with the state that may simultaneously promote more inclusive decision-making while establishing parameters around democratic participation. CSOs may only effectively exercise these new rights through state-sanctioned channels. This is unacceptable to the many Indigenous leaders who are wary of working to closely with the state. What's more, while participation had been expanded to previously excluded Indigenous actors, states resist bringing certain issues that challenge key political or economic interests into the participatory realm. Such "threatening" issues tend to include claims over land and natural resources. Here, there is a notable difference between the two Pink Tide countries. While participatory reforms have commonalities on paper, Bolivia under Morales went much further in terms of creating genuine spaces for Indigenous CSOs to engage in the policy process. As we will see, this set organizations there on a different trajectory from their Ecuadorian counterparts.

Ecuador and Bolivia also passed legislation aimed at democratizing the circulation of ideas (Lupien, Chiriboga, and Machaca 2021). Here too, there is a paradox between the normative goals of these measures and the lived reality for Indigenous organizations. The sweeping reforms appeared to support information pluralism by limiting the power of traditional elites and expanding access to the instruments of information to marginalized actors. In theory these reforms should serve to expand political opportunities for Indigenous CSOs by supporting the creation of socially controlled media as a means of ensuring the democratization of information. On the other hand, the same reforms allow the state to regulate these instruments, thus reducing space for criticism of the government. Information pluralism reforms may be tipping the balance too far in the other direction, toward excessive state control over information dissemination. Constitutional provisions and legislation surrounding communication and information in these two countries demonstrate the delicate balance between freedom of expression and information pluralism. That said, the expansion of community media and the increasing capacity to transmit using digital technologies give Indigenous actors tools for pursuing the democratization of information on their own terms.

In contrast, Chile has retained the liberal model, which restricts state interference but allows private media firms to maintain their monopoly over the circulation of ideas (Becerra and Mastrini 2009; Guerrero 2014). This leaves Indigenous groups with few options beyond using social media, which itself is subject to various laws and mechanisms that limit the usefulness of these technologies for engaging in the public sphere. Community media have not taken off to the extent that they have in Bolivia, because state legislation favors large private conglomerates.

All three countries have retained dictatorship-era laws and regulations that limit and constrain political opportunities—at least for actors who lack the resources to circumvent them—even as they established more inclusive state-society mechanisms. This wide array of antiterrorism laws and other measures, developed under Cold War–era dictatorships, are increasingly being applied to Indigenous activists who challenge extractive industries and development projects on their traditional territories.

In Bolivia and Ecuador, and to a lesser extent in Chile, Indigenous civil society was contending with these threats at the same time that states were engaging in a discourse around deepening democracy and creating new opportunities to participate in decision making, at least around "nonthreatening" issues. This forced Indigenous leaders, even those with considerable experience, to navigate a complex and ambiguous political opportunity structure that seemed to simultaneously expand and restrict opportunities. This was no easy task, and yet it encouraged them to diversify and rethink their tactical repertoires.

The political opportunity structure for Indigenous civil society is precarious and constantly evolving. By 2019 and into 2020, it had shifted once again. Right-wing governments were in place in all three countries, although they came to power through different means. Piñera was democratically elected on a right-wing platform. Moreno campaigned for the presidency under a leftist banner but moved to the right once elected. He was replaced with more committed neoliberal Guillermo Lasso in the 2021 election. Áñez became president of Bolivia by seizing power following the ouster of a left-leaning Indigenous president. These regimes moved the political sphere to the right and Indigenous CSOs in all three countries were required to adjust to this new reality. This involved a sustained return to more disruptive action across the region.

Citizenship Regimes and Social Rights

Citizenship has been at the core of Indigenous mobilization from the end of the twentieth century onward (Postero 2007; Tapia 2006; Hale and Millamán 2006; Yashar 2005). Citizenship is closely intertwined with political opportunities: it both reflects actually existing opportunities and contributes to the ability of groups to engage as equal actors in the political system.

Scholars have dubbed the citizenship model that emerged in late twentieth-century Latin America "neoliberal multiculturalism" (Hale 2002, 2004; Richards 2013; Postero 2007). Under this regime, Indigenous peoples and other minorities are granted limited rights as a means of ensuring consent for neoliberalism. Neoliberal multiculturalism promotes nonthreatening forms of cultural recognition while denying marginalized actors social rights and meaningful political participation (Hale 2002). It seeks to create what Aymara intellectual Silvia Rivera Cusicanqui (2012; and see Hale and Millamán 2006) calls the "authorized Indian": an Indigenous subject who accepts and participates in the globalized neoliberal economic arrangements promoted by elites. Those who contest this model are condemned as a violent and dangerous Other, to be ignored or repressed (Richards 2013).

Constitutional reforms in the late 2010s moved the two Pink Tide countries from a neoliberal to a postneoliberal citizenship regime. While concrete changes were far more apparent in Bolivia than in Ecuador, Indigenous leaders were not naïve enough to believe that all of these measures would be implemented. The constitutional reforms and the new citizenship regimes they established were seen as a starting point by Indigenous leaders. Neoliberal multiculturalism remains firmly entrenched in Chile, although Mapuche CSOs demanded an alternative citizenship model in the constitutional reform process launched in 2021.

But the most tangible reforms in Bolivia and Ecuador are related to the expansion of social rights. Both Morales and Correa implemented policies targeted at increasing wages, increasing welfare spending, and investing in schools and healthcare for lower-income sectors. Data from this era demonstrate a significant reduction in the income gap, unemployment, extreme poverty, and malnutrition (Fernandes and Casas 2014; Grugel and Fontana 2019; Wampler 2012). While center-left president Michelle Bachelet (2006–10, 2014–18) implemented various policies aimed at the poor, Chile retained its liberal model and did not extend social rights in the same way. We should therefore expect to see CSOs in the two Pink Tide countries working to pressure the state to respect and implement the gains they have achieved, while those in Chile continue to struggle for recognition and social rights.

If one of the reasons for the relative decline of collective action in the 2005–19 period is that many Indigenous citizens benefited from the social citizenship reforms and plurinational project of the Pink Tide governments, the retrenchment that occurred under the neoliberal administrations of the late 2010s ignited a new round of protests. The expansion of social rights lifted many Bolivians and Ecuadorians out of poverty and provided them with access to health care, education, and higher incomes. On paper at least, the new citizenship regimes in Bolivia—and to a lesser extent in

Ecuador—provided Indigenous groups with the ability to be equal on their own terms, along with tools to enforce these rights. Latin American constitutions are often more of a norm to strive toward than a strict basis for the rule of law and they represent an ideal to which those who govern and are governed aspire (Vanden and Prevost 2009). However, it would be a mistake to undervalue the importance of the momentous changes that took place in these two countries. When I first visited Bolivia and Ecuador shortly after the adoption of the new constitutions, Indigenous leaders there viewed these documents as the culmination of two decades of work. They did not view their adoption as an end to Indigenous struggles but rather as tools to be used to further enhance their position. Leaders and activists understood that groups cannot exercise rights that they do not have.

This new citizenship regime has had a positive effect on Indigenous CSOs in Bolivia and Ecuador. It authorizes them to concentrate on pursuing concrete goals aimed at implementing the citizenship rights they have already achieved with the knowledge that domestic and international law are on their side. It allows them to construct preferred imaginings of citizenship that align with the plurinational and collective citizenship regime promoted through state discourse. Almost all of the leaders I spoke to agreed that while the state does not always comply with its own laws, the new citizenship regime lends Indigenous organizations legitimacy. It allows them to point out obvious discrepancies between what is on paper and how the state engages with them in practice. They are therefore in a very different position when compared with the limited neoliberal multiculturalism of the 1980s to early 2000s.

On the other hand, the new citizenship regimes may partially explain the difficulty that organizations have faced mobilizing supporters when compared with the previous period. The protest cycle of the 1990s was dominated by the struggle over the content of citizenship, including the recognition of Indigenous peoples and social rights in the form of socioeconomic inclusion. The Pink Tide administrations in Bolivia and Ecuador made considerable strides in both of these areas. While they certainly did not address all of the demands put forward by Indigenous civil society, the political and economic reforms managed to satisfy a significant proportion of their base. In their day-to-day lives, Indigenous communities had more opportunities to "be Indigenous" and most benefited to some extent from infrastructure development, social programs, and a general increase in standard of living. The fact that Indigenous organizations may challenge the legitimacy of the government but not the boundaries of the nation-state itself leaves room for negotiation around citizenship. But those I spoke to all acknowledge that there is still much work to do. In late 2019 and into 2020, both Moreno and Áñez appeared eager to restore the neoliberal project and they challenged the social citizenship regimes put in place by their leftist predecessors. This was clearly a motivating factor in the return to large-scale mobilization in 2019.

The struggle over citizenship in Chile challenges both the content and the boundaries of citizenship. But unlike in Bolivia and Ecuador, Chile's citizenship regime remains steadfastly (neo)liberal and has not evolved over the first decades of the twenty-first century. The Chilean state retains a conception of citizenship premised on representation; citizens should be satisfied with institutions that provide a space for consultation, and with exercising their individual rights. The Mapuche CSO representatives I spoke to argue there is an underlying assumption of universality that allows no room for differentiated citizenship or the exercise of collective Indigenous rights. According to the liberal perspective, affirming one's Indigenous identity should be limited to expressions of culture: music, dance, literature, and organizing performances and festivals.

Some organizations have followed in the footsteps of their Bolivian and Ecuadorian peers by seeking recognition of Indigenous peoples and differentiated rights within a devolved Chilean state. They seek a Mapuche renaissance which will encourage the youth in particular to reengage with "being Mapuche." Others, including the most visible movements such as CAM, are challenging the very foundations of the Chilean nation-state (Millalen Paillal 2012; Pairicán 2013). Those I spoke to who identify with this vision refer to their nation as Wallmapu and dream of a united Mapuche nation across the Chile-Argentina border that would exercise a high degree of autonomy or even outright independence. Leaders and community members in the other two countries are deeply attached to their Indigenous identity but they generally consider themselves to be Bolivian or Ecuadorian. They seek autonomy and local self-governance, but separatism has not emerged as an objective. Contesting the boundaries of citizenship is even more threatening to the state than challenging the content, because it provokes struggles over national territory and borders. Chilean political leaders and much of the country's population fear that this could entail the disintegration of the state.

The result has been confrontation and little negotiation between Mapuche organizations and successive governments across the political spectrum. Neither the state nor CSOs such as CAM will budge when it comes to their conception of citizenship. This may change over the next few years as a new crop of Indigenous organizations focused on Mapuche culture and identity build their mobilizing structures through experience and as political opportunities expand through the drafting of a new constitution. But because the state has not recognized a postneoliberal citizenship regime, Indigenous organizations in Chile have less to build on than their cousins in the other two countries. They must claim citizenship by working through (or against) a system that recognizes only a universal, liberal form of citizenship. Given that the state was not open to revisiting the boundaries of citizenship during the constitutional reform process, the type of low-intensity conflict that has marked Wallmapu since 1990 will likely continue.

Mobilizing Structures

Political opportunities have unfolded differently in the three countries. We should therefore expect to see a contrast in how mobilizing structures have evolved in Bolivia, Ecuador, and Chile, as well as in the forms of multiscalar positioning that have developed. In Bolivia and Ecuador, Indigenous leaders and activists have been creating and adapting independent mobilizing structures since at least the 1960s. CSOs remained stable and active despite a relative decline in protest activity. They had considerable experience and well-established mobilizing networks and their leaders developed a high level of political skill. Indigenous groups in the twenty-first century have built on existing structures that they had gradually developed from the second half of the twentieth century onward. While both countries experienced military rule in the 1970s, their governments were less repressive than most in the region, particularly when compared with the Pinochet regime in Chile. They tolerated civil society as long as groups did not openly challenge state authority (Yashar 2005). The dictatorships also ended much earlier: 1982 in Bolivia and 1979 in Ecuador. As we saw in the previous two chapters, Indigenous organizations in these two countries gradually developed an array of structures and networks and continued to build on these foundations at the end of the twentieth century and into the twenty-first. Many of these began as rural peasant unions affiliated with the traditional left or with religious institutions. Their experience and historic achievements during the 1990s and 2000s provided them with valuable experience and political capital.

Following the decline of the protest cycle after about 2005, CSOs in Bolivia and Ecuador continued to build on prior established networks and to learn from successes and failures. They did not have to start from scratch but were able to draw on the financial resources, knowledge, experience, organizational structure, technology, and leadership skills already developed over the decades. They increasingly reoriented their work toward "civic" tactics, but without losing the ability to deploy disruptive action.

While the Mapuche had a long history of local governance institutions and practices across Wallmapu, including regional parliaments by the nineteenth century, these mechanisms fell victim to the centralizing ambitions of the Chilean state following the "pacification." Mapuche actors were deeply involved in Chilean civil society throughout the twentieth century, engaging in leftist movements, peasant councils, and professional syndicates (Cárcamo Hernández 2016; Curivil Bravo 2012; Redondo Cardeñoso 2017). But two decades of violent oppression under Pinochet served to dismantle (or drive underground) any Mapuche mobilizing structures that remained. In Chile, then, Indigenous actors had to build their networks from the ground up following the return to democracy in 1990. Most existing CSOs were founded in the late 1990s and 2000s. CAM, which is arguably the most visible Mapuche political organization in the country, was not founded until 1998. By that year, large Indigenous organizations in Bolivia and Chile had already led major uprisings and transformed the political landscapes of their respective nation-states. They had decades of experience and leadership on which to draw, as well as transversal collaborations to support their activities. Mapuche civil society has not yet had a significant impact on Chile's political institutions.

Beyond these historical differences, we can identify three distinct models for Indigenous civil society in Bolivia, Ecuador, and Chile in the 2010s and the 2020s. These models affect the forms that multiscalar positioning take in the three countries, as well as CSO mobilizing capacity. While Indigenous peoples in Ecuador are heterogeneous and the organizations that represent the different nations do not always agree, the majority of Indigenous civil society groups fall under the umbrella of CONAIE. This does not mean that they always agree with CONAIE and its leadership, nor is the relationship hierarchical. CONAIE works closely with the three large organizations representing Ecuador's main geographic regions: CONAICE on the coast, ECUARUNARI in the highlands, and CONFENAIE in the Amazon. Each coordinates activities in the respective region's provinces. While none of these are subordinate to CONAIE, the national organization takes the lead in times of crisis to achieve maximum effect.

This arrangement has several advantages. The structure of Indigenous civil society in Ecuador allows smaller regional groups to present their demands to higher-level organizations through a bottom-up process. For example, a local Kichwa organization in the province of Azuay is likely to be a member of the provincial Union of Indigenous Communities of Azuay, which is affiliated with regional ECUARUNARI, which in turn works closely with CONAIE to coordinate civil and extrainstitutional political action. This allows for the development of strong democratic practices and coordination of efforts. In some ways, this structure allows the Indigenous movement to function much like a decentralized parallel government, although the actors must still work with (or pressure) the Ecuadorian state to get decisions adopted. This also provides Indigenous leaders with an enormous mobilization capacity. For a time in the mid-2000s, it appeared as though the ill-fated alliance with the short-lived Gutiérrez administration would fracture the movement, but it has now become clear that Indigenous civil society was strong enough to withstand internal divisions. There is little doubt that the 2019 uprisings that destabilized the government and forced President Moreno to back down on his neoliberal agenda would not have been possible without the mobilizing structures that CONAIE and its allies have built over the past four decades.

In Bolivia, there was never a single umbrella organization like CONAIE, but the two largest organizations, CIDOB and CSUTCB, represent a significant proportion of the Indigenous population. To a certain extent, they function somewhat like the large regional organizations in Ecuador: CIDOB represents the interests of the diverse group of nations that inhabit the eastern lowlands, while CSUTCB supports the demands of the mostly Quechua and Aymara people of the altiplano. Both work closely with smaller, department-level, municipal, and issue-specific organizations, OTBs, and with different groups within CONAMAQ. Large organizations, working with and receiving input from smaller regional groups, are able to represent the interests and demands of a significant element of Indigenous civil society in Bolivia.

But CIDOB and CSUTCB are rooted in very different historical contexts, and the issues that divide them run deeper than those that have arisen in Ecuador. They have long been divided over land-related issues, with those in the highlands focused on obtaining access to land for use by Indigenous peasants while lowland peoples have been concerned with protecting and gaining titles to land that they already inhabit (Canessa 2012; Paige 2020).

CIDOB was also more willing to work with governments of the neoliberal era, a strategy which CSUTCB flatly rejected. CIDOB efforts to unite with CSUTCB in a national organization akin to Ecuador's CONAIE were therefore unsuccessful, although most Indigenous organizations united behind the MAS from 2005 to about 2011. Since then, however, the relatively solidarity achieved to confront the neoliberal Sánchez de Lozada administration has fractured. These tensions within Indigenous civil society may very well have been strategically encouraged by the MAS. The party was, after all, able to play Indigenous organizations off against each other in order to diminish the influence of opponents. But in the end, this fragmentation not only weakened Indigenous civil society but also helped the right-wing opposition to remove the MAS from power in 2019. When Morales was asked to resign by the military and was replaced by a nonelected senator representing Bolivia's conservative elites, Indigenous civil society was too divided to come to his rescue.

Mapuche civil society is characterized by even greater fragmentation. There has never been a national umbrella organization and even the development of unifying regional structures has been elusive. Part of this stems from the different visions that Mapuche actors have for the future. Most CSO representatives I spoke to seek some form of autonomy, and many dream of a politically independent Wallmapu. Some are willing to use violence to achieve this goal; they reject the Chilean state as illegitimate and refuse to recognize its authority. Others prefer to achieve land rights and self-governance goals through other means. These types of differences are difficult to reconcile. Another obstacle for Mapuche CSOs is their lack of experience working with other sectors of civil society. In Ecuador, CONAIE has taken a leadership role on various occasions in the fight against neoliberal austerity. In Bolivia, working-class and even some lower-middle income sectors joined with Indigenous movements and supported the MAS. Mapuche CSOs have struggled to achieve public support. Part of this may be due to their relative geographic concentration, though the relative lack of experience of their mobilizing structures is also evident. Richards (2013) notes that systematic racism and the refusal of many Chileans to recognize the existence of the Mapuche as a people are key factors; Chileans would have to first reflect on these questions and open their minds to plurinational solutions before meaningful alliances could be built.

But as I discovered through my fieldwork, there has been a gradual shift on this front. More and more Chileans recognize the common grievances they share with the Mapuche, in terms of both the failure of the neoliberal project and the quality of democracy in the country. Meanwhile, a growing number of Mapuche CSOs recognize the importance of developing alliances with supportive sectors within Chilean civil society and are taking steps in this direction. Many leaders I spoke to believe that 2019 may mark the beginning of a new era for Mapuche relations with the state. There has been a gradual diversification of the organizations that represent Mapuche interests. While CAM still dominates the headlines, there is a growing crop of organizations that are drawing on a broader tactical repertoire and are willing to work with like-minded sectors of Chilean civil society.

Evolution of Multiscalar Positioning

CSOs choose the strategies and tactics that are available to them based on their resource mobilization capacity and the domestic (and sometimes international) political opportunity structure. Groups with weak mobilizing structures and limited political opportunities have fewer options (Gamson 1990; McCarthy 1996; Piven and Cloward 1977). Given the evidence presented in the preceding pages, we would expect that Indigenous civil society in Bolivia should have been able to significantly expand its multiscalar tactical repertoire following the election of the MAS, while the Mapuche CSOs would have fewer new options and those in Ecuador should fall somewhere in between. The reality aligns with these expectations to an extent, although it is far more complex.

Indigenous movements in 2010s have operated in a different political context and have adjusted their multiscalar positioning approach accordingly. The Pink Tide regimes extended social citizenship and deepened political rights to varying degrees, while civil rights remained unchanged or were possibly curbed. Socioeconomic demands of many Indigenous citizens were met by the left-leaning regimes, despite ongoing conflict between some CSOs and the state. All of this led to a decline in the protest cycle as many communities enjoyed an improved standard of living, explored new avenues for citizenship, and had a greater number of political options at their disposal. Organizations and structures remained intact and relatively stable, although the increasing use of ICTs—by both CSOs and their opponents—had an impact on their capacity to do these things. The reforms, even if imperfect, created opportunities but also limited their capacity to mobilize and engage in protest. This forced Indigenous

CSOs in Bolivia and Ecuador to revisit strategies and tactics for political participation, communication, resource mobilization, and education. But while social citizenship was extended and the concept of plurinationality was adopted in both countries, reforms went much further in Bolivia and this led CSOs to pursue a much deeper integration with the state, a strategy that gave them access to power but may have weakened them in the long run. This strategy led to relative stability until the gains achieved were threatened.

In Chile the rigid and closed political system and an enduring neoliberal citizenship regime meant that the opportunities available to Bolivian—and to a lesser extent Ecuadorian—CSOs were simply not available. Change did occur, but very gradually. Tactics employed by the larger Mapuche CSOs evolved at a much slower pace and disruptive conflict remained the norm due to a lack of access to the state and limited political participation opportunities. But in the meantime, some CSOs decided to move in a new direction by focusing their efforts on communication, education, and nation building, believing that success in these areas would strengthen Indigenous political prospects in the long term.

There is considerable variation with respect to how multiscalar positioning strategies played out within the three countries. This is based on number of variables. Of course, size matters: the largest organizations are able to raise more revenue through *autogestión*, and therefore have more human, financial and ICT resources. They are able to hire lawyers and other professionals; CONAIE has its own full-time university-trained communications specialist. Smaller, local CSOs tend to focus on local issues and avoid national politics, although they work with larger organizations to pursue their goals and exert influence beyond their communities. In this way, they are able to pursue a diverse multiscalar positioning strategy even when their own mobilizing structures and resources are limited. This approach works best when there are strong national organizations (Ecuador) or regional bodies (Bolivia) through which smaller CSOs can engage indirectly in the political sphere. I found fewer instances of this in Chile, although smaller CSOs have used *autogestión* to develop innovative initiatives at the local level.

Geography matters as well. Indigenous communities located in territories that are rich in natural resources are far more likely to attract the attention of the state and other powerful actors, and their activism is more likely to be interpreted as a threat. This means that CSOs representing these communities generally come into conflict with the state, and their tactical repertoire must reflect this. In Bolivia and Ecuador, the Indigenous populations in the Amazon regions are smaller, more dispersed, and diverse than the large Andean Kichwa and Aymara populations. But, as their territories overlap with Ecuador's oilfields and Bolivia's natural gas deposits, they represent a significant threat to state and private economic interests. This explains why leaders of Amazonian organizations have experienced higher levels of repression and are more fearful of confrontation with the state. Similarly, the Araucanía is home to Chile's profitable forestry industry. Organizations that have the capacity to effectively use a variety of ICTs are better able to compete with powerful actors in the online world by challenging hegemonic narratives. But social media can be used by powerful actors to confuse, threaten and harass (Larson 2019; Tufekci 2017). My online content analysis shows that more the demands of a particular community threaten extractive industries, the more likely they are to be the targets of misinformation and fear campaigns. And very few if any of the CSOs I worked with have the resources to counter these efforts.

Relationship with the state is another important variable. Positive relations between civil society and government open to the door to state funding and generate significant political opportunities. But Indigenous leaders must maintain a balance; working closely with state agencies can provide them with influence on policy but may also lead to co-optation (or the appearance of co-optation among supporters). When CSOs are in opposition to the government, they are more likely to face repression or to be subjected to negative media campaigns. In this way, states in all three countries perpetuate the construct of the *indio permitido*, or authorized Indian, an Indigenous subject who plays according to the rules in opposition to the Other who does not (Hale and Millamán 2006; Rivera Cusicanqui 2013). We have seen that the construction of the "good" Indigenous subject persists even in Bolivia under the MAS, where Indigenous peoples are categorized based on their support for the government. But Indigenous CSOs are not merely passively manipulated by the state. The vast majority of leaders I spoke to are very well aware of the *indio permitido* versus terrorist discourse and of its political implications. Many CSOs strategically choose to engage with this by participating in authorized spaces and taking advantage of programs while simultaneously supporting extrainstitutional tactics. In some cases, individual CSOs do both, engaging in a tricky balancing act. Many more organizations, however, choose to proactively (but never blindly) take part in the permitted model while supporting (directly or covertly) organizations that contest the state. This is at the heart of multiscalar positioning. And there is also evidence to suggest that it is in the interest of states to provide CSOs with opportunities and mechanisms for multiscalar positioning. By restricting state-society interface mechanisms, denying Indigenous identity claims, and criminalizing Mapuche resistance, the Chilean state has contributed to the ongoing conflict. Where there are fewer channels through which to engage, the chances of violence increase as opportunities for multiscalar positioning are curtailed.

Political Participation

In the previous section, I discussed the different civil society organizational models that have developed in Bolivia, Ecuador, and Chile based on the divergent political opportunities in each jurisdiction. In this section, I examine how these structures have affected how CSOs participate in the public sphere. It would be reasonable to expect Indigenous organizations in Ecuador and (especially) Bolivia to demonstrate more diverse multiscalar positioning strategies than those in Chile but we may also anticipate that they will struggle with questions surrounding co-optation.

It is true that Indigenous civil society in Bolivia and Ecuador was less visible during this period and CSOs did not engage the in large-scale civil disobedience that rocked much of the region at the end of the twentieth century. But less visible does not mean less active. In fact, Indigenous civil society never ceased to fight for land rights, natural resources, cultural recognition, political autonomy, and a dignified standard of living. They developed a multiscalar positioning approach, adapting and diversifying their tactical repertoire to the new political and economic context. Since 2005, Indigenous CSOs in Bolivia and Ecuador have shifted their efforts from disruptive (and costly) protest and focused on engaging in the policy process through "authorized" spaces, promoting political participation in their communities, communication and public relations, alliance building, identity promotion, and education. In the 2010s, this involved a greater variety of tactics, engagement with a range of state-society mechanisms, and complex, interlocking forms of civic action. CSOs were more focused on sustained political participation than the disruptive tactics that many observers associated with Indigenous organizations. Those with the means to do so are exploring new ways of mobilizing resources and are using ICTs to reach a wider audience and to engage in the "virtual" public sphere on their own terms.

Particularly in Bolivia and to some extent in Ecuador, shifting political opportunities and citizenship regimes provided civil society actors with new opportunities to pursue. Even when what is on paper does not translate into practice, Indigenous leaders understand that they cannot exercise rights that they do not have, and working to ensure that these "on paper" rights are respected provides them with arguments and tools to pursue their interests. This has translated into a wider range of strategies and tactics they can use.

In all three countries, Indigenous CSOs engage with their communities through *trabajo en territorio,* or community work. This is a defining feature of Indigenous civil society and serves not only to meet social needs but also to shore up political support, to solidify networks, and to promote agendas. But there are also significant differences between the approaches CSOs have taken. In the two Andean countries, leftist governments' redistributive so- cial policies addressed long-neglected basic needs of large segments of the population. Constitutional reform provided an expanded set of political and cultural rights. But from this point on, the paths diverge. Unlike in Ecua- dor, Bolivian CSOs were welcomed into the national policymaking process. The MAS, which was founded through collective action, integrated these organizations into its governance structure and created numerous indi- genized state-society mechanisms that provide genuine access to power and the policy process. The party was so dependent on CSOs like CSTUCB, and its governance structure so closely intertwined with these organ- izations, that it could not govern without their support. It could, as we saw following the TIPNIS crisis, afford to cut loose less supportive CSOs, but this meant solidifying ties with allied organizations.

In Ecuador, CONAIE and the large regional associations engaged in an ongoing, sustained multiscalar positioning strategy. This included dialogue with all levels of government, working through formal and informal insti- tutions, and developing strategic relationships with certain political actors. But while they supported the Correa administration in the early years, the relationship soured by the end of the 2000s. The multiscalar position- ing approach continued, but CSOs were just as likely to work from the out- side of the system as they were to engage from within. While Indigenous Ecuadorian civil society therefore remained autonomous and continued to adapt, modify and develop their strategies over the past decade, many Bolivian groups worked directly through MAS-dominated institutions and mechanisms. They recentered their tactical repertoires around the MAS's new participatory architecture while Ecuadorian CSOs did not. For pro- MAS Indigenous CSOs, years of integration with the governing party and the growing rift may have left Bolivia's Indigenous organizations in a weaker position than those in Ecuador, particularly when the MAS was removed from power. And while most Ecuadorian leaders united against the Moreno government in October 2019, the events that transpired the following month in Bolivia appear to have had the opposite effect.

Indigenous movements in Bolivia have arguably had more success in achieving their goals than any other in the region (or perhaps the world). Yet in the long run, the strong mobilizing networks that allowed Bolivian Indigenous peoples to achieve these outcomes may have been weakened by integrating too closely into the state apparatus and depending too heavily on one party. In Ecuador, the conflict between the government and Indigenous movements maintained a clear division between the state and civil society. This meant that organizations had no choice but to continue to build on previous experience and mobilizing structures and to engage in a complex multiscalar positioning approach that included the ongoing development of innovative tactics and the use of ICTs to engage in the public sphere.

Mapuche leaders do not have as many options. Despite a change in discourse under Bachelet, political opportunities have not evolved much either on paper or in practice. Neoliberal multiculturalism remains dominant, granting limited rights and cultural recognition in exchange for compliance (Antileo Baeza et al. 2015). The Concertación's Indigenous policies refused to recognize collective rights around land or autonomy (Richards 2013). And the Concertación did not rewrite the country's outdated constitution that fails to acknowledge Chile's plurinational character, nor did it develop the participatory architecture created in Bolivia under the MAS. Chile's participatory mechanisms, such as neighborhood councils or the "Quiero mi Barrio" program, are almost entirely consultative with limited decision-making powers, and none has been designed to integrate Indigenous modes of governance (Lupien 2018a). This leaves Mapuche civil society with little to build on, although CSOs have been at the forefront of calls for constitutional reform. Furthermore, successive governments on the right and the center-left of the political spectrum have demonstrated their willingness to use violence against those constructed as threats to national interests. As a result, Indigenous CSOs are limited to engaging in either "permitted" but limited forms of cultural expression or disruptive action that exacerbates conflict with the state.

Mapuche CSOs have taken different approaches to engaging in the public sphere. The lack of access points to the state means that political participation beyond elections remains limited at best. The larger organizations, such as CAM, CTT, and ATM, have chosen to orient their participation toward resisting and confronting the state, either through disruptive actions or through litigation. But other organizations have chosen a different path. If the Chilean state will not let them in, they have chosen to (re)build their own nation, encouraging a revival of Mapuche culture and epistemologies through communication, education, and socialization. The high level of ICT access, experience, and expertise enjoyed by Mapuche civil society in comparison with their counterparts in the region should provide them with advantages in these areas. Many of these actors believe that promoting Mapuche identity and pride is a means of invigorating the movement. They are developing a longer-term strategy that seeks to instill pride in Mapuche youth, believing that this will sustain activism through the reproduction of a strong national identity.

Resource Mobilization

Indigenous organizations across the three countries employ similar resource mobilization strategies that incorporate traditional practices while adapting to twenty-first-century globalization. With state funding limited and highly politicized to favor "authorized" groups, strategies have focused on *autogestión,* a system of self-funding that revolves around soliciting and selling goods and services through contributions, donations, and pro bono work. Bolivian organizations have more options to raise revenue because of provisions that allow them to receive a percentage of the profits from resource extraction or development projects on their territories. In many cases, the management of this "taxation" system is in the hands of local Indigenous governance mechanisms. But in all three countries, communities are relying on traditional sources of revenue—agricultural products, meats, leather, clothing—to fund their activities. Others have capitalized on their reputations as environmental stewards or knowledge holders to raise revenue through sustainable tourism or education services.

What has changed from the 2010s onward is their interest in using ICTs and social media to expand their markets. Examples abound of organizations in small, isolated communities using the Internet to sell products and services to consumers who would not otherwise have access. It is now possible for someone in Seattle or Sydney to purchase a blouse produced by an Aymara seamstress in rural Bolivia directly from an organization she is affiliated with. Tourists from Berlin can book a rafting tour in the Ecuadorian Amazon with a local Shuar guide through his Facebook page, and part of the proceeds may be used by his neighbors to support a court case against oil drilling the region. Mapuche organizations in Chile have been particularly adept at using ICTs to augment their revenue. They have developed a broad range of language and culture courses that contribute to their coffers while promoting Indigenous identity and disseminating knowledge.

Finally, many organizations use ICTs for commercialization of products or services. About one-third of the CSOs in Bolivia and Ecuador and just over half in Chile use ICTs for these purposes, and many others are exploring the possibilities. Communities can announce their participation in a market or fair through social media, with information about what kind of goods will be available. Another use of ICTs involves selling specific products on social networks or on a website. Some felt that technologies could help them to export their products internationally to consumers in Western countries who were interested in purchasing Indigenous handicrafts and clothing online. Communities also create pages on sites such as Facebook to advertise services such as community tourism experiences. CSOs reported that these endeavors provided them with autonomy from both state and NGO actors, leaving them freer to pursue their own agendas.

Communication and Public Relations

Media theorists have long argued that control of the instruments of information is monopolized by powerful private economic interests that dominate domestic and transnational power structures (Herman and Chomsky 1988; McChesney 2016). The liberal model equates freedom of speech uniquely with right of commercial media to disseminate information without state interference (Asante 1997; Gunaratne 2002). But the media in Latin America is dominated by a small elite with the resources to filter the flow of information, conferring special privileges to some citizens who can dominate public debate (Fox and Waisbord 2002; Becerra and Mastrini 2009). Scholars argue that media concentration, particularly during the era of intensified globalization, has supported the creation of a Eurocentric worldview that promotes a reality that aligns with the interests of those who control the instruments of power, and ignores or devalues non-Western epistemologies (Artz 2015; Mingolo 2000). And even in the social media age, media conglomerates continue to set agendas, identify priorities, and contextualize information (Calderón and Castells 2020).

In 1980s, Chilean thinkers Juan Somavía and Fernando Reyes Matta promoted the idea that information should be valued as a social good rather than a commodity (Reyes Matta 1981; Somavía 1981). This position, which was embraced by Correa and Morales in theory if not in practice, contends that voice equalization is essential to democracy. It shifts the focus away from the markets and private press organizations as mediators of information to the diversity of sources and voices involved in their production. Voice equalization requires not only a range of sources but diverse perspectives, as well as the involvement of the public (particularly traditionally marginalized actors such as Indigenous peoples) as communicators rather than as passive recipients.

Bolivia presents us with concrete examples of why the liberal notion of press freedom is insufficient and simplistic. While the media are dominated by powerful private interests across Latin America, in the Bolivian context the contrast is particularly glaring because of a rural Indigenous majority and media dominated by a small urban white/mestizo elite. This media landscape has excluded Indigenous peoples from the public sphere and in many cases has resulted in racist representations and messages (Lupien 2013). Like other political changes in Bolivia that are the result of the interplay between social power and political action, the combination of government support in the form of legislation that levels the playing field and active civil society involvement in media creation and communication is key to achieving democratic access to media production and distribution.

Both the Morales and Correa governments, responding to civil society influence, sought to play a proactive role by promoting information pluralism through progressive communication policies. The emergence of state-owned media alternatives in countries formerly dominated by a handful of private conglomerates may be an improvement over the past. At the very least, this means that an alternative ideological position is now available to the public and that the stranglehold of the neoliberal elites over information and ideas has been weakened. Yet, absent participatory and independent CSOs, governments alone are unlikely to provide diverse and unbiased information. Reliance of state media outlets on funding from the government of the day also opens the door to manipulation and cooptation. Furthermore, the aggressive tone that emerges from both government and private media interests has a destabilizing effect on these countries by exacerbating the already deep societal divisions.

Communication for Indigenous civil society is ultimately about contesting hegemonic narratives and asserting agency (Ginsburg 2000, 2016; Turner 1995, 2002). In the early years of the World Wide Web, some dared to hope that the Internet would support information pluralism by providing marginalized groups with the tools to tell their own stories (Castells 2001). More recently, Calderón and Castells (2020) argue that new technologies can "become a counterweight opposing the power of the major media corporations." The experience of Indigenous CSOs paints a mixed picture. ICTs allow Indigenous actors to produce content on their own terms. Most leaders acknowledge that if politics is increasingly taking place in cyberspace, they must be there in order to have a voice and to contest frames that depict their communities in a negative light. But they point out that even when their organizations have access to social media and the skills to use them, they cannot compete with powerful actors such as stage agencies and mining corporations when it comes to designing public relations campaigns.

This is especially true in Bolivia, the region's least developed country. While ICTs may pose new threats to Indigenous communities, the relative lack of access and low use of these technologies by that country's CSOs appears to have been a weakness, particularly during the 2019 uprisings. Comparing the successful use of ICTs by Ecuador's CSOs to mobilize supporters and disseminate information, with the limited presence of Bolivian CSOs on social media (and the resulting hegemonic discourse controlled by the right) is a case in point. But as with the other strategic areas discussed in this book, Indigenous CSOs are learning. Mapuche CSOs have a head start on their counterparts in the other two countries. While ICTs have not really enhanced the efforts of Mapuche CSOs to engage in the political arena, they have supported their capacity to communicate with the public, to tell their own stories, to contest hegemonic discourse, and to denounce state violence. This was at least part of the reason that Mapuche symbols took on a prominent place in Chile's 2019 uprisings.

Identity, Education, and Socialization

Scholars who have studied Indigenous collective action through the lens of identity politics note that Indigenous CSOs have fostered a strong ethnic identity which drives their political strategies and enhances their mobilization capacity (Albó 2004; Lucero 2008; Postero 2007). About half of the leaders I spoke to expressed concern over a loss or diluting of Indigenous identity, particularly among the youth. Several reasons were identified to explain this trend. Since the 2000s, migration from rural Indigenous communities to urban areas has accelerated (Del Popolo, Ribotta, and Oyarce 2009; Reyes 2014). Young people are leaving their villages behind and heading to the cities either to look for economic opportunities or to pursue an education. The latter objective was facilitated by the generous bursaries created by the Correa and Morales governments, which provided thousands of Indigenous young people with the opportunity to attend university. But for many Indigenous leaders, this means that their people are more geographically dispersed and they think that living in the cities causes young people to abandon traditional practices and values. Many Elders I spoke to lamented that Indigenous youth seek to blend in with their mestizo peers and are attracted by the promises of the Westernized urban lifestyle.

Even those who remain in Indigenous rural communities are affected by the pull of globalization, which most leaders equate with Westernization. This pull is accelerated and intensified through the Internet and social media. As more and more young people in their communities become connected, the long arm of globalization reaches into even the most isolated communities (Calderón and Castells 2020). Young people, many interviewees told us, are exposed to images, values, and ideas that encourage them to question their indigeneity. If identity is key to mobilizing people for a cause, this trend will make it increasingly difficult for organizations to do to. If the development and reproduction of a strong sense of ethnic identity among disparate Indigenous groups is key to sustaining a strong civil society, and if online "networked individualism" has transformed how people engage in politics, how can Indigenous organizations adapt?

Two patterns have emerged. Some Indigenous organizations have embraced, or at least accepted, ICTs as tools that can support their efforts to promote identity. Their leaders argue that ICTs have become central to identity promotion for youth, and they must therefore be able to engage with their younger community members in online spaces. Others see digital technologies as a threat to Indigenous identity and believe that even when they are able to overcome access barriers, they cannot complete with the homogenizing culture of globalization, which they believe turns young people away from their roots.

I encountered proponents of both positions in all three countries, although there were more cyber optimists among the Mapuche. In Chile, basic access is relatively more widespread and Indigenous civil society has more experience with using these tools for a variety of purposes. Mapuche organizations have started to explore new avenues for using ICTs. But leaders were also apprehensive about the impact of social media on young people who do have access.

Nearly half of interviewees in Bolivia and Ecuador attribute a decline in their capacity to mobilize supporters to the influence of technology and the Internet on identity. Some leaders in the two countries look back with nostalgia on the 1990s, when organizations were successful in creating a strong sense of common Indigenous identity among formerly disparate peoples. They were able to channel this collective identity into large marches, roadblocks, and occupations, which led to significant political victories. In 2017, I spoke to an Ecuadorian Elder who regretted that "it is harder to mobilize than in the past because there is lack of interest, our Indigenous identity has become diluted. The Internet brings in foreign ideas that make people want to pursue a different lifestyle and leave their Indigenous culture behind. Without a strong sense of collective identity, people will not mobilize" (Freddy, interview with the author, November 27, 2017). Two years later, events in all three countries suggest that some of these concerns may have been overstated. This situation is fluid, and the perspectives of Indigenous leaders will likely evolve over time. Most CSOs still lack the resources to compete with more powerful information and entertainment industry actors, but as they gain new skills, they are discovering innovative ways of promoting identity and culture among young people.

Mobilization and Disruptive Action

During the first round of interviews that ended in March 2019, Indigenous leaders in Bolivia and Ecuador generally spoke of large-scale mobilization and protest in the past tense. Many looked back with nostalgia on the momentous protests of 1990 to the early 2000s and on their ability to mobilize heterogeneous communities across the country behind a set of believes, values, and goals. Some lamented that this mobilizing power had diminished since the mid-2000s for the reasons discussed earlier in this chapter: popular governments that provided significant (if sometimes double-edged) concessions, improvements in living standards and government services, new political spaces that provided options beyond protest, and the impact of globalization on identity.

Leaders and long-time activists also pointed to changes in the nature of the overall struggle. In the 1990s, calls to action were felt deeply because they were aimed at recovering territory and land. They were also about affirming identity and taking pride in being Indigenous after centuries of being made to feel inferior. Social organizations such as CONAIE, CIDOB, and CSUTCB presented clear goals around these issues, including demands for constitutional reform, formal recognition of land rights, and local self-governance. By the late 2000s, many of these tangible goals had been achieved, at least on paper. Despite ongoing conflict between Indigenous organizations and the Ecuadorian and Bolivian governments, these reforms, along with the investment in social spending that accompanied them, may have satisfied a wide segment of the movements' constituents. But many activists and leaders were also critical of their own organizations. They felt that in the earlier period, there was a clear and legitimate purpose and conviction to the struggle that seems to have been lost over the years. As a result, calls to action did not carry the same weight.

When I conducted follow-up interviews in late 2019 and early 2020, things had changed considerably. Ecuadorian Indigenous organizations had led the most significant protests in a generation and had forced the government to back down on its austerity package. The protests in Bolivia were still ongoing in the face of state repression. What had started as a rejection of the removal of Bolivia's first Indigenous president had morphed into a call for free and fair elections in the face of an unelected government that was using COVID-19 as a pretext for postponing the vote. By the mid-2020s, Indigenous Bolivians were once again paralyzing the nation's economy and transportation infrastructure on a massive scale. In late 2019, Mapuche CSOs joined in the nationwide protests that forced a conservative administration to finally accept constitutional reform, providing them with a unique opportunity to pressure Chile to join other Latin American states in formally recognizing their rights. By mid-2020, Mapuche citizens continued to protest in the Araucanía region and in Santiago against state violence and efforts to delay the referendum. But this time, they did so with non-Indigenous Chileans at their side.

What explains this new protest cycle? The reasons vary across the three countries. In 2019, Indigenous mobilizing structures were fully developed, particularly in the two Pink Tide countries. CSOs in Ecuador and Bolivia had diversified their tactical repertoires over the previous fifteen years, but their experience with calling for and coordinating large-scale mobilizations remained firmly entrenched in their institutional memory. Even if they had been focusing on other strategies, mobilization has remained in their arsenal as the weapon "when all else fails." This provided them with the infrastructure to play a leading role in their countries' respective uprisings. Mapuche organizations are younger, have less experience leading large-scale protests, and lack the extensive networks that give Ecuadorian and Bolivian organizations their mobilizing capacity. But their mobilizing structures have evolved and grown over the past twenty years. While they are not positioned to take the lead in nationwide resistance, they were able to coordinate Mapuche participation in the ongoing protests and to align themselves more closely with Chilean civil society.

On the surface, political opportunities were not optimal in any of these countries. The Moreno government in Ecuador had demonstrated a desire to be more conciliatory than its predecessor but deployed force against protesters early on. From the beginning, there was little doubt over the willingness of Áñez and Piñera to use violence against Indigenous citizens. But political opportunities are about more than the openness of a government to demands, they also include the presence of allies, legitimacy of those in power, and divisions among the elites. In Ecuador and Chile, Indigenous organizations had support from other sectors of society. The Ecuadorian uprising did not begin with Indigenous organizations but they were able to take the lead because of strong public support for their goals and their ability to align their frames with those of other sectors of society. Mapuche organizations were able to latch on to a massive mobilization effort by aligning with the goals that other sectors were pursuing: attacking inequality, deepening democracy, and reforming the constitution. They avoided framing their grievances uniquely around identity because they understood the need for allies. By expressing empathy for the thousands of non-Indigenous protesters injured by the police, they were able develop a sense of solidarity between the often-oppressed Mapuche and non-elite Chileans.

Moreno's popularity was at a historic low by late 2019, with most polls suggesting that fewer than 20 percent approved of his leadership and 90 percent of Ecuadorians did not trust him. Amid the unrest in Chile, only 14 percent of citizens expressed confidence in Piñera, the lowest level of support for a president since the return to democracy in 1990. Such low numbers, disseminated daily via social media, are extraordinary even in a region where people are extremely cynical when it comes to politics and politicians. The resulting lack of legitimacy opened a political opportunity window for Indigenous civil society even if the administrations themselves has closed their doors.

Indigenous identity appears to have played less of a role in mobilization than in the past, at least in Ecuador and Chile. But leaders were able to frame their calls to action around another equally important issue. At the time when the protest broke out, CSOs were faced with administrations determined to restore (Bolivia and Ecuador) or reinforce (Chile) a neoliberal agenda. In Bolivia and Ecuador, the citizenship regime and social rights that generations of Indigenous people had fought so hard for were under threat. The Áñez and Moreno regimes, by reversing policies of their predecessors, threatened to withdraw social rights through privatizations and cuts to government programs. Áñez also appeared willing to attack Indigenous political and civil rights and turn the plurinational state back into an instrument of the neoliberal project dominated by white Media Luna elites. Despite tensions between some Indigenous groups and the Morales and Correa governments, and the fact that the new citizenship regimes were only partially enacted, leaders in Ecuador understood what they had achieved and would not easily give this up. They therefore framed their calls to action around broad, cross-sectorial issues such as equality. They also focused on specific concerns that could be targeted to Indigenous peoples while also appealing to other nonelite actors, such as democracy and social rights.

Mapuche leaders did something similar, but from another direction. Rather than expressing concern about maintaining gains they had achieved, they framed their calls to action around what they needed to accomplish. Some messages were targeted at Mapuche communities but linked to questions of citizenship and participation. For example, while Camilo Catrillanca was at the center of Mapuche leaders' calls to action in late 2019, they also framed the death of an unarmed young man at the hands of police as a threat to all Chileans. They positioned the killing as a citizenship issue. The fact that so many non-Indigenous protesters were violently oppressed by security forces supported the argument that all Chileans needed to rise up and claim their own citizenship against a closed state. This is one of the reasons that Catrillanca became a symbol of the uprisings both within and outside of Mapuche communities. Mapuche leaders were also able to merge their calls for social citizenship with Chilean civil society's demand for greater equality.

Overall, then, Indigenous movements in all three countries built on existing mobilizing structures and took advantage of a set of political opportunities that presented themselves in late 2019. They also framed their struggle around citizenship and social rights in a way that was able to inspire their own communities while connecting with other sectors of society. But the protests did not play out in the same way. The October 2019 uprising against the Ecuadorian government's austerity measures brought Indigenous peoples together again. After a decade of segmented collective action relying primarily on nondisruptive tactics, CONAIE was once again able to gain the trust of Indigenous communities and to coordinate efforts to influence policy. One of the most popular hashtags used by Indigenous

CSOs throughout Ecuador during the protests was #SomosCONAIE (#WeAreCONAIE). The hashtag was used even by CSOs that do not normally work closely with the umbrella organization. In any case, the Ecuadorian Indigenous movement achieved an important victory by forcing Moreno to back down.

This did not happen in Bolivia. While Indigenous groups were far more active and visible in the protests demanding Morales be restored to power than in those that called for his resignation, Indigenous communities and the movements that represent them were split. Some Indigenous organizations did not lend their support to those who hoped to bring Morales back. Pro-MAS activists did not get what they wanted through protest; Morales was not restored to the presidency. The interim government made no concessions, and in fact began reversing MAS policies against the wishes of both pro and anti-Morales CSOs. The anti-MAS individuals we spoke to in the follow-up interviews admitted that even the *pititas* were impatient for fresh elections, although they were equally determined to ensure Morales did not return to power, depriving Indigenous CSOs of the broader support that their counterparts in the other two countries enjoyed.

Meanwhile, Mapuche civil society leaders called on their communities to support the demonstrations which had already begun. While the outcomes of the protests did not specifically address Indigenous demands, organizations can nonetheless claim an important victory. First and foremost, the Chilean government finally agreed to the need for a new constitution. While this triumph was not primarily due to the actions of Indigenous peoples, it does address a long-standing demand and provides Indigenous leaders with the opportunity to have a voice in the Constituent Assembly. They will have much work to do, but the door is now open to the possibility of enshrining Indigenous rights in the state's supreme law. Second, Indigenous protesters managed to achieve a visibility that has been denied to them in the past. Both the state and mainstream media had long associated Mapuche protest with violence and acts of "terrorism." They concentrated on CAM and its armed units but virtually ignored the growing number of organizations that sought change through a multiscalar positioning approach. In 2019, Mapuche and non-Indigenous protesters marched side by side carrying symbols of resistance such as Mapuche flags and pictures of Camilo Catrillanca. Many Santiagueños (residents of Santiago) experienced the type of state repression that Indigenous communities in the far-off Araucanía have endured for decades.

This does not mean that Chilean public opinion will suddenly shift drastically in favor of Mapuche claims to land and autonomy, but it does provide an opportunity for CSOs to contest the frames that have been used to delegitimize and criminalize them. In both Ecuador and Bolivia, visibility and legitimacy were the first achievements to emerge from the historic 1990 protests. From that point on, they were able to build on their new image. Mapuche organizations are gaining experience in building cross-sectorial alliances. It is clear now to people of all backgrounds that there are socioeconomic and political issues that unite them. There is a broad consensus outside of elite sectors that constitutional reform is nonnegotiable. These common interests provide an opportunity for Mapuche organizations to develop the types of alliances that have thus far eluded them.

Interestingly, then, it appears that Bolivian Indigenous organizations, who were in the strongest position prior to October 2019, emerged from the protests weaker than those in Ecuador and Chile. The common denominator in the latter two cases appears to be that they achieved some degree of unity between Indigenous organizations, and with non-Indigenous actors. They also managed to align their interests with those of non-elite mestizos. Ecuadorian organizations such as CONAIE had done this before. While Mapuche civil society remains fragmented, almost all CSOs agree that inequality must be addressed, the constitution must be rewritten, and a greater devolution of power is needed. They may still not agree on tactics, but the 2019 protests helped to identify these common aspirations within and beyond the Mapuche nation. This presents a unique opportunity for leaders to move ahead with a collective agenda. The ability of Mapuche CSOs to achieve tangible outcomes through multiscalar positioning was demonstrated by the integration of long standing demands into the new draft constitution in 2022, including the recognition of Indigenous peoples and certain land claims.

ICTs, Indigenous Civil Society, and Protest

October and November 2019 were the first large nationwide Indigenous uprisings of the social media age. I noted differences between Ecuador and Chile, where ICT use by Indigenous CSOs was primarily offensive, and Bolivia, where use was more limited and defensive. As we saw in the three previous chapters, leaders and activists were divided on the impact of ICTs on mobilization. Many felt that cellphones and social media facilitated and speeded up mobilization efforts. But there are disadvantages to this as well. Before the appearance of the cellphone, leaders had to go from one community to another, often on foot, to meet with people in person. In fact, mobilization as recently as the early 2000s could occur only through formal community meetings. These were often led according to traditional practices and included ceremonies, impassioned speeches, and deliberation. The personal bonds and reinforcement of identity generated through these experiences cannot be reproduced over the Internet or via a cellphone app. This is why many leaders felt that while ICTs provide tools to communicate calls for action instantaneously, they weaken the relationships and conviction that produced strong collective action in the recent past. Many others went even further, blaming ICTs, and social media in particular, for contributing to the loss of identity among young people and insisting that without a strong sense of being Indigenous, people will not respond to calls for action.

Indigenous CSOs used ICTs for three primary purposes during the 2019–20 protests. First, ICTs such as cellphones and social media aps such as WhatsApp were used extensively to support mobilization, especially among younger people. Second, Indigenous CSOs and community members used social media to inform themselves about what was going on around the country, and to disseminate their version of events to domestic and international audiences. Finally, Indigenous activists used social media to make state aggression visible.

In Ecuador, Indigenous groups took advantage of social media and other ICTs to both mobilize supporters and to show the world what they were doing and why they were doing it. While CONAIE and other organizations worked through their existing networks and used familiar tactics, the 2019 protests represented a turning point in that it was the first time they had used social media to facilitate mobilization on a large scale. The speed with which they were able to muster support and their enhanced ability to coordinate forms of action across the country may have contributed to the effectiveness of the protests, but Indigenous Ecuadorians had the mobilizing networks to carry this off without the help of technology.

What was truly novel about this protest cycle was the skillful use of ICTs to expose state violence and to seize control of the narrative. Rather than relying on Ecuadorian media to tell the story of the protests, Indigenous organizations produced their own news reports and disseminated these to Ecuadorians and the world. By live streaming while under siege, they were able to create a sense of solidarity with those who supported their cause at home and abroad. By broadcasting their meetings with government ministers, they not only demonstrated their ability to negotiate, but ensured transparency. Indigenous organizations elsewhere were watching closely. Several of the Mapuche leaders I spoke to had carefully analyzed how CONAIE and its partners used social media in October 2019, and claimed that they had learned lessons from what transpired.

We have already seen that Indigenous organizations in Chile have used ICTs to expose state violence and to promote language, culture, and identity. They have continued to use social media to contest the dominant narrative of the state and extractive industries and to make their own voices heard. That the most iconic and widely circulated image of the late 2019 protests captured a Mapuche flag atop a military statue suggests that this campaign may be starting to work. Mapuche filmmakers and artists are increasingly working with IT and communications specialists to make themselves known to the world. With their strong head start using digital technologies, Mapuche organizations are slowly but steadily gaining the type of positive visibility that can support their political agenda. The Catrillanca and Operation Hurricane fiascos demonstrate that Mapuche actors may be gaining ground when it comes to contesting online spaces against the state.

In Bolivia, the experience of pro-MAS organizations with ICTs during and after the protests is more difficult to assess. In some ways, the 2019 uprisings demonstrate the threat that digital technologies can pose to Indigenous civil society. As I mentioned in the chapter on Bolivia, many Indigenous actors closed their social media accounts entirely during the Áñez regime, some after receiving explicit threats. Under the interim government, fear of surveillance prevented them from using ICTs to mobilize supporters or even to disseminate information. Social media was used by right-wing actors to mobilize supporters against Indigenous protesters, to spread fear and misinformation, and to issue threats. These groups have better access and more experience with using ICTs and during the 2019 protests, social media clearly provided an advantage to forces that seek to turn back the clock on the progress that Indigenous peoples have made. They managed to control the dominant narrative at home and abroad, that the MAS and its supporters are violent and enemies of democracy. Unlike in the other two countries, Indigenous CSOs do not appear to have succeeded in using social media to turn this discourse around. That said, Indigenous and allied activists who fled the country, including those just across the border in Argentina, used social media to disseminate alternative news and views.

Certain acts of violence by the Áñez government and its supporters may have never come to light otherwise, because Bolivian media chose to turn a blind eye.

Social media can supply Indigenous actors with tools to disseminate messages that would otherwise not be heard. Social media provide an outlet for Indigenous CSOs to frame their political action on their own terms, to contest the discourse of powerful actors, and to make repression visible. While this may be more likely to reach those already inclined to support their agenda, in the twenty-first century, CSOs need to have an online presence or risk having their voices left out of important conversations. My research on the late 2019 protests in these three countries suggests that visual images may be more effective for Indigenous CSOs in advancing their agendas. This aligns with a growing body of research that finds that images disseminated over social media are particularly influential in political communication (Highfield and Leaver 2016; Rovisco and Veneti 2017). In particular, disseminating images of state violence and repression may achieve results. During the October 2019 uprisings in Ecuador, activists gradually increased their use of Twitter and Facebook to broadcast images of police repression. This led to widespread attention and condemnation from international organizations. The government then shifted its framing strategy, claiming to be open to negotiation. In Chile, there is strong evidence that the government was influenced by Indigenous groups' use of social media. The president and interior minister abruptly changed their tune with respect to the death of a Mapuche activist once video evidence of the young man's innocence was widely shared over social media.

But the results of my online content analysis suggest Indigenous civil society messages generally fall on deaf ears and do not change the tone or direction of dominant online conversations. Discourse surrounding Indigenous resistance in Latin America is surprisingly consistent across the three countries; it is framed in a positive light by CSOs and as dangerous by government and media sources (see table 5.2). Indigenous CSOs portray themselves as peaceful and just, in contrast to a repressive and illegitimate state that uses violence to suppress dissent and to deny Indigenous peoples rights to land, autonomy, and resources. They frame their actions thematically around indigeneity and as a legitimate response to the institutionalized racism of a colonial state. Yet while they seek to make visible the violence that their communities are subjected to, they do not portray themselves as helpless victims. They insist on Indigenous agency, arguing that their activism is organized, ongoing, and aimed at building a better society.

Messages disseminated over social media by state agencies also demonstrate consistency across the three jurisdictions in terms of themes and even words and hashtags used. They portray Indigenous protest as dangerous and threatening, and as either as spontaneous and irrational outbursts not linked to broader social goals or as manipulated and controlled by external leftist actors who seek to provoke chaos. Common frames across the three countries include security, particularly the safety of citizens not involved in collective action; Indigenous protesters as violent mobs engaged in acts of vandalism; terrorism; the state as the defender of order, rule of law, and democracy; and the police and armed forces as noble and heroic. Another consistent theme involves dividing the population between "citizens," subtly constructed as mestizos who do not disrupt public order, and subversive "delinquents," a category into which Indigenous protesters are placed. States frame themselves as concerned with preserving democracy and ensuring the safety of "citizens." Additional themes focus on property damage and injuries suffered by police officers (while failing to acknowledge state violence), as well as a tendency to divide Indigenous peoples themselves into "noble" and "dangerous" categories depending on the nature of their political action. The analysis revealed similarities even in terms of the words and hashtags used by government actors in the three counties. The word most frequently used when discussing Indigenous protesters is *delincuentes* (delinquents). Other frequently used words include *terroristas/terrorismo, violencia* and *desestabilización* (terrorists/terrorism, violence, and destabilization). There is sympathy for security forces and "peaceful citizens" but no thematic recognition of the historical and contemporary factors that motivate Indigenous political action.

Mainstream private media reporting on the events under study was primarily focused on acts of vandalism and violence while it ignored the root causes of the uprisings. Indigenous leaders and activists were rarely interviewed, although newspapers and television stations do share the perspectives of state officials and business owners. In none of the countries did mainstream media outlets quote from or share Indigenous social media content. Alternative media, including community radio and online news sources created by leftist groups, were more likely to be sympathetic to Indigenous causes and collective action. Many of these outlets reproduced the content disseminated by Indigenous CSOs and framed events thematically, with an emphasis on injustice and violence against Indigenous communities. But their circulation is limited.

While social media may have played a role in forcing governments to reverse their positions in countries where Indigenous CSOs are able to develop a coherent and united campaign and to widely disseminate images of police violence, I found little evidence that Indigenous narratives have a significant impact on the virtual public sphere or that frames disseminated by Indigenous CSOs are acknowledged beyond their allies. State actors and mainstream media outlets not only failed to engage with Indigenous narratives over social media, they also used their own platforms to attack Indigenous political action and to frame it as a threat to stability and order. This aligns with research that demonstrates that, rather than attempting to censor dissent (a difficult task in the social media age), governments are using these tools to their own ends by attacking rivals, generating misinformation, and spreading conspiracy theories (Tufekci 2017). While Indigenous groups are not the only targets of government misinformation campaigns, they are particularly vulnerable to attack because powerful actors can use social media to generate "racial scripts" and create a sense of moral panic (Flores-Yeffal, Vidales, and Martinez 2019). Social media are used as a means of reproducing frames that reduce Indigenous actors by characterizing them as either dangerous mobs or as manipulated by enemies of the state (Raynauld, Richez, and Morris 2018). In this way, social media, like "traditional media," can be used as a mechanism for othering. Table 5.2 presents a comparative summary of the data collected from the content analysis, including the most common themes and most frequently used hashtags in social media content produced by Indigenous CSOs, state agencies, and media outlets.

TABLE 5.2 Comparative summary of social media content analysis

Actors	Posts/items analyzed	Framing of Indigenous collective action	Themes	Hashtags
Ecuador: January 10 to February 2, 2019 (Cotopaxi), October 1 to November 1, 2019 (nationwide)				
Indigenous CSOs	260	heroic, peaceful, democratic	Human rights, fighting exclusion and discrimination, historic struggle for territory and self-determination, state terrorism and repression, discursive defense of victims of state violence, Indigenous movement leading the resistance against unjust state, protesters as heroes, democracy, concerning all Ecuadorians	#DaysOfResistance #WeAreCONAIE #PeoplesPower #SOSEcuador
State agencies	380	illegal, dangerous, uncivil	Citizen security; public order; heroism of soldiers and police; government as just; vandalism and violence (of protesters) criminals, delinquents, and terrorists (protesters); state defending democracy, peace, order, Indigenous actors as aggressive and threating stability; Indigenous actors spread fake news; dangerous forces led by Venezuela, Cuba and Correa	#GovernmentForAll #Peace #DialogueForPeace #Democracy #SupportThePolice
Media	150	destructive, dangerous	Property damage and disruption of business; "excesses" of protesters; Indigenous protester violence and anger; comparison to guerrillas; downplaying completely police repression; protests as unorganized and irrational; participants manipulated by leftist actors, questioning Indigenous agency; counter march protesters as "citizens"; support for the police and military; protesters rarely interviewed	n/a

(continued)

TABLE 5.2 (*continued*)

Bolivia: August 1 to September 1, 2018 (TIPNIS), October 20, 2019, to November 20 (election aftermath)

Actors	Posts/items analyzed	Framing of Indigenous collective action	Themes	Hashtags
Indigenous CSOs	73	peaceful, democratic, antiracist	Indigenous CSOs associated with peaceful protest, democracy, political rights, indigeneity, anti-racism Right-wing opposition (later government) with racism, hate, violence, not respecting the indigenous vote, coup d'état	#HandsOffBolivia #EvoWeAreWithYou #WeAreThePeople #NoToTheCoup #StopTheMassacres #EnoughRacism
State agencies (interim regime)	559	destructive, dangerous, uncivil	MAS/Indigenous supporters as mercenaries, terrorists, delinquents, subversive groups, communists, evil, hordes, radical, dirty, violent New government restoring democracy. Supporters are citizens, brave, peaceful, democratic, heroic, defenders of society and of God/the Bible	#BoliviaUnited #EvoIsFraud #NotACoup #FreeBolivia #NewBolivia #ChristHasReturned
Media	636	destructive, dangerous, uncivil	Pro-MAS protesters "sympathizers of Evo", peasants' "invasion" of cities, vandalism Anti-MAS protests "citizen protests", heroic, images of Bolivian flags; pro-MAS protesters rarely interviewed	n/a

Chile: November 14 to December 31, 2018 (#Catrillanca), October 6 to November 30, 2019 (nationwide)

Indigenous CSOs	240	peaceful, democratic, just	Catrillanca not a criminal; justice for Catrillanca; Catrillanca as the latest of many victims of repression; ending military occupation; systematic violence against the Mapuche; murder; state police as violent and repressive; state terrorism; legitimate struggle for liberation; taking back territory; historic fight	#Catrillanca #Justice #Mapuche #NewConstitution #CarabinerosMurderers
State agencies	220	destructive, dangerous, uncivil, violent	Government as truthful and just; calls for peace; violence of Mapuche protesters, terrorism, heroic job of most Carabineros; Catrillanca killed by "bad apples", rights of Carabineros to defend themselves from attacks	#ChileMovingForward #ChileAllTogether #PlanAraucania #PeaceDevelopmentIn Araucanía #SafeStreets #ThankYouCarabineros
Media	234	destructive, dangerous, uncivil	Limited coverage. Hostility toward Mapuche in Araucanía conflict; defense of Carabineros, condemnation of 'bad apples'; Catrillanca killing as an anomaly; violence and excesses of protesters; protesters as delinquents and criminals; loss of business and property; focus on security; anger over destruction of statues of colonial figures; some focus on criminal past falsely attributed to Catrillanca	n/a

Note: Social media accounts of Indigenous CSOs and state agencies/politicians were analyzed. Online news sites of media outlets were analyzed.

6 Indigenous Civil Society in the Twenty-First Century

Looking Forward

∙∙∙

Indigenous peoples have developed a distinctive civil society characterized by a unique set of claims, a variety of organizations and structures that range from local governance mechanisms to social service provision, and the deployment of multiscalar positioning repertoires based on years of experience. Indigenous CSOs have retained or reinvented many traditional practices and integrated these into their tactical repertoires, such as turning to ancestral modes of production to support resource mobilization. An understanding of contemporary Indigenous civil society reveals the limitations inherent in the liberal categories of "civic" and "uncivic" collective action. In all three countries, we observe manifestations of the complex associational landscape that René Zavaleta (1990, 1986) referred to as the *sociedad abigarrada*. Although it takes on different forms across the three countries, the concept that Zavaleta developed to understand Bolivian society is discernable in the variegated social formations that characterize Indigenous civil society, and in the shifting, porous, and often strained relationships between state power and self-determination. But this landscape is not frozen in time. While some elements of Indigenous civil society continue to employ precapitalist structures and practices that remain disconnected from the state, these too have evolved and transformed in the twenty-first century. And at the same time, some Indigenous CSOs have integrated themselves into contemporary state-society interface mechanisms and have sought innovative ways to use digital technologies to pursue their goals.

Indigenous civil society is unique, complex, and in many ways distinct from non-Indigenous civil society. Some of these differences are related to Indigenous "ways of doing," such as participatory or communitarian decision making or distinctive public sphere spaces. Indigenous civil society has developed a broad array of institutions, such as citizen assemblies, that sometimes serve as parallel governments, particularly at the local level. Other unique characteristics include the community service-oriented nature of Indigenous civil society that often fills in gaps left by the state, the diversity of institutions and associational spaces and their ability to switch to protest mode during crises. Civic-minded service provision organizations can quickly transform into mechanisms for political participation or even channeling protest in the face of a crisis.

As this book demonstrates, Indigenous actors have continued to develop multiple, overlapping forms of participation since the end of the 1990–2005 protest cycle. This multiscalar positioning approach was formulated and masterminded by Indigenous civil society and entails an evolving reconfiguration of the structure and strategies of the Indigenous sphere. In part, this is due to the unique nature of Indigenous civil society itself, which provides strong mobilizing structures and identity constructs on which to build. More so than any other sector, Indigenous actors have relocated authority to the local level and disrupted state-centric views of citizenship and sovereignty. They do so by blending Indigenous and European worldviews, governance practices, institutions within the contested but real realm of Indigenous civil society. But they have also developed a distinct relationship with the virtual world that includes experimenting with ICTs without depending on them and continuing to strengthen the structures and strategies that have served them well in the recent past.

Political Opportunities, Citizenship Regimes, and Mobilizing Structures

The presence or absence of certain conditions determines the ability of groups to mobilize and the relative success or failure of mobilization (Tarrow 1998). These conditions include the openness of the political system, the stability of political alignments, the presence of supporters or divisions within the elites, the capacity or willingness of the state to use repression, and the existence of allies at the international level (Brysk 2000; Tarrow 1998). Organizations calculate their approach based on what is available to them and what they believe will be most effective; marginalized actors are likely to engage in disruptive action because other access points are closed to them (McCarthy 1996; Piven and Cloward 1977). This explains the 1990 marches in both Bolivia and Ecuador, which drew on large-scale disruption to force governments to listen.

But this calculation also helps us to understand why tactical repertoires evolved during the Pink Tide period in Bolivia and Ecuador but less so in Chile. By the late 2000s, CSOs in Bolivia and Ecuador had gained valuable experience and political skill (which are important resources in their own right) and had pried open windows of political opportunity. This means that they were in a position to use a wider range of tactics and no longer had to rely uniquely on disruptive action. Mapuche CSOs did not have access to the same opportunities and resources, and so disruptive action remained the dominant approach to pursuing their goals, although with time this is slowly evolving. It is worth recalling Suh's (2001) argument that political opportunities also depend on how actors perceive them and the extent to which the actors attribute success to their own actions. Bolivian and Ecuadorian CSOs made significant tangible gains during the 1990s and up to the adoption of new constitutions in the late 2000s. These victories served to empower and embolden CSOs and to provide them with confidence required to expand and diversify their tactical repertoires. And if opportunity is only important when actors perceive it as such, then we can also understand why Mapuche CSOs encouraged supporters to join the uprisings against the right-wing Piñera government in late 2019. They viewed this moment as a chance to transform the image that Chileans have of the Mapuche and to shift the narrative about state security and social rights.

Yashar (2005) argues that the shift from a corporatist to a neoliberal citizenship regime in the two Andean republics encouraged mobilization by simultaneously expanding associational space while restricting access points to the state. Her arguments regarding the role of citizenship still hold; withdrawal of social rights provides part of the answer for why Indigenous CSOs in Bolivia and Ecuador engaged in large-scale mobilization in 2019 after more than a decade of preferring a less confrontational approach. New governments in these two countries began to dismantle the postneoliberal regimes established by their predecessors. As flawed as these new citizenship regimes may have been, they did expand social rights in ways that had a positive impact on people's standard of living (Calderón and Castells 2020). Attempts to reverse these reforms provided an incentive for Indigenous peoples to mobilize in both countries, but also angered non-Indigenous working-class actors in Ecuador, where Indigenous civil society was relatively united and was able to tap into public disaffection.

The research presented in this book also raises another important question about what motivates people to mobilize and to seek cross-sectoral alliances. In Ecuador and Bolivia, social citizenship was expanded during the Pink Tide years. This created expectations both within Indigenous communities and across popular sectors. We also witnessed a tension between social rights on the one hand, and political or civil rights on the other. This tension dominated the Pink Tide era from Venezuela to Bolivia and Ecuador; leftist governments intent on implementing "twenty-first-century socialism" adopted increasingly authoritarian tactics in order to push through the types of changes they believed were necessary. They maintained popular support in spite of the curtailment of civil rights as long as social investment continued to improve people's quality of life and access to services. It wasn't until 2019, when new governments began to withdraw social rights, that Indigenous CSOs returned to large-scale mobilization.

In Chile, social citizenship was never extended in the first place. But the scale of the 2019 uprisings, which were ignited by anger over socioeconomic inequality, showed Mapuche CSOs that they had allies in Chilean civil society. They jumped on board in an effort to expand social citizenship and political rights through a new constitution. In all three countries, social citizenship was at the heart of the 2019 uprisings, either because socioeconomic rights were perceived as being under attack (in Ecuador and Bolivia) or because actors sought to seize an opportunity to push for their expansion (Chile).

Many Indigenous leaders I spoke to expressed sorrow that young people in particular have become more individualistic and less attached to their roots. They generally attributed this to globalization and argued that there has been a gradual shift over the past two generations. Increasingly, people are more likely to mobilize and connect with other sectors around social rights and material issues rather than for civil or political rights. In part, this is because Indigenous and popular sector actors can agree on social rights, but political and civil rights for Indigenous peoples are distinct and therefore more contentious.

This reminds us that while identity is important, we should not abandon an understanding of the role material grievances play in mobilization. In any case, Indigenous leaders are perfectly capable of adapting their discourse and tactical repertoires to respond to what motivates their communities. In fact, the 2019 protests demonstrate that Indigenous CSOs in all three countries have done just that. In Ecuador and Chile, their calls to action over social media were largely oriented toward socioeconomic equality and their frames were tailored to align with non-Indigenous lower-income sectors. In Bolivia, Indigenous CSOs started by focusing on what they believed to be an illegal coup d'état, but pro-MAS organizations increasingly began to orient their discourse toward socioeconomic issues and the interim government's reversal of the postneoliberal project.

Evolution and Forms of Multiscalar Positioning

Comparing cases within and across these three countries tells us quite a bit about the conditions that enhance or hinder the ability of Indigenous CSOs to achieve their goals. Alliances between Indigenous CSOs and with other sectors of civil society expand political opportunities and support the development of strong mobilizing structures. Indigenous organizations in Ecuador and Bolivia were strongest when they were able to put aside differences and work together.

Ideally this solidarity is built on more than informal alliances but rather on a coherent structure that can provide direction and leadership, particularly in times of crisis. The literature supports this; social movements that are too diffuse and lack leadership are less likely to have a significant impact on the public sphere than those that have developed strong, well-organized CSOs. The remarkable ability of disparate Indigenous actors in Ecuador to form a united front in times of crisis and to work under the auspices of CONAIE is the clearest example of this. Indigenous civil society in Ecuador boasts a comprehensive political system that functions like a parallel state yet encourages bottom-up participation. Its highly democratic structure reflects the need for regional representation and accountability. It includes a strong organization at the top of the pyramid and three large and integrated CSOs that represent the country's regions, each of which works with provincial organizations. These in turn network with local associations. This structure, which is unique in Latin America, allows for a level of coordination not available to Indigenous groups in other countries. The system allowed Indigenous actors in Ecuador to take control of the protest movement against the Moreno administration, to mobilize and coordinate the actions of tens of thousands of supporters, to achieve a significant victory by forcing the government to back down, and to demonstrate the political skill of Indigenous leaders.

The lack of such a unified front in Bolivia by the end of 2019 led to a fractured Indigenous movement in which leaders worked at cross purposes. This allowed both the MAS and the right-wing interim government to divide, and therefore weaken the movement. This does not mean that pro-MAS CSOs were not able to mobilize supporters. In November 2019 and well into 2020, Indigenous activists managed to severely disrupt the country's economy by blocking roads and essential infrastructure. But Áñez, well aware of the hostility between pro- and anti-MAS CSOs, was able to use these divisions to frame her opponents as violent *masistas* in contrast to the "peaceful," civil-society organizations that did not take to the streets in support of Morales.

The fragmentation of Mapuche civil society has allowed the Chilean state to use this same strategy against more contentious CSOs. The lack of higher-level mobilizing structure makes it difficult for leaders to develop coherent and unified collective action strategies. But Lucero and García (2007) argue that evaluating the "success" of collective action on the ability to achieve a degree of national unity may divert our attention from the influence that regional organizations can develop in their respective territories. They also suggest alternative ways of assessing the impact of Indigenous collective action, including identity, scale, and tactics. And while Mapuche CSOs have not managed to achieve the scale of their counterparts in the other two countries, they have constructed a unique Mapuche national identity that challenges the geography of the colonial state itself. This is in contrast to the universal, generic, and increasingly deterritorialized Indigenous identity constructed by the larger CSOs in Bolivia and Ecuador. This Indigenous cosmopolitanism, as Canessa (2014) calls it, seeks to accommodate difference but may in fact exclude peripheral Indigenous peoples. The concrete outcomes achieved to varying degrees by Indigenous civil society in Bolivia and Ecuador have been more elusive for the Mapuche. Yet while Bolivian and Ecuadorian CSOs have achieved many tangible policy outcomes, identity is more fragmented than in Wallmapu. And as we have seen, Mapuche CSOs have used ICTs to promote identity and culture in dynamic and unique ways. The events of 2019, and the participation of prominent Mapuche actors in the 2021–22 constitutional reform process, suggest that they are also gaining experience in using them as part of their tactical repertoire to engage in the Chilean public sphere. While Chilean media and the state still tend to associate Indigenous collective action with sabotage and violence, this does not reflect reality. More and more CSOs are using a more diverse multiscalar positioning strategy that involves everything from a cultural renaissance (using ICTs) to drawing on international law. Some are engaging with new state institutions. From the killing of a young Mapuche activist in 2018 to their participation in the cross-sector uprising of 2019 and the Constituent Assembly, there is evidence that they have started to successfully deploy a counterhegemonic narrative and that at least some Chileans are listening.

Alliances with other sectors of civil society also help to expand political opportunities. Indigenous-led initiatives during the period studied in this book were most successful when CSOs were able to reach beyond core constituencies and frame issues in a way that resonates with other sectors. The ability of CONAIE and its allies to capture and channel the anger of working-class actors in Ecuador allowed it to gain considerable cross-sector support. Likewise, the efforts of some Mapuche CSOs to associate their experience with the violence directed against non-Indigenous protesters, and to align their calls for social citizenship with a broader movement, provided them with a high degree of visibility during the 2019 protests. In both cases, social media helped Indigenous CSOs to challenge state discourse and to disseminate their own narrative. In the case of Bolivia, pro-MAS CSOs had worked so closely with the state for over a decade that many had come to rely more on the party than on external allies. In some ways, the MAS and its affiliated CSOs sealed themselves off and created an adversarial relationship with other sectors, including some Indigenous CSOs. This left them isolated when power shifted. As a result, they had trouble finding allies willing to support them once the MAS's grip on the state was challenged.

As is often the case in politics, CSOs can be victims of their own success, and some may attribute the relative decline in protest to co-optation. Alvarez and her colleagues (2017) are critical of what they call the "civil society agenda," which involves the appropriation and depoliticization of social movements to produce disciplined citizen-subjects through integration of actors into the state. According to this view, civil society serves as a space where citizens willingly inherit some of the responsibilities the state has downloaded on to them through neoliberal restructuring (Baiocchi 2017). Finding the right balance between participation and co-optation is a challenge but it is also important to be critical of perspectives that associate Indigenous collective action with the latter. Elite or middle-class sectors working with the state and securing concessions is often seen as demonstrating the capacity of "civic" civil society to make government responsive to their demands (Junge 2017). When marginalized sectors do the same, it is often framed as co-option, with the underlying assumption that they have uncritically given up autonomy in exchange for handouts.

But these assumptions overlook how sophisticated Indigenous CSOs have become, as well as the experience and political shrewdness of their leaders. Most are keenly aware of the civil society agenda (although they would not use that term) and while they are not always successful, they have learned how to navigate this terrain. Furthermore, we have seen in previous chapters that it is problematic to assume that CSOs become depoliticized as they take on more of the state's responsibilities. In Indigenous communities, service provision and *trabajo en territorio* are not apolitical, nor do these roles necessarily represent co-optation. For one thing, Indigenous CSOs frequently see community service as a long-term means of building political engagement and loyalty. Furthermore, the same organizations used to deliver services can be quickly transformed into mobilizing structures or can lend support to more politically oriented CSOs during protest events. This happened in all three countries in late 2019. "Civic" CSOs worked with politically oriented social movement organizations to disseminate calls to action, information, and political messages to their communities.

The relationship that developed between social movements and the MAS was far more equal and "push and pull" than a "civil society agenda" assessment would account for. Assuming that CSOs that work closely with the MAS have been uncritically incorporated into the party is condescending and does not reflect reality. The CSOs that I worked with were not only able to maintain a critical stance toward the government but were able to exert considerable pressure on the policy process. This is not co-option; it reflects the strength of CSOs and is the result of decades of political experience. That said, close integration into state-society mechanisms, particularly when that state is dominated by a single party (as with the MAS), may provide CSOs with influence for a time but can become a weakness when that party no longer holds power. Indigenous CSOs in Ecuador created their own parallel government-like institutions, while many in Bolivia integrated their structures into the MAS state, and this influence collapsed when the MAS was temporarily removed from power. But Indigenous CSOs are built on a strong foundation and have considerable experience to draw on. They were able to quickly to reorient themselves to focus on extrainstitutional strategies after fifteen years of working through institutional channels.

Multiscalar positioning, which Indigenous CSOs have pioneered, includes participating in disruption (outside, but sometimes from the inside), state institutions (inside, while keeping a foot outside), service provision and *trabajo en territorio* (which often has a political dimension), participatory mechanisms that straddle institutional and extrainstitutional participation, and the virtual world (not really inside or outside, everywhere and nowhere). Local (municipal) politics is also important as an area of Indigenous participation, and given the devolved nature of some Indigenous local governments, this cannot be defined as either inside or outside. How does one categorize the Bolivian *ayllu*, which is based on traditional communitarian governance practices but is acknowledged by the state, or the Indigenous communal council in Ecuador that receives state recognition as a decentralized local government but incorporates uniquely local ways of doing?

Multiscalar positioning also includes reaching out to and engaging with non-Indigenous sectors by promoting mutual demands or framing Indigenous demands in ways that resonate with other sectors. The strategic ebbs and flows are based on mobilizing resources, political opportunities, and threats to citizenship and social rights. But successful Indigenous groups have learned how and when their tactics need to be adjusted, and they are engaging in ongoing, sustained work outside of protest cycles.

Unlike many non-Indigenous civil society groups, Indigenous organizations have retained the ability to disrupt. But even during the 2019 uprisings, their leaders drew not only on extrainstitutional tactics but also on constitutional rights and the citizenship regime established in the late 2000s to support their arguments. They also demonstrated the skill and experience they had acquired over the preceding decades as civil society actors capable of deploying a multifaceted approach to collective action.

ICTs and Balance of Power

Throughout this book, we have seen that in the twentieth century, Indigenous civil-society actors pioneered the use of technologies such as radio and video for self-representation and political action. These ICTs were used to counter hegemonic discourse produced by mainstream media, to reclaim spaces in the public sphere, to promote identity, to mobilize communities, and to produce and disseminate critical pedagogy. Research suggests that these experiences were largely positive (Ginsburg 1991, 2000; Salazar 2002, 2011; Turner 1992, 1995, 2002). The impact of twenty-first-century technologies such as social media on the capacity of Indigenous actors to achieve their goals is far more complicated.

The ubiquity of ICTs and social media is the most significant difference between the late twentieth-century protest cycle and the political landscape that Indigenous organizations must navigate going forward. These technologies affect CSOs' resource mobilization capacity and political opportunities, and they play a key role in how they participate in politics, communicate, promote identity, and mobilize supporters. According to Calderón and Castells (2020), these changes are intertwined with a broader societal shift toward individualization and the relative decline of collectivism and traditional structures. This, they believe, is redefining values and identities, especially among youth, who are products of a new culture of "technosociability" that fosters fluid individual identities and relocates political participation to the web. But like others, they apply their analysis to Latin America without taking into account the distinct features of Indigenous civil society.

The evidence presented in this book suggests that ICTs have both a positive and a negative impact on Indigenous civil society. Indigenous CSOs gained momentum in the final decades of the twentieth century based on their success at uniting different groups through the promotion of a sense of collective identity, their capacity to build on existing structures and mobilize resources, their experience with defending social citizenship, and their ability to take advantage of new political opportunities. Social media and other ICTs support these activities in some ways and hinder them in others.

Perhaps the most significant potential outcome of using the Internet for the purpose of selling products and services is political autonomy. Relying on state or NGO subsidies limits organizations' autonomy and puts them at a disadvantage vis-à-vis both government departments and privately funded groups that do not depend on public funding. Increasing business opportunities by promoting Indigenous products, services, and experiences to a worldwide audience is a means of gaining revenue to replace external subsidies, and this should in turn decrease dependence on outsiders. None of this suggests that Indigenous organizations are well resourced. Competing with powerful actors on this front remains a struggle, but these strategies at least provide a degree of independence.

Calderón and Castells (2020) write that new technologies have completely transformed the public sphere, creating new networked spaces that allow for the representation of more diverse interests and alternative voices. The research presented in this book suggests that ICTs allow Indigenous actors to perform, represent, debate, and reconceptualize indigeneity in new and innovative ways. They provide tools for cultural positioning and survival, for countering essentialized understandings of indigeneity, as well as for new expressions of culture and identity. Having a social media presence can allow Indigenous actors to tell their stories without an intermediary, promote their activities and join conversations beyond their communities.

But this matters only if there is an audience willing to receive, interpret, internalize, and reproduce these messages. According to Indigenous representatives in countries such as Bolivia and Ecuador, many individuals in their communities are still unable to benefit from the products of these efforts. It may be that Indigenous organizations are increasingly reaching international audiences through social media, which may help CSOs to develop political capital and support. But if the development and reproduction of a strong sense of ethnic identity among disparate Indigenous peoples is key to sustaining a strong civil society, and ICTs have become central to identity promotion, Indigenous CSOs must also be able to engage with their own communities and with domestic audiences. My analysis of social media during the 2019 protests suggests that content produced by Indigenous CSOs was either ignored or contested by government and media actors. Indigenous collective action continues to be framed as dangerous and threatening, despite positive messages disseminated by CSOs over social media. While ICTs allow Indigenous actors to produce content on their own terms, they do not necessarily have the resources to compete with well-financed, powerful actors.

The current political opportunity structure in Latin America does not facilitate the use of ICTs by Indigenous civil society. Many organizations identify threats including cyber surveillance and the spread of misinformation designed to discredit Indigenous communities or frame them as threats to national security. There was variation between the three countries, but a majority of interviewees in each jurisdiction expressed these concerns. Latin American governments have different capacities with respect to cybersecurity but there is a clear trend emerging. Governments are spending significant sums of money to purchase and maintain security software, including surveillance systems, biometric data and identification registries, CCTV, and drones. State intelligence agencies appear to be using these technologies without regard for the law or constitutional provisions (Scott-Railton et al. 2015).

Social media may expand certain capabilities for Indigenous CSOs but, as Tufekci (2017) and Larson (2019) argue, governments have learned how to respond and have adapted their own tactical repertoires, sometimes borrowing from CSOs. Rather than traditional censorship, they muddy the waters with a glut of information and spread false information, confusion, harassment, intimidation, and abuse, frequently directed against minority groups. They can also use social media to mobilize their own supporters against challengers.

Indigenous organizations generally lack the technical expertise and resources to detect and counter espionage and cyberattacks, which narrows the opportunities available to them. This should be seen as yet another factor in the digital divide. ICTs may reinforce marginalized actors' position of vulnerability, exposing them to threats in ways that they may not have anticipated. This concern is exacerbated in commodity-rich regions where Indigenous organizations are in conflict with the state and powerful private interests. While social media may in theory provide a means for Indigenous peoples to make their voices heard, there remains an imbalance with respect to political opportunities between those with the power, skills, and resources to develop expensive online campaigns free from state surveillance and those who do not.

The range of affordances available through twenty-first-century digital technologies is vastly different from those associated with ICTs that Indigenous actors used successfully in the recent past. Affordances are the properties of technologies that determine how they can be used by individuals, or the "mutuality of actor intentions and technology capabilities that provide the potential for a particular action" (Faraj and Azad 2012). An affordance lens therefore helps us to understand the relationship between technology and its users (Majchrzak et al. 2013). Social media affordances include visibility, editability, and associations between people and information (Treem and Leonardi 2013). The bidirectional, interactive nature of social media—the ability to engage in ongoing conversations by reacting online to others—is a key affordance that distinguishes it from earlier technologies (Majchrzak et al. 2013). These affordances interact with how Indigenous CSOs are able to use twenty-first-century technologies for critical tasks such as identity promotion, political participation, and mobilization. We have seen that in some circumstances, such as during the 2019 protests in Ecuador, Indigenous activists were able to use these features to their advantage by engaging with domestic and international audiences in real time to call attention to state repression. The activities, tasks and connections that social media facilitates stand in sharp contrast to the more unidirectional, managed, and insulated affordances of radio and video.

The interactive nature of social media is an opportunity and a threat. It allows for the expression of voice that goes well beyond the limited reach of community radio. A small, rural CSO, assuming it has access and skills to use social media effectively, can interact with members that have migrated to the cities or abroad. It can also promote its culture to audiences around the world. Bidirectional communication should support the (re)construction of a sense of community and dialogue. But this interactivity also has a downside, as powerful actors are able to interrupt, challenge and misinterpret Indigenous voices, in some cases before these messages are able to reach their intended audiences. State agencies and business interests can hire skilled communications specialists to neutralize Indigenous narratives in real time. The evidence I presented from the 2019–20 uprisings suggests that the success of such efforts depends on a number of factors, including CSOs' ICT-related resource mobilization capacity, political opportunities, and how they negotiate identity. In Ecuador, relatively well-resourced CONAIE was able to outmaneuver the state by drawing on its experience with and access to ICTs, public dissatisfaction with the government, and its ability to align Indigenous with working-class grievances. In Bolivia, the relative absence of these advantages allowed hostile actors to use social media against Indigenous civil society, effectively shutting them out of a virtual world dominated by the urban middle class and right-wing elites.

When the infrastructure and knowhow are in place, digital media affordances can recreate communities and build a virtual public sphere in ways that radio could not do. The Mapuche have excelled at this through the creation of Mapudungun language classes, cultural exhibits, and even virtual worlds that allow young Mapuche in Santiago to experience their homeland by "visiting" Wallmapu. But these tools also facilitate connections well beyond Indigenous civil society. They allow young Indigenous people in particular to immerse themselves in a globalized, Western culture to an extent that would have been impossible in the recent past. Loss of identity among youth was one of the greatest concerns among interviewees (including youth leaders). Many of them claim that ways of thinking are changing rapidly, that political and social action is becoming more individualized, that engagement with the community is wavering, and that these changes have an impact on organizations' ability to mobilize. Even when Indigenous CSOs are able to use digital technologies to construct Indigenous spaces, they cannot compete with the types of cultural offerings produced by U.S. and other foreign conglomerates. Many Indigenous leaders I spoke to stressed the ongoing importance of community radio as a medium through which they can create a counterhegemonic space free of foreign influences. Yet they lament that young people who have access to social media and the Internet are less likely to tune in.

In contrast to messages produced by unidirectional media such as radio and video, social media allow state actors, extractive industries, and right-wing political parties to manipulate and interfere in Indigenous online public spheres. They do so by using their resources to overpower Indigenous voices, creating fake profiles and disseminating misinformation. Misinformation existed long before the advent of social media. Private and state actors regularly used legacy media to attack Indigenous civil society, but it was clear where the information was coming from. Social media makes it more difficult to know who is behind a given message. We have seen, for example, attempts to discredit Indigenous leaders by impersonating them online and to discourage mobilization by exaggerating the numbers of casualties or by generating confusion about calls to action. While Indigenous CSOs do use ICTs to mobilize supporters, they continue to rely on radio because their communities know that this is a trusted source of information.

The state has always had the capacity to regulate ICTs and all three countries have attempted to censor community radio. But everyone understood that radio was a public medium, and that messages broadcast were monitored by government agencies. With social media and digital platforms, it is not clear who is listening. While social media expand possibilities for collaboration, Indigenous actors are very aware of the capacity of state agencies to spy on online activities, and of their own inability to detect and disrupt cyber espionage. Social media affordances therefore simultaneously expand and limit how Indigenous CSOs are able to use these platforms for their work. These affordances are not available to all actors in the same ways. Well-resourced state and private actors, with their vast networks, their armies of communications specialists (and trolls), and their access to monitoring systems, can benefit from the capabilities of digital tools while interfering with the ability of less powerful actors to do the same.

But the full picture is more complex than a digital "haves versus have-nots" binary can account for. We must also interrogate the literature on social media and twenty-first-century "networked" politics in light of this book's findings. If social media is replacing "on the ground" mobilization, if digital inequality remains a fact of life in Indigenous communities, and if the state and other powerful actors are better positioned to take advantage of ICTs, have Indigenous CSOs lost some of the advantages they had in late twentieth century? Or do they enjoy certain advantages that the networked movements lack?

The networked movements literature fails to capture the evolving and unique nature of Indigenous civil society. Indigenous actors in the 2010s challenge the distinction between "new" and "old" forms of collective action. We need to integrate Indigenous experiences into the social movement and social media research, as these can make important theoretical contributions to this growing body of literature. Indigenous movements do not fit into the diffuse, nonsituated, tech-savvy model described in a growing number of studies on collective action in the Internet age. Indigenous CSOs use ICTs but look nothing like the "networked" movements identified by Castells, Tufekci, and others. ICTs are a part of the tactical repertoire of Indigenous civil society organizations but they are not at the heart of their strategies. Some of the greatest strengths of Indigenous civil society (strong organizations, community decision-making mechanisms, experienced leaders, the need for in-person contact, ethnic identity) seem to clash with the "networked" characteristics that many authors believe define "new movements" that are largely ICT-enabled. Yet Indigenous CSOs are thoroughly modern despite a (relatively) limited reliance on ICTs and social media. This is another unique characteristic of Indigenous civil society and should compel us to challenge the very notion of what "modern" collective action looks like. Indigenous CSOs demonstrate that by not becoming fully "networked" movements, and by adapting and updating "traditional" tactics that made them strong in the past, they have a lot to teach us about engaging in politics. They can in fact reveal some of the weakness of the "networked" movements.

When I first visited Ecuador and Bolivia in 2009, most Indigenous activists I met used very basic cellphones. A handful of larger organizations had static websites, but few used social media to engage in the public sphere. This was evolving rapidly by the time I began the fieldwork presented in this book. Almost all of the Indigenous organizations I worked with recognized the importance of the Internet and social media for supporting their work, but none of the organizations I encountered could be considered part of a "networked movement." Bennett (2014) labels collective action that relies on centralized coordination and community organizing as "old-fashioned," but does not being "networked" mean that organizations have not evolved or that they are somehow less "modern" than those that are "born digital"? This book demonstrates that this is certainly not the case. There are profound differences between Indigenous organizations and the types of networked movements described as the new face of political struggle. Some of these may be identified as potential weaknesses, but others are in fact strengths. Indigenous CSOs have evolved and matured while using technology to the extent possible but they have not become engulfed by it.

Technology alters the landscape in which state-civil society interaction takes place, but it is never the only factor that shapes the power dynamic. As Tufekci (2017) points out, the strength of social movements lies in their narrative, disruptive, and electoral capacities. But capacity also includes collective strategizing and deploying the right tactics on an ongoing basis. Many of the strengths of Indigenous movements are based on place, human contact, strong organizations, leadership, and the importance of traditional practices, the very components that "new" movements downplay. The relatively limited use of digital technologies by Indigenous CSOs does not reflect a rejection of "modernity." They are perfectly willing to use digital tools when they support a task but not when they fundamentally alter important and proven ways of doing things. Traditional collective action tactics have worked in the past, and leaders rightly do not want to abandon these to orient their activities around unproven technologies. Rather, digital technologies, when and where they are available to Indigenous CSOs, are seen as complementing rather than replacing their growing tactical repertoire.

Tufekci (2017) agrees that even for the new networked movements, ICTs and social media are not everything. Successful movements must be built on something else, including structures and tactical experience. Indigenous movements already have that "something else" in place: a complex, evolving architecture of "real" organizations, strong leadership combined with participatory practices, a wide array of tactics developed over decades, and a capacity for tactical innovation. In many ways, their collective action is more sophisticated, and certainly more multiscalar, than those that are born digital. They encompass a range of the "old" but proven, and the "new" and operate at various, overlapping scales. Western activists could learn a great deal from Indigenous civil society in Latin America.

The Path Ahead: Right-Wing Resurgence, COVID-19, and Economic Crisis

At the time of this writing, the political situation in Latin America is extremely fluid. For one thing, the COVID-19 pandemic continues to have a profound economic, political, and social impact. In Bolivia and Chile, far-right movements embrace xenophobia, racism, and a nostalgia for the authoritarian military regimes of the 1970s. These forces are inspired and enabled by the likes of Brazilian president Jair Bolsonaro and former U.S. president Donald Trump. But in the Latin American context, their hostility takes on a particularly anti-Indigenous tone.

By mid-2020, it was clear that COVID-19 was not an equal-opportunity pandemic. Indigenous peoples, who remain among the most marginalized population groups in the region, are affected by two important dimensions of the pandemic: unequal access to health care and the measures implemented by governments to contain the virus. During our follow-up interviews, many participants expressed concern about the health, social protection, and civil rights dimensions of the pandemic. Indigenous peoples in the three countries tend to have limited access to health care at the best of times, and several communities were already suffering the effects of over-burdened hospitals and lack of medication. Leaders and Elders like Salomé, whom we met in chapter 2, said that their friends and families were forced to choose between their work—which often involves close contact with others—and putting food on the table. The limited benefits offered by their governments were barely enough to buy a month's groceries for a small family, much less pay the rent. Several of Salomé's friends, who earn their living selling food in streets and plazas, were fined for being in public spaces while others had gotten sick from COVID-19. And interviewees in the three countries argued that COVID-19 was used as a pretext to quash protest throughout 2020 and 2021.

But Indigenous CSOs are flexible and are accustomed to adapting to changing circumstances. Many organizations, particularly local ones, had shifted their efforts to enhancing their *trabajo en territorio* efforts by supporting community members in need. Their well-developed *autogestión* resource mobilization strategies have served them well during the pandemic. Communities are exchanging food for clothing, or pooling resources to ensure that basic needs are met. The larger CSOs continue to engage in politics, although their ability to mobilize is limited by public health measures. But this has not stopped them from pursuing the multiscalar positioning approach developed throughout the 2010s.

In Bolivia, the discourse and actions of the unelected Áñez regime demonstrate that rather than engaging in a process of renewal, the Bolivian right remains dedicated to excluding Indigenous voices from government. Equally disturbing for pro- and anti-MAS Indigenous organizations was the regime's apparent determination to reverse many of the gains they had achieved during Morales's mandate. Beyond retrenchment of social rights, many of the most prominent actors and parties on the Bolivian right, primarily based in the Media Luna departments, reproduce the racist discourse that has permeated Bolivian society from the colonial era to the present. Hostility toward the MAS and its leaders is tinged with resentment toward Indigenous peoples and a rejection of being governed by them. These groups became emboldened once Morales was removed from power and they engaged in unprovoked attacks against Indigenous CSOs and communities.

According to Indigenous leaders I spoke to in 2020, Áñez and members of her cabinet enabled and tacitly supported violence against Indigenous peoples. Her government's supporters engaged in performances that include burning the colorful wiphala flag, a symbol of Indigenous identity that had been embraced by the Morales administration. Indigenous interviewees agreed that far-right sectors have become emboldened, and most have witnessed physical or verbal violence since the November 2019 coup. The offices of one of the CSOs I had worked with was vandalized with racist graffiti days before I spoke to its leader on the phone. In the Media Luna, interviewees witnessed an increase in acts of violence committed by members of the Santa Cruz Youth Union (Unión Juvenil Cruceñista, UJC), a fascist movement that regularly targets Indigenous citizens. While anti-Indigenous racism is nothing new, Indigenous leaders did not hesitate to connect contemporary events to a broader worldwide trend. Some of the Indigenous CSOs speculated that their role may shift to defending their communities against racist violence.

When fresh elections were held in October 2020, Bolivians delivered a decisive rebuke to the right-wing actors who had seized power nearly a year earlier. Morales's former economy minister Luis Arce was elected with 55 percent of the vote and the MAS secured majorities in both chambers of the Plurinational Legislative Assembly. This should provide opportunities for pro-MAS CSOs to resume the institutional action side of their multiscalar positioning strategy, but one hopes it will allow Arce, seen as more conciliatory and pragmatic than Morales, to rebuild relationships with peripheral sectors of Indigenous civil society.

In April 2021, Ecuadorians elected conservative banker Guillermo Lasso as their new president. Lasso, a staunch neoliberal, narrowly defeated former Correa cabinet minister Andrés Arauz. The Pachakutik party's candidate, a Kichwa environmental lawyer, university professor, and former ECUARUNARI president called Yaku Pérez, came in third following the first round in February of the same year. His relatively conservative economic proposals, and the support of some Indigenous actors for Lasso over Arauz, demonstrate the homogeneity of Indigenous civil society despite CSOs' ability to unite in the face of a crisis. While Ecuador has not experienced the rise of far-right groups like the UJC, and Indigenous CSOs earned respect among working-class sectors in 2019, interviewees were quick to point out that their communities are victims of violence from the state and from private actors, especially in resource-rich areas. Most argued that the result of the presidential elections will not change much for Indigenous Ecuadorians but insisted that their CSOs will be ready to fight any attempts to withdraw political or social rights. Given Lasso's ideological proclivities, he has used the economic crisis exacerbated by COVID-19 to pursue his neoliberal agenda and to deepen the cuts imposed by his predecessor. This has generated conflict with both Indigenous and non-Indigenous civil society. In June 2022, CONAIE and its allies launched a new series of protests and a national strike that destabilized the country and led Lasso to declare a state of emergency.

During my fieldwork, Mapuche participants expressed concern about the rise of far-right politicians such as José Antonio Kast. Their fears were not unfounded; Kast took the lead in the first round of the 2021 general election. A member of the Chamber of Deputies from 2002 to 2018, he openly expresses admiration for the Pinochet dictatorship and made the Mapuche conflict one of the central themes of his presidential campaign, promising to "restore order." Kast is from the Araucanía and has deliberately cultivated an acrimonious relationship with the region's large Mapuche population. He exacerbated this situation by supporting the Carabineros following the killing of Catrillanca. Mapuche leaders I spoke to label him as the "Chilean Bolsonaro" in reference to the racist, far-right views he shares with the Brazilian president. Despite a tight race, Kast was decisively defeated by Gabriel Boric, a progressive former student leader who assumed the presidency in March 2022. The Araucanía voted heavily in favor of Kast, which suggests that the new president will have little support from the region's non-Indigenous majority. Boric, who initiated his victory speech by greeting supporters in Mapudungun, has pledged to respect the rights of Indigenous peoples and to pursue reconciliation with the Mapuche. He will have to seek a balance between working closely with moderate Mapuche civil society and maintaining peace in Araucanía while avoiding repression against the dissidents he has vowed to respect. Yet in May 2022, just two months after his government initiated a military withdrawl process, Boric declared a state of emergency in the Araucanía and redeployed soldiers to the region. This reversal followed a series of roadblocks and arson attacks carried out by groups such as CAM. Mapuche CSOs that reject these tactics and participated in the Constituent Assembly worry that these developments will undermine support for the new draft constitution which, if accepted by voters, would confer unprecedented rights on Indigenous peoples in Chile.

And there have been other disturbing developments in the Araucanía. On June 4, 2020, Mapuche leader Alejandro Treuquil was shot and killed days after denouncing police violence against his community to the National Institute of Human Rights. In August 2020, groups of right-wing extremists violently attacked Mapuche protesters who had peacefully occupied mayoral offices in four Araucanía municipalities to demand the release of individuals they identified as political prisoners. The attackers, coordinated by the far-right Association for Peace and Reconciliation of Araucanía (Asociación por la Paz y la Reconciliación de la Araucanía, APRA), hurled racist insults and beat the protesters with sticks and stones. An APRA spokeswoman took to Twitter to call on the people of her region to "rise up against the Mapuche" (Jofré 2020). Witnesses affirm that the Carabineros stood by and allowed the attacks to proceed, even though a COVID-19 curfew was supposed to be in effect. Participants insisted that this is in spite of the fact that Carabineros had previously broken up Mapuche demonstrations due to the public health orders. Isolated attacks by groups of citizens against Mapuche communities appeared to be intensifying throughout 2021 and 2022. Like some of their counterparts in Bolivia, CAM, ATM and other CSOs told us that they are currently refocusing their efforts on developing defense measures. While Indigenous and popular sector movements in Bolivia and Ecuador will likely spend the next decade fighting to maintain their gains, those in Wallmapu will be working to transform Chile's political institutions. The constitutional reform process presented an opportunity for Indigenous peoples to finally be recognized in the state's supreme law. President Boric and his team pledged that the new constitution would recognize the rights of Indigenous peoples. They faced ferocious opposition from the right, and Mapuche CSOs that reject the authority of the Chilean state stayed out of the process. Mapuche leaders who seek greater autonomy within Chile sought to cooperate with each other and with allies in Chilean civil society. The result is a new draft constitution that for the first time in the country's history defines Chile as a plurinational state, recognizes Indigenous peoples, and incorporates key demands such as land claims.

Prospects

In the coming years, CSOs will have to reorient their strategies once again. On the one hand, those in Bolivia and Ecuador will be fighting to retain hard-won gains while continuing to push demands that have not yet been realized. Those in Chile will continue the struggle for rights they never had to begin with. At the time of this writing, the political opportunity structure is not particularly favorable. The global political climate is marked by a wave of xenophobic, right-wing populist sentiment that has trickled into Latin America. Many leaders express concern about governments using excessive and extrajudicial force to enforce quarantines and curfews. They worry that COVID-19 will continue to be used as a pretext by authoritarian leaders to cement their grip on power, and that restrictive measures become the "new normal" as a means of quashing dissent.

As of 2022, Indigenous civil society in Ecuador has maintained a comprehensive and coherent structure and a unified front despite differences between individual CSOs. This has allowed prominent Indigenous CSOs to adopt a leadership role, uniting popular sectors in contesting efforts of the government to reverse social citizenship and restore the neoliberal project. This explains why in Ecuador the political power of Indigenous civil society outweighs the demographic size of the Indigenous population.

Indigenous civil society in Bolivia appears to have been seriously weakened. It temporarily lost access to power when the MAS was overthrown and actors remained divided even in the face of violence from the interim regime. But there is more that unites pro- and anti-MAS CSOs than divides them. They all wish to preserve the social and political gains they have made. President Arce will need to repair damaged relationships with Indigenous CSOs that split with his party under Morales. This is particularly true in the face of uncertain economic conditions; the MAS will need the support of its traditional base more than ever in order to govern. This means fostering a spirit of compromise, consensus, and collaboration in which both the government and Indigenous civil society will have to work together. The MAS is too closely integrated with Indigenous civil society to allow any leader to abandon its core principles. Arce cannot follow in the footsteps of Ecuador's Lenín Moreno but in the face of declining state revenue, he will certainly be under pressure to reduce spending and this may lead to conflict with core elements of the base. It may also exacerbate underlying differences within the MAS itself.

Mapuche civil society is at a crossroads. It has historically been relatively weak when it comes to achieving policy outcomes and remains politically fractured. But Mapuche CSOs demonstrate important advantages. First, they are developing innovative ways of using ICTs to share their stories, teach their language and culture, and connect communities across the region. They are becoming more strategic at using symbols and constructing narratives to promote their perspectives and counter discourse that seeks to frame them in a negative light. Second, the 2019 uprisings made it clear to many Mapuche and Chilean popular-sector CSOs that they have much in common.

Shared interests include extending social citizenship, redrafting the constitution, decentralizing the state, and holding relevant authorities accountable for state violence. Finally, there is a growing consciousness among Mapuche leaders that their CSOs must develop stronger horizontal alliances, as well as mechanisms to coordinate political action. The revival of a Mapuche parliament may be one step in this direction. In December 2021, Chileans decisively rejected Kast's intolerance in favor of a progressive message and elected an Indigenous woman to preside over the body charged with rewriting their constitution. These are encouraging signs of hope for a path toward reconciliation.

But at the time of this writing, the final outcome of the constitutional reform process remains unclear. While a significant majority of Chileans supported a new constitution in 2019 and 2020, polls released following the unveiling of the draft constitution suggested that voters may reject it when a pelecite is held in September 2022. This would deal a devastating blow to sectors of Mapuche civil society that seek to empower the Mapuche within the Chilean nation state, and would force them to re-evaluate the value of their multiscalar positioning approach. It may also increase support for the types of "uncivic" tactics that will prolong the conflict in Wallmapu.

Indigenous actors are active at many levels: in Indigenous civil society, but also within the broader public sphere and political institutions. The sustained multiscalar positioning approach will likely have the most significant long-term impact in terms of advancing these groups' claims, and research should engage with these sustained, ongoing, and diverse forms of participation. On a practical level, it means that organizations are no longer forced to choose between (ultimately unsustainable) disruptive action and co-optation but can now engage in the development of a multiscalar positioning strategy and a range of tactics with the knowledge that domestic and international law are on their side. This type of collective action on many fronts does not yield instant results. It requires time, skill and practice. It is this type of ongoing, sustained multiscalar positioning strategy that will likely ensure the long-term integration of Indigenous demands into the political system.

Notes

Introduction

1. Estimating the Indigenous population of Latin American countries is difficult for a number of reasons, including overlapping and fluid identities, internal migration, and the wording of censuses. The most commonly cited figure for Bolivia is 62.2 percent and for Chile it is 10 percent. In Ecuador, the Indigenous population ranges from 7 to 35 percent, according to estimates from the Ecuadorian government and the Coordinadora Andina de Organizaciones Indígenas, respectively. See Economic Commission for Latin America and the Caribbean, https://www.cepal .org/en/infografias/los-pueblos-indigenas-en-america-latina.

Chapter 2

1. The Ecuadorian state claims that 7 percent of the population is Indigenous based on census data, while CONAIE estimates that it is closer to 25 percent.

Chapter 3

1. The *chasqui* was an important Inca official charged with delivering important messages throughout the empire via a sophisticated relay system. He would do this using the *quipu*, an elaborate information recording device fashioned from strings. The *chasqui* was trained to read and interpret *quipus*.

Chapter 4

1. The Freedom in the World 2020 report can be found at: https://freedomhouse .org/country/chile/freedom-world/2020.

2. United Nations Office of the High Commissioner, October 6, 2017: https://www .ohchr.org/en/NewsEvents/Pages/DisplayNews.aspx?NewsID=22209&LangID=E.

3. Inter-American Court of Human Rights, 2014, Case of Norín Catrimán et al. v. Chile, Judgment of May 29, 2014: https://www.corteidh.or.cr/corteidh/docs/casos /articulos/seriec_279_ing.pdf.

4. Brújula, for Subsecretaría de Telecomunicaciones de Chile, "IX Encuesta de Acceso y Usos de Internet: Informe Final," December 2017: https://www.subtel.gob .cl/wp-content/uploads/2018/07/Informe_Final_IX_Encuesta_Acceso_y_Usos _Internet_2017.pdf.

5. El Ciudadano, "Se inicia Escuela para el Autogobierno Mapuche": https://www .elciudadano.com/organizacion-social/se-inicia-escuela-para-el-autogobierno -mapuche/01/13/.

References

Aguilera, Carolina. 2007. "Participación ciudadana en el gobierno de Bachelet: Consejos asesores presidenciales." *América Latina Hoy* 46: 143–99.

Aguirre, Daniela, Susana Aravena, Maria González, Nelson Morales, and Alejandro Sandoval. 2008. "Progama quiero mi barrio: Avances y desafíos." *Temas Sociales* 60: 1–12.

Albó, Xavier. 2004. "Ethnic Identity and Politics in the Central Andes." In *Politics in the Andes: Identity, Conflict, Reform*, edited by Jo-Marie Burt and Philip Mauceri, 17–37. Pittsburgh: University of Pittsburgh Press.

Altschuler, Daniel, and Javier Corrales. 2012. "The Spillover Effects of Participatory Governance: Evidence from Community-Managed Schools in Honduras and Guatemala." *Comparative Political Studies* 45: 636–66.

Alvarez, Sonia, Jeffrey W. Rubin, Millie Thayer, Gianpaolo Baiocchi, and Agustín Laó-Montes, eds. 2017. *Beyond Civil Society: Activism, Participation, and Protest in Latin America*. Durham, NC: Duke University Press.

Amenta, Edwin, Neal Caren, Elizabeth Chiarello, and Yang Su. 2010. "The Political Consequences of Social Movements." *Annual Review of Sociology* 36: 287–307.

Antileo Baeza, Enrique, Luis Cárcamo-Huechante, Margarita Calfío Montalva, and Herson Huinca-Piutrin. 2015. *Violencias coloniales en Wajmapu*. Temuco: Comunidad Historica Mapuche.

Arauz, Andrés, Mark Weisbrot, Andrew Bunker, and Jake Johnston. 2019. *Bolivia's Economic Transformation: Macroeconomic Policies, Institutional Changes, and Results*. Washington, DC: Center for Economic and Policy Research.

Artz, Lee. 2015. "Animating Transnational Capitalism." *Journal of Intercultural Communication Research* 44: 93–107.

Asante, S. K. B. 1997. *Regionalism and Africa's Development: Expectations, Reality, and Challenges*. New York: Macmillan.

Assies, Willem. 2004. "Bolivia: A Gasified Democracy." *Revista Europea de Estudios Latinoamericanos y del Caribe/European Review of Latin American and Caribbean Studies* 76: 25–43.

Atun, Rifat, Luiz Monteiro de Andrade, Gisele Almeida, Daniel Cotlear, T. Dmytraczenko, Patricia Frenz, et al. 2015. "Health-System Reform and Universal Health Coverage in Latin America." *The Lancet* 385: 1230–47.

Avritzer, Leonardo. 2002. *Democracy and the Public Space in Latin America*. Princeton, NJ: Princeton University Press.

———. 2017. "Civil Society in Brazil: From State Autonomy to Political Interdependency." In *Beyond Civil Society: Activism, Participation, and Protest in Latin America*, edited by Sonia E. Alvarez, Jeffrey W. Rubin, Millie Thayer,

Gianpaolo Baiocchi, and Agustín Laó-Montes, 45–62. Durham, NC: Duke University Press.

Baiocchi, Gianpaolo, 2017. "A Century of Councils: Participatory Budgeting and the Long History of Participation in Brazil." In *Beyond Civil Society: Activism, Participation, and Protest in Latin America*, edited by Sonia E. Alvarez, Jeffrey W. Rubin, Millie Thayer, Gianpaolo Baiocchi, and Agustín Laó-Montes, 27–44. Durham, NC: Duke University Press.

Banaszak, Lee Ann. 2010. *The Women's Movement Inside and Outside the State.* Cambridge: Cambridge University Press.

Barber, Benjamin. 1984. *Strong Democracy: Participatory Politics for a New Age.* Berkeley: University of California Press.

Basanta, Juan José. 2013. "Comunicación y TIC en organizaciones indígenas de Argentina." *Revista Argentina de Estudios de Juventud*, 7. Retrieved from: http://www.perio.unlp.edu.ar/ojs/index.php/revistadejuventud/article/view /2032.

Bastías Rebolledo, Julián. 2009. *Memorias de la lucha campesina.* Vol. 1, *Cristiano, Mestizo y Tomador de Fundo.* Santiago: LOM Ediciones.

———. 2016. *Memorias de la lucha campesina.* Vol. 2, *Mapuches, Mestizos y Estudiantes.* Santiago: LOM Ediciones.

Becerra, Martín, and Guillermo Mastrini. 2009. *Los dueños de la palabra.* Buenos Aires: Prometeo.

Becker, Marc. 1999. "Comunas and Indigenous Protest in Cayambe, Ecuador." *The Americas* 55: 531–59.

———. 2008. *Indians and Leftists in the Making of Ecuador's Modern Indigenous Movements.* Durham, NC: Duke University Press, 2008.

Beckwith, Karen. 2000. "Beyond Compare? Women's Movements in Comparative Perspective." *European Journal of Political Research* 37: 431–68.

Bennett, W. Lance. 2014. "Connective Action: The Public's Answer to Democratic Dysfunction." *The Conversation*, October 23, 2014.

Bennett, W. Lance, and Alexandra Segerberg. 2011. "Digital Media and the Personalization of Collective Action: Social Technology and the Organization of Protests against the Global Economic Crisis." *Information, Communication and Society* 14: 770–99.

———. 2013. *The Logic of Connective Action: Digital Media and the Personalization of Contentious Politics.* Cambridge: Cambridge University Press.

Biekart, Kees, and Alan Fowler. 2013. "Transforming Activisms 2010+: Exploring Ways and Waves." *Development and Change* 44: 527–46.

Bimber, Bruce. 1998. "The Internet and Political Transformation: Populism, Community, and Accelerated Pluralism." *Polity* 31 (1): 133–60.

———. 2017. "Three Prompts for Collective Action in the Context of Digital Media." *Political Communication* 34: 6–20.

Breuer, Anita, and Jacob Groshek. 2014. "Online Media and Offline Empowerment in Democratic Transition: Linking Forms of Internet Use with Political Attitudes and Behaviors in Post-Rebellion Tunisia." *Journal of Information Technology and Policy* 11: 25–44.

Brysk, Alison. 1994. "Acting Globally: Indian Rights and International Politics in Latin America." In *Indigenous Peoples and Democracy in Latin America*, edited by Donna Lee Van Cott, 29–51. New York: St. Martin's.

———. 2000. *From Tribal Village to Global Village: Indian Rights and International Relations in Latin America*. Stanford, CA: Stanford University Press.

Budka, Philipp. 2019. "Indigenous Media Technologies in 'The Digital Age': Cultural Articulation, Digital Practices, and Sociopolitical Concepts." In *Ethnic Media in the Digital Age*, edited by Sherry S. Yu and Matthew D. Matsaganis, 162–72. New York: Routledge.

Calderón, Fernando, and Manuel Castells. 2020. *The New Latin America*. New York: John Wiley and Sons.

Cameron, Maxwell A. 2009. "Latin America's Left Turns: Beyond Good and Bad." *Third World Quarterly* 30, no. 2: 331–48.

Cameron, Maxwell A., Eric Hershberg, and Kenneth E. Sharpe. 2012. "Voice and Consequence: Direct Participation and Democracy in Latin America." In *New Institutions for Participatory Democracy in Latin America: Voice and Consequence*, edited by Maxwell A. Cameron, Eric Hershbert, and Kenneth E. Sharpe, 1–20. New York: Palgrave Macmillan.

Canessa, Andrew. 2007. "A Postcolonial Turn: Social and Political Change in the New Indigenous Order of Bolivia." *Urban Anthropology and Studies of Cultural Systems and World Economic Development* 36: 145–59.

———. 2012. "New Indigenous Citizenship in Bolivia: Challenging the Liberal Model of the State and Its Subjects." *Latin American and Caribbean Ethnic Studies* 7: 201–21.

———. 2014. "Conflict, Claim and Contradiction in the New 'Indigenous' State of Bolivia." *Critique of Anthropology* 34: 153–73.

Cárcamo Hernández, Ovidio. 2016. "Movimiento Campesino Revolucionario y Consejos Comunales Campesinos de base: Una experiencia de poder popular en Chile." *Desacatos* 52: 94–111.

Cárcamo-Huechante, Luis. 2013. "Indigenous Interference: Mapuche Use of Radio in Times of Acoustic Colonialism." *Latin American Research Review* 48, special issue: 50–68.

Cárcamo-Huechante, Luis, and Elías Paillan Coñuepan. 2012. "Taiñ pu amulzugue egvn: Sonidos y voces del Wajmapu en el aire." In *Ta Iñ Fijke Xipa Rakizuameluwün: Historia, colonialismo y resistencia desde el país Mapuche*, 335. Temuco: Ediciones Comunidad de Historia Mapuche.

Carrera, Patricio. 2010. "Ex Farc reconoce a miembros de la CAM y dice que fueron instruidos en Colombia." *La Tercera*, July 19.

Castellaro, Sebastián. 2015. "La criminalización de la protesta: El caso Norín Catrimán y otros (Dirigentes, miembros y activista del pueblo indígena Mapuche) vs. Chile." *Anuario de Derechos Humanos* 11: 123–33.

Castells, Manuel. 2001. *The Internet Galaxy*. Oxford: Oxford University Press.

———. 2009. *Communication Power*. Oxford: Oxford University Press.

———. 2015. *Networks of Outrage and Hope. Social Movements in the Internet Age*. Cambridge, MA: Polity.

Castañeda, Jorge G., and Marco A. Morales. 2008. "The Current State of the Utopia." In *Leftovers: Tales of the Latin American Left*, edited by Jorge G. Castañeda and Marco A. Morales, 3–18. New York: Routledge.

Cayuqueo, Pedro. 2018. *Porfiada y rebelde es la memoria: Crónicas mapuche.* Santiago: Catalonia.

Cerbino, Mauro, and Francesca Belotti. 2016. "Medios comunitarios como ejercicio de ciudadanía comunicativa: Experiencias desde Argentina y Ecuador." *Revista Científica de Educomunicación* 47: 49–56.

Cleuren, Herwig. 2007. "Local Democracy and Participation in Post-Authoritarian Chile." *European Review of Latin American and Caribbean Studies* 83: 3–18.

Cohen, Jean, and Andrew Arato. 1992. *Civil Society and Political Theory.* Cambridge, MA: MIT Press.

Cohen, Joshua, and Archon Fung. 2004. "Radical Democracy." *Swiss Journal of Political Science* 4: 23–34.

Collier, Ruth, and Samuel Handlin. 2009. *Reorganizing Popular Politics: Participation and the New Interest Regime in Latin America.* University Park: Penn State University Press.

Colloredo-Mansfeld, Rudi. 2009. *Fighting Like a Community: Andean Civil Society in an Era of Indian Uprisings.* Chicago: University of Chicago Press.

Córdova, Amalia. 2014. "Reenact, Reimagine: Performative Indigenous Documentaries of Bolivia and Brazil." In *New Documentaries in Latin America*, edited by Vinicius Navarro and Juan Carlos Rodríguez, 123–44. New York: Palgrave Macmillan.

———. 2018. "Wallmapu Rising: Re-envisioning the Mapuche Nation through Media." In *From Filmmaker Warriors to Flash Drive Shamans: Indigenous Media Production and Engagement in Latin America*, edited by Richard Pace, 59–74. Nashville, TN: Vanderbilt University Press.

Cornia, Giovanni. 2014. *Falling Inequality in Latin America: Policy Changes and Lessons.* Oxford: Oxford University Press.

Crow, Joanna. 2013. *The Mapuche in Modern Chile: A Cultural History.* Gainesville: University Press of Florida.

Cruz, Melquiades, and Tommaso Gravante. 2018. "Comunalizar la tecnología para una democracia participativa: La experiencia de la comunidad indígena zapoteca." In *Ciudadanía digital y democracia participativa*, edited by Francisco Sierra, Salvador Leetoy, and Tommaso Gravante, 127–44. Salamanca: Comunicación Social.

Curiel, Jack, and John Williams. 2020. *Analysis of the 2019 Bolivia Election.* Washington, DC: Center for Economic and Policy Research.

Curivil Bravo, Felipe. 2012. "Contra la dispersión: Territorios de reconstrucción sociopolítica: Asociatividad Mapuche en el espacio urbano. Santiago, 1940–1970." In *Ta Iñ Fijke Xipa Rakizuameluwün: Historia, colonialismo y resistencia desde el país Mapuche*, 155–86. Temuco: Ediciones Comunidad de Historia Mapuche.

Dangl, Benjamin. 2007. *Price of Fire: Resource Wars and Social Movements in Bolivia.* Edinburgh: AK.

De la Peña, Guillermo. 2005. "Social and Cultural Policies toward Indigenous Peoples: Perspectives from Latin America." *Annual Review of Anthropology* 34: 717–39.

Della Porta, Donatella. 2013. "Protest Cycles and Waves." In *The Wiley-Blackwell Encyclopedia of Social and Political Movements*, edited by David A. Snow, Donatella della Porta, Bert Klandermans, and Doug McAdam. Malden, MA: Wiley-Blackwell.

———. 2014. "Democratization from below: Civil Society versus Social Movements?" In *Civil Society and Democracy Promotion*, edited by Timm Beichelt, Irene Hahn-Fuhr, Frank Schimmelfennig, and Susan Worschech, 137–49. London: Palgrave Macmillan.

Della Porta, Donatella, and Mario Diani. 2006. *Social Movements: An Introduction.* Malden, MA: Blackwell.

Della Porta, Donatella, and Dieter Rucht. 2002. "Comparative Environmental Campaigns." *Mobilization* 7: 1–95.

De la Torre, Carlos. 2016. "Left-Wing Populism: Inclusion and Authoritarianism in Venezuela, Bolivia, and Ecuador." *Brown Journal of World Affairs* 23: 61–76.

Del Popolo, Fabiana, Bruno Ribotta, and Ana María Oyarce. 2009. "Indígenas urbanos en América Latina: Algunos resultados censales y su relación con los Objetivos de Desarrollo del Milenio." *Notas de Población* 86: 99–138.

Diani, Mario. 1997. "Social Movements and Social Capital: A Network Perspective on Movement Outcomes." *Mobilization: An International Quarterly* 2: 129–47.

Do Alto, Hervé. 2011. "Un partido campesino en el poder: Una mirada sociológica del MAS boliviano." *Nueva Sociedad* 234: 95–111.

Duarte, Marisa Elena. 2017. *Network Sovereignty: Building the Internet across Indian Country.* Seattle: University of Washington Press.

Duno, Luis. 2011. "The Color of Mobs: Racial Politics, Ethnopopulism and Representation in the Chávez Era." In *Venezuela's Bolivarian Democracy: Participation, Politics, and Culture under Chávez*, edited by David Smilde and Daniel Hellinger, 271–94. Durham, NC: Duke University Press.

Eckert, Stine. 2018. "Fighting for Recognition: Online Abuse of Women Bloggers in Germany, Switzerland, the United Kingdom, and the United States." *New Media and Society* 20 (4): 1282–302.

Ellner, Steve. 2012. "The Distinguishing Features of Latin America's New Left in Power: The Chávez, Morales, and Correa Governments." *Latin American Perspectives* 39: 96–114.

Exeni Rodríguez, José Luis. 2012. "Elusive Demodiversity in Bolivia: Between Representation, Participation and Self-Government." In *New Institutions form Participatory Democracy in Latin America: Voice and Consequence*, edited by Maxwell A. Cameron, Eric Hershberg, and Kenneth E. Sharpe, 207–300. New York: Palgrave Macmillan.

Fabricant, Nicole, and Bret Gustafson, eds. 2011. *Remapping Bolivia: Resources, Territory, and Indigeneity in a Plurinational State.* Santa Fe, NM: School for Advanced Research Press.

Fabricant, Nicole, and Kathryn Hicks. 2013. "Bolivia's Next Water War: Historicizing the Struggles over Access to Water Resources in the Twenty-First Century." *Radical History Review* 116: 130–45.

Fabricant, Nicole, and Nancy Postero. 2013. "Contested Bodies, Contested States: Performance, Emotions, and New Forms of Regional Governance in Santa Cruz, Bolivia." *Journal of Latin American and Caribbean Anthropology* 18: 187–211.

Faraj, Samer, and Bijan Azad. 2012. "The Materiality of Technology: An Affordance Perspective." In *Materiality and Organizing: Social Interaction in a Technological World*, edited by Paul M. Leonardi, Bonnie A. Nardi, and Jannis Kallinikos, 237–58. Oxford: Oxford University Press.

Faris, James C. 1992. "Anthropological Transparency: Film, Representation and Politics." In *Film as Ethnography*, edited by Peter Ian Crawford and David Turton, 171–82. Manchester: Manchester University Press.

Fernandes, Gabriel, and Pedro Casas. 2014. *Rethinking Integration in Latin America: The "Pink Tide" and the Post-Neoliberal Regionalism*. Buenos Aires: FLACSO.

Fernandes, Sujatha. 2010. *Who Can Stop the Drums? Urban Social Movements in Chávez's Venezuela*. Durham, NC: Duke University Press.

Ferree, Myra Marx, and Beth Hess. 1994. *Controversy and Coalition: The New Feminist Movement across Three Decades of Change*. New York: Twayne, 1994.

Field, Les. 1994. "Who Are the Indians? Reconceptualizing Indigenous Identity, Resistance, and the Role of Social Science in Latin America." *Latin American Research Review* 29: 237–48.

Flores-Yeffal, Nadia Y., Gudalupe Vidales, and Girsea Martinez. 2019. "#WakeUpAmerica, #IllegalsAreCriminals: The Role of the Cyber Public Sphere in the Perpetuation of the Latino Cyber-Moral Panic in the US." *Information, Communication and Society* 22 (3): 402–19.

Fox, Elizabeth, and Silvio Waisbord. 2002. *Latin Politics, Global Media*. Austin: University of Texas Press.

Frenkel, Alejandro. 2011. "Los actores de la derecha boliviana: Tipos, fundamentos y lógicas de la acción política en el escenario nacional, 2000–2008." *Theomai* 23: 205–15.

Fuchs, Christian. 2009. "Information and Communication Technologies and Society: A Contribution to the Critique of the Political Economy of the Internet." *European Journal of Communication* 24: 69–87.

Fundamedios. 2017. *Censura y autocensura en medios e internet en Ecuador*. December 26. https://www.fundamedios.org.ec/censura-y-autocensura-en -medios-e-internet-ecuador/.

Fung, Archon. 2011. "Reinventing Democracy in Latin America." *Perspectives on Politics* 9: 857–71.

Gamson, William A. 1990. *The Strategy of Social Protest*. Belmont, CA: Wadsworth.

———. 2003. "Defining Movement 'Success.'" In *The Social Movements Reader: Cases and Concepts*, edited by Jeff Goodwin and James M. Jasper, 350–52. Malden, MA: Wiley.

García-Guadilla, María Pilar. 2007. "Social Movements in a Polarized Setting: Myths of Venezuelan Civil Society." In *Venezuela: Hugo Chávez and the Decline of an "Exceptional Democracy"*, edited by Steve Ellner and Miguel Tinker Salas, 140–54. Boulder, CO: Lynne Rienner.

———. 2008. "La praxis de los consejos comunales en Venezuela: ¿Poder popular o instancia clientelar?" *Revista Venezolana de Economía y Ciencias Sociales* 14: 125–51.

García Linera, Álvaro. 2008. *Sociología de los movimientos sociales en Bolivia.* La Paz: Plural Editores.

Ginsburg, Faye. 1991. "Indigenous Media: Faustian Contract or Global Village?" *Cultural Anthropology* 6: 92–112.

———. 2000. "Resources of Hope: Learning from the Local in a Transnational Era." In *Indigenous Cultures in an Interconnected World*, edited by Claire Smith and Graeme K. Ward, 22–47. Vancouver: UBC Press.

———. 2008. "Rethinking the Digital Age." In *Global Indigenous Media: Cultures, Poetics, and Politics*, edited by Pamela Wilson and Michelle Stewart, 287–306. Durham, NC: Duke University Press.

———. 2016. "Indigenous Media from U-matic to Youtube: Media Sovereignty in the Digital Age." *Sociologia y Antropologia* 6: 581–99.

Goldfrank, Benjamin. 2011. *Deepening Local Democracy in Latin America: Participation, Decentralization, and the Left.* University Park: Penn State University Press.

González Lorenzo, Eva María. 2009. "Nuevas fórmulas, nuevos medios: La comunicación de los pueblos indígenas andinos." *Actas del I Congreso Internacional Latina de Comunicación Social.* http://www.revistalatinacs.org/09/Sociedad/actas/104evag.pdf.

Grillo, Oscar. 2006. "Políticas de identidad en Internet. Mapuexpress: Imaginario activista y procesos de hibridación." *Razón y Palabra* 54. https://www.redalyc.org/pdf/1995/199520736010.pdf.

Grugel, Jean, and Lorenza Fontana. 2019. "Human Rights and the Pink Tide in Latin America: Which Rights Matter?" *Development and Change* 50: 707–34.

Gruzd, Anatoliy, Philip Mai, and Andrea Kampen. 2016. "A How-to for Using Netlytic to Collect and Analyze Social Media Data: A Case Study of the Use of Twitter During the 2014 Euromaidan Revolution in Ukraine." *The SAGE Handbook of Social Media Research Methods*, edited by Luke Sloan and Anabel Quan-Haase, 513–29. Thousand Oaks, CA: SAGE Publications.

Guerrero, Manuel. 2014. "The 'Captured Liberal' Model of Media Systems in Latin America." In *Media Systems and Communication Policies in Latin America*, edited by Manuel Alejandro Guerrero and Mireya Márquez-Ramírez, 43–65. London: Palgrave Macmillan.

Gunaratne, Shelton A. 2002. "Freedom of the Press: A World System Perspective." *International Communication Gazette* 64: 343–69.

Gustafson, Bret. 2009. *New Languages of the State: Indigenous Resurgence and the Politics of Knowledge in Bolivia.* Durham, NC: Duke University Press.

———. 2017. "Oppressed No More? Indigenous Language Regimentation in Plurinational Bolivia." *International Journal of the Sociology of Language* 246: 31–57.

Hale, Charles. 2002. "Does Multiculturalism Menace? Governance, Cultural Rights and the Politics of Identity in Guatemala." *Journal of Latin American Studies* 34 (2002): 485–524.

——. 2004. "Rethinking Indigenous Politics in the Era of the 'Indio Permitido.'" *NACLA Report on the Americas* 38: 16–21.

Hale, Charles, and Rosamel Millamán. 2006. "Cultural Agency and Political Struggle in the Era of the *Indio Permitido*." In *Cultural Agency in the Americas*, edited by Doris Sommer, 281–304. Durham, NC: Duke University Press.

Heiss, Claudia. 2017. "Legitimacy Crisis and the Constitutional Problem in Chile: A Legacy of Authoritarianism." *Constellations* 24: 470–79.

Herman, Edward, and Noam Chomsky. 1988. *Manufacturing Consent: The Political Economy of the Mass Media.* New York: Pantheon.

Highfield, Tim, and Tama Leaver. 2016. "Instagrammatics and Digital Methods: Studying Visual Social Media, from Gelfies and GIFs to Memes and Emoji." *Communication Research and Practice* 2: 47–62.

Hinzo, Angel, and Lynn Clark. 2019. "Digital Survivance and Trickster Humor: Exploring Visual and Digital Indigenous Epistemologies in the# NoDAPL Movement." *Information, Communication and Society* 22: 791–807.

Hoetmer, Rafael. 2017. "'This is No Longer a Democracy . . .': Thoughts on the Local Referendums on Mining on Peru's Northern Frontier." In *Beyond Civil Society: Activism, Participation, and Protest in Latin America*, edited by Sonia E. Alvarez, Jeffrey W. Rubin, Millie Thayer, Gianpaolo Baiocchi, and Agustín Laó-Montes, 226–51. Durham, NC: Duke University Press.

Homedes, Nuria, and Antonio Ugalde. 2005. "Why Neoliberal Health Reforms Have Failed in Latin America." *Health Policy* 71: 83–96.

Howard, Philip. 2010. *The Digital Origins of Dictatorship and Democracy: Information Technology and Political Islam.* Oxford: Oxford University Press.

Howard, Philip N., and Muzammil M. Hussain. 2013. *Democracy's Fourth Wave? Digital Media and the Arab Spring.* Oxford: Oxford University Press.

Human Rights Watch (HRW). 2020. "Ecuador: Lessons from the 2019 Protests." April 6. https://www.hrw.org/news/2020/04/06/ecuador-lessons-2019 -protests.

Jofré, Pablo. 2020. "Racismo y militarización en el Wallmapu." *Diario UChile*, August 8.

Junge, Benjamin. 2017. "Uncivil Subjects, Uncivil Women: Civic Participation, Ambivalence, and Political Subjectivity among Grassroots Community Leaders in Porto Alegre, Brazil." In *Beyond Civil Society: Activism, Participation, and Protest in Latin America*, edited by Sonia E. Alvarez, Jeffrey W. Rubin, Millie Thayer, Gianpaolo Baiocchi, and Agustín Laó-Montes, 81–100. Durham, NC: Duke University Press.

Kauffman, L. A. 1990. "The Anti-Politics of Identity." *Socialist Review* 90: 67–80.

Kitzberger, Philip. 2017. "The Media Politics of the 'Citizens' Revolution': Communicative power redistribution and democratization." In *The Pink Tide: Media Access and Political Power in Latin America*, edited by Lee Artz, 87–110. Lanham, MD: Rowman and Littlefield.

Kowalczyk, Anna María. 2013. "Indigenous Peoples and Modernity: Mapuche Mobilizations in Chile." *Latin American Perspectives* 40: 121–35.

Landzelius, Kyra. 2006. *Native on the Net: Indigenous and Diasporic Peoples in the Virtual Age.* London: Routledge.

Langman, Lauren. 2005. "From Virtual Public Spheres to Global Justice: A Critical Theory of Internetworked Social Movements." *Sociological Theory* 23 (1): 42–74.

Laó-Montes, Agustín. 2017. "Mapping the Field of Afro-Latin American Politics: In and Out of the Civil Society Agenda." In *Beyond Civil Society: Activism, Participation, and Protest in Latin America*, edited by Sonia E. Alvarez, Jeffrey W. Rubin, Millie Thayer, Gianpaolo Baiocchi, and Agustín Laó-Montes, 103–21. Durham, NC: Duke University Press.

Larrea, Carlos, and Natalia Greene. 2018. "Concentration of Assets and Poverty Reduction in Post-Neoliberal Ecuador." In *Dominant Elites in Latin America: From Neoliberalism to the "Pink Tide"*, edited by Liisa L. North and Timothy D. Clark, 93–118. Cham: Palgrave Macmillan.

Larson, Jennifer. 2019. "Collective Action in the Information Age: How Social Media Shapes the Character and Success of Protests." In *Protest and Democracy*, edited by Moisés Arce and Roberta Rice, 71–91. Calgary: University of Calgary Press.

Laruta, Carlos Hugo. 2008. "Organizaciones y Movimientos Sociales en el Proceso Político Actual. In *Los Actores Políticos en la Transición Boliviana*, edited by Roberto Moscoso and Horst Grebe López. La Paz: Instituto Prisma.

Laserna, Roberto. 2011. "Mire, la democracia boliviana en los hechos." *Latin American Research Review* 45: 27–58.

Lempert, William. 2018. "Indigenous Media Futures: An Introduction." *Cultural Anthropology* 33: 173–79.

León, Jorge. 2001. "Conflicto étnico, democracia y Estado." *Íconos-Revista de Ciencias Sociales* 10: 48–56.

Lilleker, Darren, and Karolina Koc-Michalska. 2017. "What Drives Political Participation? Motivations and Mobilization in a Digital Age." *Political Communication* 34: 21–43.

Linabary, Jasmine, and Danielle Corple. 2018. "Privacy for Whom? A Feminist Intervention in Online Research Practice." *Information, Communication and Society* 22: 1447–63.

Lozada, Fernando, and Gridvia Kúncar. 2004. "Miners' Radio of Bolivia: A Historic Experience of Self-Managed Communication." In *Community Radio in Bolivia: The Miners' Radio Stations*, edited by Alan O'Connor, 317–23. Lewiston, NY: Edwin Mellen Press.

Lucero, Jose A. 2007. "Barricades and Articulations: Comparing Ecuadorian and Bolivian Indigenous Politics." In *Highland Indians and the State in Modern Ecuador*, edited by Marc Becker and A. Kim Clark, 209–33. Pittsburgh, PA: University of Pittsburgh Press.

———. 2008. *Struggles of Voice: The Politics of Indigenous Representation in the Andes.* Pittsburgh, PA: University of Pittsburgh Press.

Lucero, Jose A., and Maria García. 2007. "In the Shadows of Success: Indigenous Politics in Peru and Ecuador." In *Highland Indians and the State in Modern Ecuador*, edited by Marc Becker and A. Kim Clark, 234–47. Pittsburgh, PA: University of Pittsburgh Press.

Lupien, Pascal. 2011. "The Incorporation of Indigenous Concepts of Plurinationality into the New Constitutions of Ecuador and Bolivia." *Democratization* 18: 774–96.

———. 2013. "The Media and Attacking the 'Bad Left' from below in Venezuela and Bolivia." *Latin American Perspectives* 40: 226–46.

———. 2017. "Bolivia: New Information and Power Dynamic and Information Pluralism." In *The Pink Tide: Media Access and Political Power in Latin America*, edited by Lee Artz, 63–86. Lanham, MD: Rowman and Littlefield.

———. 2018a. *Citizens' Power in Latin America: Theory and Practice.* Albany: SUNY Press.

———. 2018b. "Participatory Democracy and Ethnic Minorities: Opening Inclusive New Spaces or Reproducing Inequalities?" *Democratization* 25: 1251–69.

———. 2020. "Indigenous Movements, Collective Action, and Social Media: New Opportunities or New Barriers?" *Social Media + Society* April–June: 1–11.

Lupien, Pascal, and Gabriel Chiriboga. 2019. "Use of Information and Communications Technologies by Indigenous Civil Society Organizations in Ecuador." *Information, Communication & Society* 22 (8): 1029–43.

Lupien, Pascal, Gabriel Chiriboga, and Soledad Machaca. 2021. "Indigenous Movements, ICTs and the State in Latin America." *Journal of Information Technology and Politics* 18 (4): 387–400.

Luna, Laura, Consuelo Telechea, and Natalia Caniguan. 2018. "Mapuche Education and Situated Learning in a Community School in Chile." *Intercultural Education* 29: 203–17.

Lyall, Angus, Rudi Colloredo-Mansfeld, and Malena Rousseau. 2018. "Development, Citizenship, and Everyday Pppropriations of Buen Vivir." *Bulletin of Latin American Research* 37: 403–16.

Machado, Cristiani. 2018. "Health Policies in Argentina, Brazil and Mexico: Different Paths, Many Challenges." *Ciencia y Saude Coletiva* 23: 2197–212.

Majchrzak, Ann, Samer Faraj, Gerald C. Kane, and Bijan Azad. 2013. "The Contradictory Influence of Social Media Affordances on Online Communal Knowledge Sharing." *Journal of Computer-Mediated Communication* 19, no. 1: 38–55.

Mallon, Florencia E. 1992. "Indian Communities, Political Cultures, and the State in Latin America, 1780–1990." *Journal of Latin American Studies* 24, no. S1: 35–53.

Marimán, José A. 2012. *Autodeterminación: Ideas políticas mapuche en el albor del siglo XXI.* Santiago: LOM Ediciones.

Marimán Quemenado, Pablo. 2012. "La República y los Mapuche: 1819–1828." In *Ta Iñ Fijke Xipa Rakizuameluwün: Historia, colonialismo y resistencia desde el país Mapuche*, 63–88. Temuco: Ediciones Comunidad de Historia Mapuche.

Marshall, Thomas H. 1950. *Citizenship and Social Class.* New York, NY: Cambridge University Press.

Masala, Roberta, and Salvatore Monni. 2019. "The Social Inclusion of Indigenous Peoples in Ecuador Before and during the Revolución Ciudadana." *Development* 62: 167–77.

Mason, Ashley. 2012. "Violence, Criminal Defamation, and Censorship Laws: Threatening Freedom of Expression in Chile and Ecuador." *Law and Business Review of the Americas* 18: 369–99.

Matrone, Davide. 2019. "Cómo la pedagogía crítica de P. Freire fue interpretada por parte del Monseñor Leónidas Proaño durante la implementación de la radiofónica del Chimborazo en términos educativos." Master's thesis, Quito, Ecuador: Flacso Ecuador.

McAdam, Doug. 1996. "Conceptual Origins, Current Problems, Future Directions." In *Comparative Perspectives on Social Movements: Political Opportunities, Mobilizing Structures, and Cultural Framings*, edited by Doug McAdam, John D. McCarthy, and Mayer N. Zald, 23–40. Cambridge: Cambridge University Press.

———. 1999. *The Biographical Impact of Activism*. Minneapolis: University of Minnesota Press.

McAdam, Doug, John D. McCarthy, and Mayer N. Zald. 1996. "Introduction: Opportunities, Mobilizing Structures and Processes—Toward a Synthetic, Comparative Perspective on Social Movements." In *Comparative Perspectives on Social Movements: Political Opportunities, Mobilizing Structures, and Cultural Framings*, edited by Doug McAdam, John D. McCarthy, and Mayer N. Zald, 1–22. Cambridge: Cambridge University Press.

McCarthy, John D. 1996. "Constraints and Opportunities in Adopting, Adapting, and Inventing." In *Comparative Perspectives on Social Movements: Political Opportunities, Mobilizing Structures, and Cultural Framings*, edited by Doug McAdam, John D. McCarthy, and Mayer N. Zald, 141–51. Cambridge: Cambridge University Press.

McCarthy, John D., and Mayer N. Zald. 1977. "Resource Mobilization and Social Movements: A Partial Theory." *American Journal of Sociology* 82 (6): 1212–41.

McChesney, Robert. 2016. *Rich Media, Poor Democracy: Communication Politics in Dubious Times*. New York: New Press.

McVeigh, Rory, Michael Welch, and Thoroddur Bjarnason. 2003. "Hate Crime Reporting as a Successful Social Movement Outcome." *American Sociological Review* 68: 843–67.

Melucci, Antonio. 1989. *Nomads of the Present*. Philadelphia, PA: Temple University Press.

Meyer, David, and Suzanne Staggenborg. 1996. "Movements, Countermovements, and the Structure of Political Opportunity." *American Journal of Sociology* 101: 1628–60.

Meyer, David, and Sidney Tarrow. 1998. *The Social Movement Society: Contentious Politics for a New Century*. Lanham, MD: Rowman and Littlefield.

Meyer, David, and Nancy Whittier. 1994. "Social Movement Spillover." *Social Problems* 41: 277–98.

Mijeski, Kenneth, and Scott Beck. 2011. *Pachakutik and the Rise and Decline of the Ecuadorian Indigenous Movement*. Athens: Ohio University Press.

Millalen Paillal, José. 2012. "Taiñ mapuchegen: Nación y nacionalismo Mapuche: construcción y desafío del presente." In *Ta Iñ Fijke Xipa Rakizuameluwün: Historia, colonialismo y resistencia desde el país Mapuche*, 235–56. Temuco: Ediciones Comunidad de Historia Mapuche.

Miller, David. 2000. *Citizenship and National Identity*. Cambridge: Polity.

Mingo, Elisa García. 2014. "Persiguiendo la utopía. Medios de comunicación Mapuche y la construcción de la utopía del Wallmapu." *Deusto Journal of Human Rights* 12: 161–84.

Mingolo, Walter. 2000. *Local Histories/Global Designs: Coloniality, Subaltern Knowledge and Border Thinking*. Princeton, NJ: Princeton University Press.

Monasterios, Gloria. 2003. "Usos de Internet por organizaciones Indígenas de Abya Yala." *Comunicación, Centro Gumilla de Estudios Venezolanos de Comunicación* 22: 60–69.

Moscoso, Roberto. 2008. "Los Partidos, Hacia el Nuevo Sistema Político. In *Los Actores Políticos en la Transición Boliviana*, edited by Roberto Moscoso and Horst Grebe López. La Paz: Instituto Prisma.

Muñoz-Pogossian, Betilde. 2008. *Electoral Rules and the Transformation of Bolivian Politics; The Rise of Evo Morales*. New York: Palgrave Macmillan.

Murschetz, Paul Clemens. 2018. "Political Engagement of Individuals in the Digital Age." In *Handbook of Communication for Development and Social Change*, edited by Jan Servaes, 1–14. Singapore: Springer.

O'Connor, Alan. 1990. "The Miners' Radio Stations in Bolivia: A Culture of Resistance." *Journal of Communication* 40: 102–10.

Oxhorn, Philip. 2010. *Organizing Civil Society: The Popular Sectors and the Struggle for Democracy in Chile*. University Park: Penn State Press.

——. 2011. *Sustaining Civil Society: Economic Change, Democracy and the Social Construction of Citizenship in Latin America*. University Park: Penn State University Press.

——. 2012. "Understanding the Vagaries of Civil Society and Participation in Latin America." In *Routledge Handbook of Latin American Politics*, edited by Peter Kingstone and Deborah J. Yashar, 248–61. London: Routledge.

——. 2017. "Civil Society from the Inside Out: Community, Organization, and the Challenge of Political Influence." In *Re-Imagining Community and Civil Society in Latin America and the Caribbean*, edited by Gordana Yovanovich and Roberta Rice, 20–46. London: Routledge.

Pace, Richard. 2018. *From Filmmaker Warriors to Flash Drive Shamans: Indigenous Media Production and Engagement in Latin America*. Nashville, TN: Vanderbilt University Press.

Paige, Jeffrey. 2020. *Indigenous Revolution in Ecuador and Bolivia, 1990–2005*. Tucson: University of Arizona Press.

Pairicán, Fernando. 2013. "Lumaco: La cristalización del movimiento autodeterminista mapuche." *Revista de Historia Social y de las Mentalidades* 17: 35–59.

Pallares, Amalia. 2017. "Refounding the Political: The Struggle for Provincialization in Santa Elena, Ecuador." In *Beyond Civil Society: Activism, Participation, and Protest in Latin America*, edited by Sonia E. Alvarez, Jeffrey W. Rubin, Millie Thayer, Gianpaolo Baiocchi, and Agustín Laó-Montes, 238–60. Durham, NC: Duke University Press.

Pateman, Carole. 1970. *Participation and Democratic Theory*. Cambridge: Cambridge University Press.

Pérez De Acha, Gisela. 2016. *Hacking Team Malware Para la Vigilancia en América Latina*. Santiago, Chile: Derechos Digitales.

Petray, Theresa. 2013. "Self-Writing a Movement and Contesting Indigeneity: Being an Aboriginal Activist on Social Media." *Global Media Journal: Australian Edition* 7: 1–20.

Pichinao Huenchuleo, Jimena. 2012. "Los parlamentos hispano-Mapuche como escenario de negociación simbólico-político durante la colonia." In *Ta Iñ Fijke Xipa Rakizuameluwün: Historia, colonialismo y resistencia desde el país Mapuche*, 25–42. Temuco: Ediciones Comunidad de Historia Mapuche.

Picq, Manuela. 2018. *Vernacular Sovereignties: Indigenous Women Challenging World Politics*. Tucson: University of Arizona Press.

Pilco, Sami. 2000. "La Red Internet y los Pueblos Indígenas en América Latina: Experiencias y Perspectivas." Master's thesis, Institute for Media Studies, University of Bergen.

Piven, Frances, and Richard Cloward. 1977. *Poor People's Movements: Why They Succeed, How They Fail*. New York: Pantheon.

Platt, Tristan. 1982. *El estado boliviano y el Ayllu Andino: Tierra y tributo en el Norte de Potosí*. Lima: IEP Ediciones.

Postero, Nancy. 2004. "Articulations and Fragmentations: Indigenous Politics in Bolivia." In *Struggle for Indigenous Rights in Latin America*, edited by Nancy Postero and Leon Zamosc, 189–216. Brighton: Sussex Academic Press.

———. 2007. *Now We Are Citizens: Indigenous Politics in Postmulticultural Bolivia*. Stanford, CA: Stanford University Press.

Postero, Nancy, and Leon Zamosc. 2004. "Indigenous Movements and the Indian Question in Latin America." In *Struggle for Indigenous Rights in Latin America*, edited by Nancy Postero and Leon Zamosc, 1–31. Brighton: Sussex Academic Press.

Ragan, Steve. 2015. "Hacking Team Hacked, Attackers Claim 400GB in Dumped Data." *CSO Online*, July 5.

Ramírez, Franklin, and Yanina Welp. 2011. "Nuevas instituciones participativas y democráticas en América Latina." *Íconos* 39: 11–20.

Rawls, John. 1993. *Political Liberalism*. New York: Colombia University Press.

Raynauld, Vincent, Emanuelle Richez, and Katie Boudreau Morris. 2018. "Canada Is #IdleNoMore: Exploring Dynamics of Indigenous Political and Civic Protest in the Twitterverse." *Information, Communication, Society* 21: 626–42.

Redondo Cardeñoso, Jesús Ángel. 2017. "Conflictos campesinos e indígenas en el sur de Chile (la provincia de Cautín, 1967–1973)." *Historia Crítica* 63: 159–79.

Reid, Michael. 2019. "Lenín Moreno's New Economic Policy." *The Economist*, April 11.

Reyes, Andrea. 2014. "Identidad indígena en Chile en contexto de migración, urbanización y globalización." *Amérique Latine Histoire et Mémoire. Les Cahiers ALHIM* 27.

Reyes Matta, Fernando. 1981. *Comunicación alternativa como respuesta democrática*. Santiago: Instituto Latinoamericano de Estudios Transnacionales.

Rice, Roberta. 2012. *The New Politics of Protest: Indigenous Mobilization in Latin America's Neoliberal Era*. Tucson: University of Arizona Press.

——. 2016. "How to Decolonize Democracy: Indigenous Governance Innovation in Bolivia and Nunavut, Canada." *Bolivian Studies Journal / Revista de Estudios Bolivianos* 22: 220–42.

Richards, Patricia. 2010. "Of Indians and Terrorists: How the State and Local Elites Construct the Mapuche in Neoliberal Multicultural Chile." *Journal of Latin American Studies* 42: 59–90.

——. 2013. *Race and the Chilean Miracle: Neoliberalism, Democracy, and Indigenous Rights*. Pittsburgh, PA: University of Pittsburgh Press.

Rivera Cusicanqui, Silvia. 1987. *Oppressed but not Defeated: Peasant Struggles Among the Aymara and Qhechwa in Bolivia, 1900–1980*. Geneva: United Nations Research Institute for Social Development.

——. 2012. "Ch'ixinakax utxiwa: A Reflection on the Practices and Discourses of Decolonization." *South Atlantic Quarterly* 111: 95–109.

——. 2013. "Etnicidad estratégica, nación y (neo) colonialismo en América Latina." *Alternativa: Revista de Estudios Rurales* 3.

——. 2020. *Ch'ixinakax utxiwa: On Decolonising Practices and Discourses*. Cambridge: Polity.

Rocha Fuentes, Verónica. 2015. "Redes Sociales Virtuales. ¿Reconfigurando todo?" In *Comicios Mediáticos II: Medios de difusión y redes sociales digitales en las elecciones 2014 en Bolivia*, edited by José Luis Exeni Rodríguez, Karina Herrera Miller, and Verónica Rocha Fuentes, 119–44. La Paz: IDEA Internacional.

Rodríguez, Katitza. 2016. *Comparative Analysis of Surveillance Laws and Practices in Latin America*. San Francisco: Electronic Frontier Foundation.

Roncken, Theo. 2019. "Nonviolent Resistance in Plurinational Bolivia: The TIPNIS Case." In *Civil Resistance and Violent Conflict in Latin America*, edited by Cécile Mouly, Esperanza Hernández Delgado, 205–26. London: Palgrave Macmillan.

Rovisco, María, and Anastasia Veneti. 2017. "Picturing Protest: Visuality, Visibility and the Public Sphere." *Visual Communication* 16: 271–77.

Salazar, José Manuel, and Juan Chacaltana. 2019. "Formalization Policies in Latin America." Presentation to the Seminar "New and Old Forms of Informality," ECLAC, Santiago, April 2019. https://www.cepal.org/sites/default/files /presentations/201904-04_11._chacaltana.pdf.

Salazar, Juan Francisco. 2002. "Activismo indígena en América Latina: Estrategias para una construcción cultural de las tecnologías de información y comunicación." *Journal of Iberian and Latin American Studies* 8: 61–79.

——. 2003. "Articulating an Activist Imaginary: Internet as Counter Public Sphere in the Mapuche Movement." *Media International Australia* 107: 19–30.

———. 2011. "Indigenous Media in Latin America." *Encyclopedia of Social Movement Media*, edited by John D. H. Downing, 253–57. Thousand Oaks, CA: Sage.

———. 2015. "Social Movements and Video Indígena." In *Media, Anthropology and Public Engagement*, edited by Sarah Pink and Simone Abram, 122–43. New York: Berghahn.

Salazar, Juan Francisco, and Amalia Córdova. 2008. "Imperfect Media and the Poetics of Indigenous Video in Latin America." In *Global Indigenous Media: Cultures, Poetics, and Politics*, edited by Pamela Wilson and Michelle Stewart, 39–57. Durham, NC: Duke University Press.

Sánchez-López, Daniela. 2015. "Reshaping Notions of Citizenship: the TIPNIS Indigenous Movement in Bolivia." *Development Studies Research* 2: 20–32.

Saxton, Gregory, Jerome Niyirora, Chao Guo, and Richard Waters. 2015. "#AdvocatingForChange: The Strategic Use of Hashtags in Social Media Advocacy." *Advances in Social Work* 16: 154–69.

Schiwy, Freya. 2009. *Indianizing Film: Decolonization, the Andes, and the Question of Technology*. Brunswick, NJ: Rutgers University Press.

Scott-Railton, John, Morgan Marquis-Boire, Claudio Guarnieri, and Marion Marschalek. 2015. *Packrat: Seven Years of a South American Threat Actor*. Toronto: Citizen Lab. https://citizenlab.ca/2015/12/packrat-report/.

Seawright, Jason, and John Gerring. 2008. "Case Selection Techniques in Case Study Research." *Political Research Quarterly* 61: 294–308.

Seligman, Adam. 1992. *The Idea of Civil Society*. Princeton, NJ: Free Press.

Selverston-Scher, Melina. 2001. *Ethnopolitics in Ecuador: Indigenous Rights and the Strengthening of Democracy*. Coral Gables, FL: North-South Center Press at the University of Miami.

Sepúlveda, Nicolás. 2018. *Los periodistas que fueron objeto de espionaje electrónico de Carabineros*. Santiago: CIPER Chile Available at: https://ciperchile.cl/2018/03/07/los-periodistas-que-fueron-objeto-de-espionaje-electronico-de-carabineros/.

Shirky, Clay. 2008. *Here Comes Everybody: The Power of Organizing without Organizations*. New York: Penguin.

Silva, Eduardo. 2009. *Challenging Neoliberalism in Latin America*. New York: Cambridge University Press.

Snow, David, and Robert Benford. 1988. "Ideology, Frame Resonance, and Participant Mobilization." *International Social Movement Research* 1: 197–217.

Solimano, Andrés. 2005. "Political Instability, Institutional Quality and Social Conflict in the Andes." In *Political Crises, Social Conflict and Economic Development: The Political Economy of the Andean Region*, edited by Andrés Solimano, 15–44. Cheltenham: Edward Elgar.

Somavía, Juan. 1981. "Towards a New World Information and Communication Order." *Development Dialogue* 2 (1981): 13–29.

Soriano, Cheryll. 2012. "The Arts of Indigenous Online Dissent: Negotiating Technology, Indigeneity, and Activism in the Cordillera." *Telematics and Informatics* 29: 33–44.

Spronk, Susan. 2008. "Pink Tide? Neoliberalism and Its Alternatives in Latin America." *Canadian Journal of Latin American and Caribbean Studies* 3: 173–86.

Srinivasan, Ramesh. 2013. "Re-thinking the Cultural Codes of New Media: The Question Concerning Ontology." *New Media and Society* 15: 203–23.

Stern, Steve J. 1987. "New Approaches to the Study of Peasant Rebellion and Consciousness." In *Resistance, Rebellion, and Consciousness in the Andean Peasant World, 18th to 20th Centuries*, edited by Steve J. Stern, 3–28. Madison: University of Wisconsin Press.

Suh, Doowon. 2001. "How Do Political Opportunities Matter for Social Movements? Political Opportunity, Misframing, Pseudosuccess, and Pseudofailure." *Sociological Quarterly* 42: 437–60.

Tapia, Luis. 2006. *La invención del núcleo común: Ciudadanía y gobierno multisocietal.* La Paz: Muela del Diablo Editores.

———. 2007. *La igualdad es cogobierno.* La Paz: CIDES-UMSA.

Tarrow, Sidney. 1989. *Democracy and Disorder: Protest and Politics in Italy, 1965–1975.* Oxford: Oxford University Press.

———. 1996. "States and Opportunities: The Political Structuring of Social Movements." In *Comparative Perspectives on Social Movements: Political Opportunities, Mobilizing Structures, and Cultural Framings*, edited by Doug McAdam, John D. McCarthy, and Mayer N. Zald, 41–61. Cambridge: Cambridge University Press.

———. 1998. *Power in Movement: Social Movements, Collective Action and Politics.* Cambridge: Cambridge University Press.

———. 2011. "Why Occupy Wall Street Is Not the Tea Party of the Left." *Foreign Affairs* October 10.

Taylor, Charles. 1990. "Modes of Civil Society." *Public Culture* 3 (1): 95–118.

Thomson, Sinclair. 2002. *We Alone Will Rule: Native Andean Politics in the Age of Insurgency.* Madison: University of Wisconsin Press.

Thomson, Sinclair, and Forrest Hylton. 2007. *Revolutionary Horizons: Past and Present in Bolivian Politics.* New York: Verso.

Tibán, Lourdes, and Raúl Ilaquiche. 2008. *Jurisdicción indígena en la constitución política del Ecuador.* Latacunga, Ecuador: Fundación Hanns Seidel.

Tilly, Charles. 1987. *From Mobilization to Revolution.* Reading, MA: Addison-Wesley.

———. 2004. *Social Movements, 1768–2004.* Boulder, CO: Paradigm.

Torres, María Belén. 2019. "Comunicación popular y comunitaria en el Levantamiento Indígena de 1990: Escuelas Radiofónicas Populares del Ecuador en la disputa del sentido político y comunicacional." *Kairós: Revista de Ciencias Económicas, Jurídicas y Administrativas* 3: 38–50.

Treem, Jeffrey W., and Paul M. Leonardi. 2013. "Social Media Use in Organizations: Exploring the Affordances of Visibility, Editability, Persistence, and Association." *Annals of the International Communication Association* 36 (1): 143–89.

Trujillo, Jorge. 2010. "Las organizaciones indígenas y el gobierno de Rafael Correa." *Íconos: Revista de Ciencias Sociales* 37: 13–23.

Tufekci, Zeynep. 2017. *Twitter and Tear Gas: The Power and Fragility of Networked Protest.* New Haven, CT: Yale University Press.

Turner, Terence. 1992. "Defiant Images: The Kayapo Appropriation of Video." *Anthropology Today* 8 (6): 5–16.

———. 1995. "Representation, Collaboration, and Mediation in Contemporary Ethnographic and Indigenous Media." *Visual Anthropology Review* 11: 102–6.

———. 2002. "Representation, Politics, and Cultural Imagination in Indigenous Video: General Points and Kayapo Examples." In *Media Worlds: Anthropology on New Terrain*, edited by Faye D. Ginsburg, Lila Abu-Lughod, and Brian Larkin, 75–89. Berkeley: University of California Press.

Urban, Greg, and Joel Sherzer. 1991. *Nation-States and Indians in Latin America.* Austin: University of Texas Press.

Van Cott, Donna Lee. 1994. *Indigenous Peoples and Democracy in Latin America.* New York: St. Martin's.

———. 2005. *From Movements to Parties in Latin America: The Evolution of Ethnic Politics.* Cambridge: Cambridge University Press.

Vanden, Harry, and Gary Prevost. 2009. *Politics of Latin America: The Power Game.* New York: Oxford University Press.

Vargas, Mauricio, and Santiago Garriga. 2015. *Explaining Inequality and Poverty Reduction in Bolivia. IMF Working Paper.* Washington, DC: International Monetary Fund.

Villanueva, Erick. 2008. "The Media in Bolivia." In *The Media in Latin America,* edited by Jairo Lugo-Ocando, 29–45. New York: Open University Press.

Virtanen, Pirjo. 2015. "Indigenous Social Media Practices in Southwestern Amazonia." *AlterNative: An International Journal of Indigenous Peoples* 11: 350–62.

Wagner, Sarah. 2018. "Cultural Revitalization and the Ontology of Communicative Spaces: 'Mobile Coordinating' among Guaraní." *International Journal of Cultural Studies* 22: 417–33.

Wagner, Sarah, and Mireia Fernández-Ardèvol. 2019. "Decolonizing Mobile Media: Mobile Internet Appropriation in a Guaraní Community." *Mobile Media and Communication* 8, no. 1: 83–103.

Walzer, Michael. 1989. "Citizenship." In *Political Innovation and Conceptual Change*, edited by Terence Ball, James Farr, and Russell L. Hanson, 211–20. Cambridge: Cambridge University Press.

Wampler, Brian. 2012. "Participation, Representation, and Social Justice: Using Participatory Governance to Transform Representative Democracy." *Polity* 44: 666–82.

Warren, Sarah. 2013. "A Nation Divided: Building the Cross-Border Mapuche Nation in Chile and Argentina." *Journal of Latin American Studies* 45, no. 2: 235–64.

Weisbrot, Mark. 2008. "Poverty Reduction in Venezuela: A Reality-Based view." *ReVista: Harvard Review of Latin America* 8: 1–8.

Weisenhaus, Doreen, and Simon Young. 2017. *Media Law and Policy in the Internet Age.* London: Bloomsbury Publishing.

Williams, Raymond. 1983. *Keywords: A Vocabulary of Culture and Society.* New York: Oxford University Press.

Wilson, Alex, Bronwyn Carlson, and Acushla Sciascia. 2017. "Reterritorialising Social Media: Indigenous People Rise Up." *Australasian Journal of Information Systems* 21: 1–4.

World Bank. 2015. *Indigenous Latin America in the Twenty-First Century.* http://documents1.worldbank.org/curated/en/145891467991974540/pdf/Indigenous-Latin-America-in-the-twenty-first-century-the-first-decade.pdf.

Wortham, Erica C. 2013. *Indigenous Media in Mexico: Culture, Community, and the State.* Durham, NC: Duke University Press.

Yashar, Deborah. 1998. "Contesting Citizenship: Indigenous Movements and Democracy in Latin America." *Comparative Politics* 31: 23–42.

———. 2005. *Contesting Citizenship in Latin America: The Rise of Indigenous Movements and the Postliberal Challenge.* Cambridge: Cambridge University Press.

———. 2007. "Resistance and Identity Politics in an Age of Globalization." *Annals of the American Academy of Political and Social Science* 610: 160–81.

Zavaleta, René. 1986. *Lo nacional-popular en Bolivia.* Mexico City: Siglo XXI.

———. 1990. *El estado en América Latina.* La Paz: Los Amigos del Libro.

Zegada, María Teresa, Clauda Arce, Gabriela Caneda, and Alber Quispe. 2011. *La democracia desde los márgenes: Transformaciones en el campo político boliviano.* La Paz: Muela del Diablo / CLACSO.

Index